PRAISE FOR THE GLUTEN-FREE ON A SHOESTRING SERIES

"With plenty of wisdom and easy instructions, *Gluten-Free on a Shoestring* is a must for any gluten-intolerant health-conscious cook."
—MIDWEST BOOK REVIEW

"Hunn has not only bestowed her readers with a complete cookbook . . . but she shows us how to save money, and time, on our meals . . . It's well worth a bite."
—SAN FRANCISCO BOOK REVIEW

"Blogger-turned-cookbook author Hunn successfully tackles a chief complaint voiced by special-diet newbies: sticker shock. Her practical tips for shopping and cooking to save time and money are a gift to all of us who are paying too much for too little."
—LIVING WITHOUT

"This book is written for real people, facing real economic issues, that can't afford to dedicate a whole paycheck to groceries. It is a great resource for preparing whole foods at home and not spending all weekends and evenings in the kitchen."
—PORTLAND BOOK REVIEW

"[Hunn's] engaging writing style makes it seem like you have a good friend in the kitchen helping you along."
—GLUTEN-INTOLERANCE GROUP MAGAZINE

"I highly recommend this cookbook. The recipes are accessible and especially geared for people with busy lifestyles."
—TUCSON CITIZEN

GLUTEN-FREE ON A SHOESTRING BAKES BREAD

ALSO BY NICOLE HUNN:

Gluten-Free on a Shoestring

Gluten-Free on a Shoestring Quick & Easy

GLUTEN-FREE ON A SHOESTRING BAKES BREAD

BISCUITS, BAGELS, BUNS, AND MORE

· · · · · · · · · ·

by Nicole Hunn

Da Capo
LIFE LONG

A Member of the Perseus Books Group

Designed by Lisa Diercks
Set in 10.5 point Abril

Cataloging-in-Publication data for this book is available from the Library of Congress.
First Da Capo Press edition 2013
ISBN: 978-0-7382-1685-0 (paperback)
ISBN: 978-0-7382-1686-7 (e-book)

Published by Da Capo Press
A Member of the Perseus Books Group
www.dacapopress.com

Note: The information in this book is true and complete to the best of our knowledge. This book is
intended only as an informative guide for those wishing to know more about health issues. In no way is this
book intended to replace, countermand, or conflict with the advice given to you by your own physician.
The ultimate decision concerning care should be made between you and your doctor. We strongly recommend you follow his or her advice. Information in this book is general and is offered with no guarantees
on the part of the authors or Da Capo Press. The authors and publisher disclaim all liability in connection
with the use of this book. The names and identifying details of people associated with events described in
this book have been changed. Any similarity to actual persons is coincidental.

Da Capo Press books are available at special discounts for bulk purchases in the U.S. by corporations, insti-
tutions, and other organizations. For more information, please contact the Special Markets Department at
the Perseus Books Group, 2300 Chestnut Street, Suite 200, Philadelphia, PA, 19103, or call (800) 810-4145,
ext. 5000, or e-mail special.markets@perseusbooks.com.

10 9 8 7 6 5 4 3 2 1

CONTENTS

Rolls and Other Shaped Breads: Smaller Breads Shaped into Bagels, Rolls, English Muffins, Knots, and Hoagies 117

INTRODUCTION

OURS IS A BREAD-OBSESSED CULTURE. WHETHER WE'RE EATING IT at every meal or refusing to eat it altogether, bread defines almost every American diet and way of life. Perhaps no one group is more bread-obsessed than the gluten-free community, yet I say this with reverence, not judgment. You are my people! So why, despite the recent proliferation of gluten-free cookbooks, the near-absence of gluten-free bread books? Fear of baking it. Plain and simple. I have been asked many, many times, even by other gluten-free cookbook authors, why a gluten-free bread book? It's so hard! To which I answer this: Exactly. Plus, we deserve a seat at the cultural table, just like everyone else.

Until now, we have found ways to get by. We know where to get gluten-free packaged bread and we know what it costs (do we ever!). Most of us have chosen a favorite brand, and have come up with a way to rationalize the price we must pay for it. When we're using it for our children's school lunch, we want it to look as "normal" as possible. We wouldn't dream of making it into bread crumbs (too expensive!), so we get used to using crushed cereal instead (which, admittedly, has its own flavor profile and undoubtedly its own place as breading). We buy bread mixes and bread makers in a vain attempt to avoid the mystery of how to make gluten-free bread at home altogether.

Enter *Gluten-Free on a Shoestring Bakes Bread.*

Forget everything you've ever heard before about baking gluten-free bread. What you will learn in this book is nothing short of revolutionary. Not only will you learn to make gluten-free yeast bread that rises beautifully and reliably, but even working with the dough will be a pleasure. You can save your ice-cream scoop for when you're eating, well, ice cream. You won't be needing it to portion weepy, wet mounds of dough that look more like they should be used to make cookies than bread. The recipes in this book make dough that you will learn to knead until it's smooth. Then, you'll shape it into everything from baguettes to cinnamon swirl bread using little more than a bench scraper and your own able, floured hands. And I will be there to guide you every step of the way, with accessible instructions in plain language, plus process photos of my own two practiced, flour-covered hands doing it right alongside you. Are you thinking about Demi Moore and Patrick Swayze in *Ghost* now, or is it just me?

No more settling for only the types of packaged, mostly frozen bread for sale in natural foods stores or, worse, pretending that a leaf of lettuce makes just as good a sandwich as real, fresh bread does (it doesn't, because it's lettuce). You'll be amazed at how quickly you become nimble and practiced enough at gluten-free bread baking to make enough to rely upon for your family's lunches. Before you know it, you'll be stocking your freezer with enough bread for thick slices of French toast, and you might even be willing to sacrifice a loaf or two in the name of fresh, gluten-free panko-style bread crumbs. And it won't even feel like a sacrifice!

We'll start by describing the few simple gluten-free flour blends you'll need to make every recipe in this book (with some alternatives, as I know you like alternatives), plus a thorough explanation of how and why they are necessary. Then, we'll move on to defining some bread-baking lingo, just to ensure that we're all on the same page. Don't worry. On a Nerd Scale of 1 to 10, it's maybe a 5. We will also review the basic home appliances and equipment you'll need—plus the items you'll want, in descending order, along with my arguments in favor of acquiring those items if you are willing and able. Next, in Chapter 2, I will teach you in detail what to expect from gluten-free bread dough and gluten-free bread baking. We'll cover basic principles for creating and handling gluten-free bread dough, how to store gluten-free bread, and finally, troubleshooting—where I'll aim to anticipate your questions and reassure you that all is, hopefully, not lost. And in Chapter 3, the final chapter before digging into the recipes themselves, you'll find full-color, step-by-step photos and detailed descriptions of how to shape everything from baguettes and boules to small, round rolls and sandwich bread.

I have acquired the knowledge and the tools, and it is my privilege and pleasure to impart it to you. You can do this. There's so much to anticipate. From loaf breads for slicing (some light and fluffy, others with a chewy crumb) to wild yeast breads with a true, pure sourdough flavor, nothing is out of reach any longer. Breads you roll flat, such as pizza, tortillas, and naan, will become everyday staples in your home. So will shaped rolls and buns, such as bagels and soft hamburger buns and hoagie rolls. Through carefully worded instructions and plenty of full color photographs, you'll come to know what the dough should look, feel, and smell like at every interval. If you didn't believe before that it was possible to create bakery-quality gluten-free bread in your own home, you will now. There are plenty of yeast-free options as well, from cream puffs and muffins to zucchini bread and flaky, layered biscuits. We will close with the most classic uses for all of this amazing dough and bread. Take it from me—once you have turned out a perfect loaf of No-Rye "Rye" Bread (page 101), you won't want another day to pass without a classic Reuben Sandwich (page 263). Or a Monte Cristo (page 264), for that matter. Classic comfort food for everyone!

Remember that life is sweet and fun. And good bread is too good to live without. Gluten is expendable.

With love,
Nicole

1 BEGINNING ESSENTIALS

GLUTEN-FREE FLOUR BLENDS, KITCHEN EQUIPMENT, AND BREAD GLOSSARY

IF YOU ASK ME (AND, TO BE FAIR, IF YOU'RE READING THIS, YOU KIND of did), hands down, the biggest thing since sliced gluten-free bread is the use of whey protein isolate in gluten-free bread baking. How's that for a tortured metaphor? The yeast bread recipes in this book will speak for themselves when you bake them—and eat them. But what they won't do is tell you the story of how they came to be. That task falls, happily, to me.

In almost all gluten-free baking, because we have removed a protein (gluten), we must replace it in one way or another. To date, the most common ingredient used to replace gluten's elasticity is the hydrocolloid xanthan gum. I do still find xanthan gum to be essential to gluten-free bread baking (and frankly, to most other gluten-free baking), so we will need some of that. But, after much trial and error, I discovered that the addition of whey protein isolate to gluten-free bread baking goes a long, long way toward more effectively replacing gluten in bread. It not only allows us to use considerably less xanthan gum, but it creates a dough that looks, behaves, and tastes much more like the bread that we remember—without nearly as much moisture as we have come to expect was necessary in gluten-free bread dough.

If you have ever attempted to make gluten-free bread with a typical all-purpose gluten-free flour blend and not added plenty of extra moisture, you know that it yields a very, very tight and unpleasant, arid crumb. I reasoned that, if I'm able to add back in a protein that behaves similarly to gluten, maybe I could make bread dough that wasn't quite so wet and weepy. And bread dough that has enough surface tension to shape into smooth loaves and rolls—not to mention is a pleasure to handle (spoiler: I did it! And now so can you).

During recipe development for this book, I tried so many protein powders: hemp protein, rice protein, rice protein isolate, egg white protein, soy protein, vegetable protein, protein isolate, and still others. Some worked better than others, but none of them had the Midas touch. At the risk of sounding melodramatic (who, me?), I was nearly inconsolable. I could have developed a hundred recipes for amazing-tasting gluten-free bread made in the conventional way that would delight us all. But the process simply would not have been truly enjoyable unless I solved our flour problem.

The bread-baking process itself is a main focus of this book for three reasons. First, bread baking has always fulfilled something of a romantic ideal to me, particularly today, in the do-it-yourself artisan world. Process is at least half the pleasure I get from even the *idea* of homemade bread. If the process of making the dough, allowing the flavors to develop with relatively simple ingredients, and then shaping the bread into everything from sandwich loaves and rolls to baguettes and bagels isn't enjoyable, then there goes half the magic.

Second, you aren't going to save any money or reclaim any feeling of normalcy in your gluten-free life if you buy this book but don't actually bake from it. I am counting on you to not only bake from this book, but to make an unholy mess of it with dog-eared pages and flour sprinklings. If the process is pleasurable, and you know that from the start, aren't you much more likely to try your hand at that first recipe? And once you try that first recipe, I predict that you will be hooked. It won't be long before you're bragging to your friends about what you can do in the kitchen.

My final reason for elevating the process of baking gluten-free bread to such importance is that it allows us to stand on the shoulders of the bread-baking giants who came before, such as Peter Reinhart, Rose Levy Berenbaum, and Nick Malgieri. Although the proportions are somewhat different, and the methods differ to a certain extent, many of the same principles that these masters have taught us through the years are still guideposts. So much of gluten-free baking is new. That's exciting, but it can also be a tremendous barrier. When I began baking gluten-free in 2004, I had Bette Hagman's books and little else as my shepherds. I scarcely understood what I was doing or why I was doing it, and I was terribly frightened. Plus, if I didn't like what I turned out, I felt powerless to do anything about it. We have come so, so far in the years since, but I believe we can go all the way. This is the next step.

Although most of those proteins I tested were dismal failures, I did finally arrive at whey protein isolate. When you use whey protein isolate in what I am referring to as Gluten-Free Bread Flour in the pages that follow, it comes closer to mimicking conventional bread dough than anything I have ever seen before—or thought I would ever see. This formula works better, by far, than any other combination I have tried (and believe me when I tell you I was exhaustive in testing various proportions). I purchase NOW Foods brand unflavored whey protein isolate, and I'm pretty sure it's for bodybuilders. It's available at Amazon.com and from many other online sources. The source with the best price seems to rotate, but it's often Netrition.com.

On the next page is my formula for Gluten-Free Bread Flour. Please note that all of the flour blends in this chapter are best measured by weight, with a simple digital scale. However, for your convenience, I have included the approximate volume measurements that correspond to each weight amount, where appropriate. Your results will almost certainly not be the same, though, as there is simply too much human error involved in measuring dry ingredients such as these by volume.

GLUTEN-FREE BREAD FLOUR
MAKES 1 CUP (140 G) FLOUR

100 grams (about 11½ tablespoons) all-purpose gluten-free flour (71%)
25 grams (about 5 tablespoons) unflavored whey protein isolate (18%)
15 grams (about 5 teaspoons) Expandex modified tapioca starch (11%)

In a moment, you'll find that I've provided you with two recipes for all-purpose gluten-free flour, either of which will work in building your gluten-free bread flour repertoire as well as any recipe that calls for an "all-purpose gluten-free flour." Please note that every recipe that calls for an "all-purpose gluten-free flour" in this book was formulated to work with one of the two blends, both of which necessarily contain a small amount of xanthan gum. The first, which I have dubbed "High-Quality All-Purpose Gluten-Free Flour," is a copycat of the blend that Better Batter.org uses in its all-purpose gluten-free flour. I generally prefer it, but it is no doubt more complex than the second blend. You can, of course, simply use Better Batter's product itself. This first all-purpose blend is appropriate to use whenever a recipe in this book, including the Gluten-Free Bread Flour above, calls for "all-purpose gluten-free flour."

The second blend, which I have dubbed the "Make-It-Simpler All-Purpose Gluten-Free Flour," is, well, simpler, with only four components. It is a good substitute for the High-Quality All-Purpose Gluten-Free Flour blend. It does tend, however, to absorb a bit more moisture than the "High Quality" blend.

A note about component flours: Typically, I insist upon a superfine rice flour for even what I would call "good" results in gluten-free baking, and it certainly is best here as well. Authentic Foods (authenticfoods.com) is currently the only source I know for truly superfine rice flours that are reliably gluten-free. However, in any of the bread recipes that call for a long, slow rise in the refrigerator (which is most yeasted recipes in this book), even a rice flour that is not ground as superfine as the one from Authentic Foods is fine. As the flour sits in the dough, it absorbs moisture and softens considerably. For other recipes, such as those in Chapter 8 (my yeast-free quick breads), your rice flour must be superfine or it will taste gritty, at least to some. The other component flours can be purchased from any number of reputable sources (www.bobsredmill.com, www.amazon.com, or www.nuts.com, to name a few), except the tapioca starch, which I only buy from www.nuts.com or Authentic Foods to avoid a metallic aftertaste or simply poor baking performance. Flours purchased at Asian markets are typically poor quality and may not work at all in these recipes. I must recommend against their use entirely.

Please note that although tapioca starch is the same as tapioca flour, potato starch and potato flour are two different ingredients and should not be substituted for each other.

HIGH-QUALITY ALL-PURPOSE GLUTEN-FREE FLOUR
MAKES 1 CUP (140 G) FLOUR

42 grams (about ¼ cup) superfine brown rice flour (30%)
42 grams (about ¼ cup) superfine white rice flour (30%)
21 grams (about 2⅓ tablespoons) tapioca starch (15%)
21 grams (about 2⅓ tablespoons) potato starch (15%)
7 grams (about 1¾ teaspoons) potato flour (5%)
4 grams (about 2 teaspoons) xanthan gum (3%)
3 grams (about 1½ teaspoons) pure powdered pectin (2%)

MAKE-IT-SIMPLER ALL-PURPOSE GLUTEN-FREE FLOUR
MAKES 1 CUP (140 G) FLOUR

90 grams (about 9 tablespoons) superfine white rice flour (64%)
31 grams (about 3½ tablespoons) potato starch (22%)
15 grams (about 5 teaspoons) tapioca starch (11%)
4 grams (about 2 teaspoons) xanthan gum (3%)

In certain recipes, such as Crepes (page 209) and in the wild yeast starter (pages 83–90), you will need a basic gum-free blend. It is only appropriate when specifically instructed in a recipe. That blend is as follows:

BASIC GUM-FREE GLUTEN-FREE FLOUR
MAKES 1 CUP (140 G) FLOUR

93 grams (about 9⅓ tablespoons) superfine white rice flour (66%)
32 grams (about 3½ tablespoons) potato starch (23%)
15 grams (about 5 teaspoons) tapioca starch (11%)

In recipes with added whole grains, such as the Whole-Grain Pizza Crust (page 191) and Lean Whole-Grain Pizza Crust (page XXX), this is the blend to use:

WHOLE-GRAIN GLUTEN-FREE FLOUR
MAKES 1 CUP (140 G) FLOUR

105 grams (about 11½ tablespoons) sweet white sorghum flour (75%)
35 grams (about ¼ cup) teff flour (25%)

Finally, Gluten-Free Pastry Flour is called for in such recipes as the Extra-Flaky Buttermilk Biscuits (page 227). It is made as follows:

GLUTEN-FREE PASTRY FLOUR
MAKES 1 CUP (140 G) FLOUR

112 grams (about 13 tablespoons) High-Quality All-Purpose Gluten-Free Flour (80%)
14 grams (about 2¼ tablespoons) nonfat dry milk, ground finely in a blender or food processor (10%)
14 grams (about 1½ tablespoons) cornstarch (10%)

A Note about Dairy-Free Alternatives

If you are dairy-free, you have no doubt noticed that the main flour innovation in this book, Gluten-Free Bread Flour, contains dairy in the form of whey protein isolate. However, I have not forgotten nor would I ever forsake those of you who are also dairy-free! I have had some success substituting one or the other of two nondairy protein powders in place of whey protein isolate, increasing the total liquid content in the recipe to 150 percent of the liquid content in the recipe as written. The two non-dairy protein powders I recommend are NOW Foods Pea Protein (just read the description to ensure that it is, in fact, a protein isolate) and Growing Naturals Rice Protein Isolate (Original Flavor), both of which are readily available online. For example, if the recipe calls for a total of 1 cup of water, you would use 1½ cups of water, adding the additional water in the dough stage (if the recipe begins with a starter). Then, due to the extra moisture content, you will need to bake the bread for longer than the original recipe calls for, usually by 25 percent. Therefore, a recipe that calls for about 40 minutes of baking time will need to be baked for closer to 50 minutes or more, taking care to ensure that the internal temperature of the bread has reached that specified in each particular recipe before you remove it from the oven.

Not only does the dough require more water, but it won't display the same glutenlike stretchy qualities, I'm afraid. It will, however, allow you to use the recipes in this book, with varying degrees of success.

In addition, when a bread recipe calls for unsalted butter, the nondairy substitute that I favor is Spectrum brand nonhydrogenated vegetable shortening, which is made from organic palm oil.

Glossary: How to Speak Bread

Baguette: A long, thin loaf of crusty bread. The longer and thinner you make it, the more crust you will have. However, you will be limited by the size of your oven.

Batard: Simply a loaf of bread that is shaped like a torpedo.

Boule: A loaf of bread shaped like a ball. It is shaped with the goal of having the loaf rise up, rather than out.

Brotform, banetton, or proofing basket: A coiled basket made of natural cane that is used for proofing shaped dough.

Bulk fermentation: The first rising of bread dough, prior to shaping.

Couche: Heavy linen fabric that can be used to hold bread in the proper shape during proofing.

Enriched bread: Bread that has enrichments, such as eggs, fats, sugars, butter, and yogurt. It tends to have a more tender crust and crumb, and, if butter or another fat is one of the enrichments, it tends to have a smoother mouthfeel. Bread made with enrichments may have a darker crust, but the crust should soften as the bread cools.

Hydration: The ratio of total liquid ingredients to total flour ingredients in the dough, by weight. For example, bread that has a total liquid weight of 273 grams and a total flour weight of 420 grams has a hydration of $^{273}/_{420}$ grams, or 65 percent. Bread dough that has higher hydration (e.g., focaccia) is wetter and usually stretchier, and bread dough with lower hydration (e.g., bagels) is drier and stiffer.

Lame: A straight razor blade attached to a handle, used for scoring or slashing bread dough before baking.

Lean bread: Refers to bread with few or no enrichments, such as eggs, fats, sugars, butter, or yogurt. It tends to have a more brittle, hard crust that has not been made tender by enrichments. The flavor of lean bread comes from yeast development.

Oven spring: The sudden rise in yeasted bread dough that occurs in the first minutes of baking. The high heat of the oven creates a rapid rise in yeast fermentation.

Proofing: The final rise of bread after it has been shaped.

Starter: There are other, more precise, technical terms for a starter (biga, poolish, sponge) used in bread baking. The nomenclature is related to the hydration and percentage of total yeast in the starter. In this book, rather than get overly technical, I simply use the general term starter to refer to any pre-ferment used in a given recipe. Do not skip this step in recipes that call for it! It makes an enormous difference in flavor development and structure in the final product (and in the dough itself, greatly assisting in making bread baking more enjoyable).

Yeast: The recipes in this book call for instant yeast (bread maker or rapid-rise yeast will also work). If you would like to substitute active dry yeast for instant yeast, multiply the weight of the instant yeast called for in the recipe by 125 percent or 1.25. A note about yeast and rising temperatures: there is actually quite a wide temperature range for reconstituted yeast to be active. The optimal temperature for rapid yeast development is about 80°F, but reconstituted yeast will live up until about 130°F and will still develop in the cold temperature of the refrigerator—just more slowly. When in doubt, err on the side of a cooler temperature instead of a hotter one, but keep in mind that the point of thermal death for yeast (between 130° and 140°F) is very high and would be terribly uncomfortable to the touch.

Equipment and Bakeware: What You Need and What You'll Want

Other than the ingredients specified in each recipe, there isn't too much you will absolutely *need* for bread-baking success. These simple items are listed here. In addition there area few gems that you will want very, very much. You must have a birthday coming up, right?

Needs

❧ **An oven thermometer:** Most ovens are improperly calibrated. My own is off by 50°F, sometimes more. I could have it calibrated properly, but I would still consider my oven thermometer the only accurate indicator of the temperature of my oven. After all, I could never be sure when my properly calibrated oven was no longer properly calibrated. Remember that all ovens have hot spots (you probably already know where yours is, and most likely account for it already by rotating baked goods during the baking cycle). So, be sure to place the oven thermometer close to the area of the oven in which you plan to place the bread as it bakes. Otherwise, the reading will not be accurate. I have a decidedly low-tech oven thermometer. It costs about $6.

❧ **A digital food scale:** Wherever possible, the recipes in this book contain both volume and weight measurements. However, in building a wild yeast starter (pages 83–90), a simple digital food scale is necessary, as volume measurements simply are insufficient. But it couldn't be easier! I promise. My digital scale is an Escali Primo multifunctional digital scale. I purchased it at Amazon.com for about $25, but I have also seen it everywhere I have ever seen digital food scales for sale, for about the same price. To use a digital food scale, simply turn on the scale with the push of an On/Tare/Off button. Then, place any bowl on top of the scale, "zero out" the weight of the bowl itself by pushing On/Tare/Off once more, select grams or ounces by pressing the button that usually says G/Oz, place an ingredient in the bowl until the digital counter reaches the desired weight, and then press On/Tare/Off once more to reset to zero before adding the next ingredient. And so on . . . That's it. A digital scale is not essential for building the gluten-free flour blends that we use in this book (see pages 8–10), but it does make for much greater accuracy. Plus, it makes clean up much easier!

❧ **A liquid measuring cup and a set of measuring spoons:** All liquid measurements in the book are given in teaspoons, tablespoons, or cups. Spoonfuls should be level, using measuring spoons, not dining cutlery. When measuring liquid in a cup, use a clear liquid measuring cup and check the accuracy of the measurement at eye level with the marking on the side of the cup.

❧ **A home proofer . . . or a heating pad:** With only a few exceptions, the first rise of bread dough (or bulk fermentation) in this book will happen in the refrigerator. This slows down yeast fermentation, and slower fermentation allows for more flavor development. Plus, it liberates the baker from having to babysit the bread dough after the small initial investment of time necessary to make the dough. However, the second rise after shaping (or proofing) is another matter entirely and requires a warm, draft-free environment, ideally a moist one. Likewise, those recipes that call for a starter require a warm, draft-free environment. In almost every instance, you can turn on your oven to about 250°F and place the shaped dough, covered as directed in the recipe, on the stovetop. The ambient heat will suffice to speed yeast production. However, when creating a wild yeast starter (pages 83–90), you will need a warm, draft-free environment that lasts for days on end. Leaving the oven on for all that time is simply impractical. There are two possible solutions. First, a Brød & Taylor Folding Proofer, a relatively new invention, allows you to create a controlled warm, moist, draft-free environment in your home. It is also great for tempering chocolate and making yogurt at home and folds flat for easy storage. I set it to 78°F when I am using it for bread dough or for growing a wild yeast starter (pages 83–90). I do set it a bit higher, around 85°F, if I'm using it to get a starter to rise. However, the Brød & Taylor is kind of spendy. If you are unable or unwilling to buy a home proofer, you can use a heating pad on its lowest setting, lined with at least two thick towels on top of which you will set the container with the developing starter. Be careful, though, if the starter mixture gets too hot, it will kill the yeast and spoil everything!

❧ **Digital calculator:** You only need a basic digital calculator, and it should cost less than $10. Buy one around back-to-school time and it might just set you back $2. Although I use my calculator more often in recipe development than I do when I'm simply following a recipe I've already created, it is way up on top of my list of most-used kitchen gadgets. Now, with three school-aged children, I have had ample opportunity in recent years to hone my "mental math" skills. Even so, when I am scaling a recipe up or down (all the recipes in this book are scalable up to at least a multiple of three) or just building a simple gluten-free flour blend, I still reach for my digital calculator. Knowing that I'm much less likely to make a simple, careless error that can torpedo a whole recipe, it's easier to relax and really enjoy baking yeasty, fragrant gluten-free bread. Nerdy? Perhaps. But geek . . . is chic.

❧ **Glass jar and wooden spoon:** Speaking of the wild yeast starter and levain recipes in Chapter 5, you will need a large glass jar and a wooden (or other nonmetal, nonreactive) spoon for making the wild yeast starter.

❧ **Mixing bowls and whisks:** Lots of mixing bowls, lots of whisks.

❧ **Bench scrapers:** Ideally, you'll need a traditional metal scraper and a more flexible one like those used for icing cakes. They are essential for folding and kneading gluten-free bread dough, as well as for transferring it from place to place.

❧ **Instant-read thermometer:** I went back and forth about whether to describe an instant-read thermometer as a "want" or a "need." I settled on "need," as it takes much of the guesswork out of bread baking and will increase your level of confidence and your chances for early success.

❧ **Rimmed baking sheets:** I own no cookie sheets, and haven't for years. I rely exclusively on rimmed baking sheets, in quarter, half, and 10 by 15-inch sizes. Whatever is along the perimeter of a baking sheet gets hotter and bakes faster, but the rims on the baking sheet tend to even out baking over the entire surface.

❧ **Unbleached parchment paper:** Unbleached parchment paper is much thinner and more flexible than bleached white parchment paper, and can withstand high oven temperatures better. If You Care brand is my favorite.

❧ **French rolling pin:** When rolling out dough, a French rolling pin (the kind that has no distinct handles and tapers on both ends) allows for much better precision and control.

❧ **8½ by 4½-inch loaf pans:** All the loaf breads in Chapter 4 call for this size loaf pan. It's juuuuuuust right. I have long recommended USA Pans loaf pans, and they are still wonderful baking tools. However, the striations on all of their loaf pans started to bother me a bit. They really do help with even baking, but not always enough to justify the impressions those striations leave on the outside of every loaf of bread I bake. Especially not for the photo shoot for this very book! For that purpose, I have begun using Williams-Sonoma Goldtouch nonstick 1-pound loaf pans.

❧ **Sharp knife or lame for slashing:** When bread bakes in the oven, it expands and will split at somewhat random points of expansion—unless you slash it. Then it should "bloom," or separate in a more controlled manner at the point of slashing.

❧ **Cooking oil spray:** Cooking oil spray is extremely useful in bread baking. It acts as a barrier between plastic wrap and rising dough so the dough does not stick to the plastic. It can also prevent shaped bagel dough from sticking to the parchment paper as it rises and before boiling, and is extremely useful in scraping down sometimes sticky dough from the sides of a mixing bowl. If you can, find a spray that contains only olive oil and a propellant—or use a Misto and add your own simple oil.

❧ **Large serrated bread knife:** For slicing into your beautiful gluten-free bread after baking, nothing beats a large serrated bread knife for sawing through that gorgeous crust.

Wants

❧ **Stand mixer:** A powerful stand mixer, such as a KitchenAid, is at the very top of the "wants" list. Not only will it make the process of making bread dough easier, but machine-kneading is essential to creating the smooth elasticity that is designed to mimic the stretchiness of conventional, gluten-containing bread dough. If you don't have a stand mixer, please don't try to use a regular, three-speed hand mixer with beater attachments. It won't work; you may even burn out your hand mixer in the process. Just use a large bowl, a wooden spoon, and some good old-fashioned elbow grease! One exception: As described on page 27, try getting a five-speed hand mixer with dough hooks. I tested out the five-speed KitchenAid "ultra power" hand mixer with dough hooks and was pleased with the results.

❧ **Pizza stone:** A pizza stone is essential for making crisp pizza, and nearly essential for making pita bread. It is also very useful for making any sort of bread in the oven because it retains heat very well, helping to maintain a consistent oven temperature. Once a pizza stone is hot, it tends to stay hot.

✤ **Pizza peel:** If you use a pizza stone, you are going to need a reliable way to slide dough quickly onto the hot pizza stone that is already in the oven. A pizza peel is simply a stiff, flat, heat-resistant surface with a long handle. It need be neither fancy nor expensive.

✤ **Banetton/brotform/proofing baskets:** Proofing baskets are typically made of natural cane and come in various shapes and sizes. They can either be lined with a specially fitted linen liner (similar to the fabric of a couche, but thinner) or just floured generously. I much prefer using them unlined. That way, when dough proofs in the proofing basket, it emerges with those gorgeous concentric circles (or ovals, depending upon your choice of shape) you see in the No-Rye "Rye" Bread (page 101). And the smoothness and evenness of the rise that is achieved through use of a proofing basket is the stuff of legends. Be sure not to wash them with soap! Just tap out the excess flour after rising, rinse with water if necessary, and then allow to dry completely and totally before storing. I like to keep mine very visible. It makes me look like a hipster. (Does, *too*.)

✤ **Dutch oven:** This round, heavy, lidded cast-iron pot is unique in its ability to guarantee a crisp crust on a round loaf of No-Rye "Rye" Bread (page 101) that literally sings as hits the cool air outside the oven when it is finished baking. A Dutch oven traps both the heat and the moisture of bread as it bakes, creating its own hot but moist environment, perfect for a crisp crust. Make sure that all of the parts of your Dutch oven are heat-safe to a high heat, including the handle on the lid. If you'd like to make another shape loaf in a Dutch oven, just be sure the size and shape of the loaf will fit inside your pot.

✤ **Lidded plastic proofing buckets:** I get tremendous use out of Cambro brand 2-quart, round, lidded, translucent plastic storage containers. They are inexpensive and are large enough to accommodate almost every dough in this book with enough room for the dough to double in size. The relatively stiff lid stays secure under pressure (which is important, as the fermenting yeast will give off gas that, over time, may fill the bucket). Oh, and the 2-quart size is relatively short and wide, so it fits easily on every shelf in my refrigerator. I also have some of the taller, 4-quart proofing buckets. They require some rearranging to fit in the refrigerator, but the extra room is sometimes necessary.

✤ **Silicone spoonulas:** You can use a basic nonstick spatula for all the scraping down of bowls that is necessary, but a silicone spoonula is like a cross between a spatula and a large spoon, so it holds the dough as you scrape down the sides of your bowl. Believe it or not, I have had a hard time finding these and most often buy them at www.kohls.com.

❧ **Large, plastic bakery freezer bags:** How you store the bread you bake is really important, because you most likely won't be able to bake bread fresh every single day (or will you?). I buy double-size bread bags online from King Arthur Flour. They prevent freezer burn better than anything else I have tried, short of buying one of those long-term food storage contraptions, which frankly scare the life out of me because I'm certain I'm going to melt myself in that thing. For more information on these bread bags, please see "Rules for Storing Gluten-Free Bread" on page 23.

❧ **Couche:** A baker's couche is a large, heavy, rectangular piece of untreated, unbleached flax linen. Having a couche is relatively low on the list of "wants," but still kind of nice to have. I don't use mine often, but I really love the way a couche will coax a baguette into rising up without rising out. It is the best way to ensure that baguettes maintain the shape I created before proofing. But you can't wash a couche with soap, and it certainly cannot be cleaned in the washing machine. You must dust it off well, fold it up, and store it until next time. My clean-freaky nature means that I find this somewhat unnerving.

2 WHAT TO EXPECT FROM GLUTEN-FREE BREAD

HOW THIS GLUTEN-FREE BREAD DOUGH IS BETTER, AND HOW TO WORK WITH IT

GLUTEN-FREE BREAD DOUGH OF YORE (AND BY "YORE," I MEAN just yesterday) was always heavy and slick with moisture, and almost always enriched with some combination of eggs, fats, sugars, butter, and yogurt. There really wasn't any sort of gluten-free bread that rightly could be described as "lean," meaning bread without most of those enrichments. The extra moisture was required because many of the gluten-free flours absorbed extra moisture, and the ever-present enrichments added structure, mouthfeel, taste, and, in some cases, more moisture. If you have ever heard gluten-free bread dough described as being similar to cookie dough, then you know exactly what I'm talking about. Can I get an Amen?

The cookie dough reference, an apt one, is not only based on the moisture of the raw dough. It is also based on the texture and lack of cohesion in the dough, as it broke apart from itself in shards, much as you would expect from, well, cookie dough. In conventional, gluten-containing bread baking, a recipe might instruct us to pull off a piece of dough for shaping, and we expect the dough to resist being separated from itself, at least a bit. It is the elasticity in the well-developed gluten strands in the dough (and then in the bread itself) that is responsible for this resistance. It makes shaping the dough in any manner of ways possible. This is not to say that it is impossible to shape gluten-free "cookie dough" bread dough. It most certainly is possible, with either well-floured or wet hands and the aid of such tools as a spring-loaded ice-cream scoop for portioning dough. I've done it many times myself, and I bet you have, too.

But now is the time for us to move forward, in the direction of the tried-and-true methods and principles developed in the realm of conventional gluten-containing bread baking. By incorporating Gluten-Free Bread Flour (page 8) in the recipes in this book, according to the simple, plain-spoken techniques expressed in the recipe instructions, we begin to reclaim the romance of baking bread. The dough may not feel exactly like conventional bread dough (it is, indeed, its own breed of dough), but it will exhibit many of its most important characteristics.

You will be able to shape a round of gluten-free bread dough and have the top maintain its smoothness and shape as the dough rises (instead of dimpling, as we have come to expect from gluten-free "cookie dough" bread dough). If you consider Gluten-Free Bread Flour to be a single ingredient, as I hope you will come to think of it, you will be able to create lean bread (see Lean Crusty White Sandwich Bread, page 43) with only a few ingredients. Rather than enrichments, such as butter and eggs, being the source of flavor, the yeast development that happens during a long, slow rise in the refrigerator will provide all the flavor, just as it does in conventional gluten-containing lean bread. I began to realize that it had been years since I had tasted the full flavor of yeast bread in all the corners of my mouth. Years since I had experienced the blistered crust and chewy center of a real bagel. Years since I had had real, wild yeast sourdough in all its flavor complexity. It's good to be back, and even better to take you with me!

Basic Principles for Creating and Handling This Bread Dough

🍂 Particularly when baking lean bread, you will need to begin with a starter. The difference between lean bread dough made with a starter and lean bread dough made without a starter is dramatic, even though the ingredients stay precisely the same. The dough made with a starter has significantly more structure and is markedly easier to handle.

❧ Particularly when baking lean bread, you will need to allow the dough a long, slow rise in the refrigerator. Not only will you have dough that is bursting with complex flavor, but you'll also find that shaping the dough straight from the refrigerator will really help to minimize its stickiness.

❧ Again when making the lean bread recipes in this book, I have found that building Gluten-Free Bread Flour (page 8) with the Make-It-Simpler All-Purpose Gluten-Free Flour (page 9) yields a dough that is somewhat easier to handle. In the enriched bread recipes, I prefer the High-Quality All-Purpose Gluten-Free Flour (page 9) when building Gluten-Free Bread Flour (page 8).

❧ When making yeast bread dough, always err on the side of creating a dough that is slightly more wet than may ultimately be necessary. It is significantly easier to work more flour into the dough during shaping than it is to add more moisture.

❧ Enriched gluten-free bread doughs are typically smoother, less sticky, and easier to handle than lean gluten-free bread doughs.

❧ If you have past experience baking gluten-free bread, you may be tempted to add egg whites to the yeast bread recipes in this book, as they are such a common ingredient in other gluten-free bread recipes. However, resist the urge, unless egg whites are called for in the recipe as written. Although they help add structure, egg whites are paradoxically quite drying to the baked bread. Bread made with egg whites tends to dry out much more quickly.

❧ Keep in mind that wet dough is not a thing of the past, entirely. In conventional, gluten-containing bread baking, certain types of dough are made with very high levels of hydration, and the same holds true for some of the gluten-free bread doughs in this book. For example, the Herb Focaccia (page 198) has 80 percent hydration, which is what is responsible for the beautiful, large holes in its crumb. There is also generally an inverse relationship between the amount of moisture in the dough and the amount of yeast in the recipe—more moisture, less yeast, and vice versa. Less yeast with a long, slow rise in a high hydration dough yields a truly historic, complex flavor.

Rules for Storing Gluten-Free Bread

❧ When it's freshly baked and cooled, if possible, store homemade gluten-free bread in a breadbox. And make sure the bread has enough empty space around it so that the air can circulate. A closed breadbox retains some moisture in the box, so the bread doesn't dry out, but doesn't hold that moisture so close to the bread that it turns soggy.

❧ Never store your gluten-free bread in a paper bag. The paper bag will itself become moist from humidity in the surrounding air, and your bread will become soggy.

❧ Never store gluten-free bread (homemade or store-bought) in the refrigerator. The refrigerator is designed to keep moisture at bay, as moisture tends to spoil food. Storing bread in the refrigerator will dry out your bread in a hurry.

❧ Store leftover gluten-free bread that is older than 3 to 4 days (depending upon humidity levels in your kitchen and the type of bread) in the freezer. To prevent freezer burn due to loss of moisture, use heavy-duty plastic bakery/bread bags for storage. I buy double-size bread bags online from King Arthur Flour. They do a great job of preserving bread, and they are less expensive than resealable plastic freezer bags. Plus, resealable plastic freezer bags are heavy but tend to be stiff, making it difficult to remove all of the air surrounding the bread, which leads to more freezer burn.

❧ If you don't expect to use all of the gluten-free bread you are freezing at once, consider slicing it before wrapping and freezing it. That way, you should be able to defrost just what you need without compromising the rest of the loaf. If you are slicing and storing English Muffin Bread (page 74), you may want to place small pieces of unbleached parchment paper between the slices before freezing. When a loaf of bread has very high hydration, like English Muffin Bread does, the slices tend to stick to one another during freezing.

❧ Let homemade gluten-free bread cool almost completely before placing it in a breadbox or other container, and before freezing it. Otherwise, the moisture in the bread that would have evaporated upon cooling will instead condense and ruin any hope of crispness in the crust.

❧ Never slice into a loaf of homemade gluten-free bread while it is still hot. It won't hold its shape, so you won't get a clean slice. Some smaller, shaped breads only need to cool for a short time before you can enjoy them, but a loaf must be completely cool.

❧ Unless you plan to freeze it, leave a fresh loaf of homemade gluten-free bread whole, unsliced, until you are ready to use it. The crust will help keep the bread from going stale.

❧ Once you have sliced into a loaf of homemade gluten-free bread, when you place it in a breadbox, store it with the cut side down, to minimize staleness.

Troubleshooting Gluten-Free Bread Baking

I can't get my bread to rise.

🌿 Try waiting longer during the final proofing stage. There are only a few recipes where overproofing is a real risk, such as with shaped breads and levain breads, which may result in a distorted or blown out shape if they overproof. Otherwise, because the rate at which yeast is active is so dependent upon its internal environment (the combined temperatures of the various ingredients plus the moisture level) and its ambient environment (the temperature and moisture level of the surrounding environment in your kitchen), rising times given in a recipe are a guide. And keep in mind that both the internal and ambient environments will differ from season to season, recipe to recipe, and sometimes due to human error. But most of these conditions can be cured with time. Be patient.

🌿 If your yeast is within the freshness date indicated on the package, the problem almost certainly isn't the yeast. But if you have opened a jar of yeast and left it at room temperature rather than refrigerating it, or otherwise mishandled the yeast, it may no longer be good. Try a fresh batch.

🌿 Your other ingredients may have killed the yeast. Be sure that you didn't add any ingredients to the dough that were near 130°F, the thermal death point for yeast. In addition, recipe instructions will always indicate that the yeast should be whisked into the other dry ingredients separately from the salt, as salt can kill yeast when the two come into direct contact.

🌿 Your process may be killing the yeast. If your preferred method of getting bread to rise is by putting your oven on its lowest temperature and allowing the dough to rise inside the oven, it may get too hot and kill the yeast. Most ovens are not properly calibrated below 150°F, and it is impractical to sit in front of the oven watching your oven thermometer for spikes in temperature that could kill your yeast.

My bread rose in the oven and then sank in the middle as it cooled.

🌿 Are you using an oven thermometer? As discussed on page 13, most ovens are improperly calibrated, and more often run hot than cold. If you bake bread (or any baked good) in a too-hot oven, it will rise too quickly and give the appearance of being done before the inside of the bread has the structure necessary to support the rise on the outside. So, as the bread cools and steam escapes from the inside, the bread sinks in the middle. Monitor that oven temperature!

My dough is too sticky to shape.

❧ Make sure you allow the starter to double in size before using it to make the bread dough. Also be sure to allow the bread a long, slow rise in the refrigerator, and then begin shaping it while it is still cold. If a recipe calls for a refrigerator rise of twelve hours to five days, wait closer to five days.

❧ Use a bit more Gluten-Free Bread Flour (page 8) for shaping. All the yeast bread recipes in this book begin with a relatively wet dough (even the lower-hydration recipes, such as bagels) for one reason: to make them easier to shape without too much fear of drying out the dough. Just be sure to use a light touch when shaping, which will prevent the dough from absorbing too much of the extra sprinkling flour.

My bread looks okay, but it's bland.

❧ If it is a lean bread, most of its flavor comes from yeast development, which happens during a long, slow rise in the refrigerator. Next time, try allowing for a longer first rise in the refrigerator.

❧ As many times as I have made yeast bread, there are still times when I simply neglected to add salt. Even when it's a recipe that I had long ago perfected and have made countless times. Sometimes, I just forget to add salt. Sadly, bread without salt is bread for the trash heap.

My pastry didn't rise much, even though I did all the "turns" you recommend.

❧ Did you process your butter until it was the size of small peas? Most recipes for biscuits and pastry will direct readers to cut the butter into the dry ingredients "until the mixture resembles small peas." That is *not* what I recommend. Biscuits rise for two reasons: because of the chemical leaveners in the recipe (e.g., baking powder and baking soda), and because of the architecture. The cold chunks of butter are surrounded by flour. When the raw pastries hit the heat of the oven, the butter expands and swells the flour around it, creating rise and flakiness. If your butter is the size of small peas, it is much more likely to merely melt into its surroundings without putting any pressure on the flour to puff and become flaky. A bonus of using large, flattened chunks of butter is that your dough will be less sensitive to being handled. The heat of your hands may melt the chunks of butter a bit, but when the dough is chilled again after shaping, it will firm back up and should still create the proper architecture.

🌿 Were your ingredients cold? See above for why that matters so much.

🌿 Was your baking powder and/or baking soda fresh? Chemical leaveners should be used within their freshness dates, and within 4 to 6 months of being opened, regardless of freshness date. After that point, they become much less effective.

I don't have or don't like [X ingredient]. Can I still make the recipe?

🌿 I'm afraid, except as otherwise indicated, I have not tested these recipes with any substitutions. As much as I would like to be able to accommodate every food intolerance, allergy, and taste-preference, it isn't possible. But, as always, I hope you'll feel free to experiment. You are the one who knows best what it's like to bake for yourself and your family!

🌿 That said, please see my note on page 10 about a dairy-free suggestion for how to make something like my Gluten-Free Bread Flour. It doesn't behave quite the same, but it is possible to approximate the results!

I don't have a stand mixer, but I want the smooth dough that you say requires one.

🌿 Well, well, well. I *may* just have some good news for you. I recently discovered that there are dough hook attachments for some hand mixers. I purchased the dough hook attachments for the five-speed "ultra power" KitchenAid hand mixer (available online), and experimented. In other words, I took one for the team. And I'm pleased to report similar results to my stand mixer with the dough hook attachment!

🌿 Some tips and disclaimers before you go shopping: I have not tested any other manufacturers' hand mixer with dough hook attachments, although many others also have dough hooks available. I cannot guarantee that repeated use of the dough hook attachments with heavy bread dough will not burn out your hand mixer's motor. Be sure to use a large, deep bowl that is somehow prevented from slipping around on the counter as you use the mixer (try a moist tea towel under the bowl). First, mix the dough ingredients together with a large spoon or spatula before you begin kneading with the dough hooks. The dough will climb up the hooks. Just keep mixing, and periodically stop the mixer, allow the dough to fall off the hooks, and begin again at another location on the dough. For best results, spray the dough hooks with cooking oil spray before using them.

I want to bake my bread in a bread machine, but your recipe instructions don't tell me how.

❧ I do not own, use, or recommend use of a bread machine for a number of reasons. First, bread machines vary significantly from brand to brand, so one set of instructions would be woefully insufficient. Second, I find that even the "best" bread machines yield inconsistent results. Third, even bread machines that make a horizontal loaf make an odd-shaped loaf, and clearly cannot make shaped breads. Finally, baking yeast bread should not require an expensive, bulky, single-use piece of kitchen equipment. It is not precious or unattainable. It's absolutely within your reach. And you can do it without much time or even much attention—particularly with the recipes in this book, which nearly all require a long, slow, first rise in the refrigerator.

Your recipes don't calculate nutrition facts. I need to know all the information I possibly can about the nutrition content of everything I make!

❧ You can calculate the nutrition facts for every recipe on this site with any of the nutrition calculators available on the Internet. Unfortunately, I do not have the resources available to me to do all of the calculations for you, but rest assured that they are just a few clicks away!

❧ Please see the Resources section of this book (pages 269–271) for suggested sites for online nutrition calculation.

SHOESTRING SAVINGS

GLUTEN-FREE PACKAGED BREAD IS MUCH MORE WIDELY available today than, well, than I ever thought it would be. Yes, it is of varying levels of quality and accessibility, but overall I am thrilled that I am able to purchase ready-made gluten-free bread. The very fact that it is as available as it is means that we are making serious progress. However (this is a book about making your own gluten-free bread—you knew there had to be a "however"!), much of what you can buy ready-made is significantly more expensive than anything you can make at home, and often it simply cannot compete with the taste of the breads in this book. Following are a few ways in which you will enjoy Shoestring Savings when you make your own gluten-free bread with the recipes in this book.

First, when it comes to loaves of bread like those in Chapter 4, you have to be sure to compare like to like. For example, a loaf of Lean Crusty White Sandwich Bread (page 43) costs about $5.68 to make, and a comparable type loaf of Udi's packaged bread costs around $6.15 to buy. But when you take into account the diminutive size of a loaf of packaged gluten-free bread, as compared to the full-size loaf that you made yourself, the Shoestring loaf costs 19¢ an ounce to Udi's 51¢ an ounce. The Lean Crusty Whole-Grain Bread (page 55) costs about 20¢ an ounce to make. To buy it? A whopping 67¢ an ounce. That's more than three times as expensive!

Second, when you make your own bread at home, you'll have exactly what you want. No settling for a plain packaged dinner roll when what you really want is a pure sourdough dinner roll, such as the Levain Dinner Rolls (page 97). In fact, almost every single pure sourdough recipe in Chapter 5 is nearly without equal in the world of packaged gluten-free breads. And when there is an exception, such as the Pain au Levain (page 91), the price is fully double for a packaged loaf.

Third, the single-serve shaped breads in Chapter 6 are also quite a good argument for baking bread at home. Examples include the English Muffins (page 118) that cost about 36¢ each to make and a full $1.25 each to buy packaged, the Plain (or Seeded) Bagels (page 123) that cost about 75¢ each to make and a full $1.74 each to buy, and Pita Bread (page 133) that costs about 42¢ each to make and $1.50 each to buy.

Fourth, and perhaps most compelling, are the flatbreads in Chapter 7. Pizza crust is one of the easiest gluten-free breads to make at home (particularly with the recipes in this book), and also the most cost-effective: the Thin-Crust Pizza Dough (page 189) is about 20¢ per ounce to make and 80¢ per ounce to buy. But even more significant than the dramatic price difference is the quality of the product. If you want fresh-tasting gluten-free pizza, you have to make it yourself at home. And when you see just how easy it is to make your whole house smell like the best pizzeria in town, you'll do it every week (every single Friday night is pizza night in my house). Flour Tortillas (page 203) are another good example, coming in at about 13¢ each to make and $1.11 each to buy. That's almost nine times as expensive to buy as to make!

Next, pastries, such as the Strawberry Scones (page 225) will cost three times as much to buy as to make, and the taste and quality of freshly baked pastries simply cannot be beat. Carrot Muffins are about 16¢ per ounce to make and 67¢ per ounce to buy. Plus, packaged gluten-free baked goods are almost always sold frozen, as they simply do not sell often enough for stores to justify selling them fresh. Can you even compare fresh to frozen?

And finally, the method of baking gluten bread that we employ in this book is, by its very nature, cost-effective. Our lack of reliance on a bread machine makes the overall cost more affordable. And although a stand mixer is expensive to buy, it is not essential to making the recipes in this book. Plus, it turns out that a hand mixer with dough hooks attached is happily a fine substitute for the more expensive stand mixer (see page 27). And a hand mixer (or even a stand mixer) has many more potential uses than a bread machine.

3 SHAPING BREAD DOUGH

EVERYTHING YOU NEED TO KNOW TO CREATE EVERY SHAPE OF BREAD IN THIS BOOK

General Shaping Tips

UNLESS OTHERWISE NOTED, ALWAYS BEGIN ON A WELL-FLOURED surface with floured hands.

❧ With the help of an oiled bench scraper, keep moving the dough as you shape it, particularly if it begins to stick to the surface or your hands. The process of kneading the dough in this book will be done using the scrape-and-fold method: Scrape the dough off the floured surface with the bench scraper, then fold the dough over itself. Sprinkle the dough lightly with flour, scrape the dough up again, and fold it over itself again. Repeat scraping and folding in this manner until the dough has become smoother.

❧ Keep the outside of the dough and the surface covered in a light coating of flour as you shape the dough. Handle the dough with a light touch to avoid kneading the flour into the dough, which might dry it out and result in a tight, unpleasant crumb.

❧ It bears repeating: A light touch is the key. Repeat that to yourself as a mantra as you first learn to shape this bread dough. It's the most important rule in shaping. More technique, less muscle.

❧ You'll notice that the recipes do not include instructions to allow dough that has been rising in the refrigerator to come to room temperature before shaping. Always begin with cold dough when shaping the dough in this book. It is much easier to shape.

❧ If you are frustrated that your dough isn't as easy to shape as you'd like because it always seems sticky, allow it a longer rise in the refrigerator before shaping. It just takes some more planning, but no more effort. If a recipe says to allow the dough to rise for anything from 12 hours to 5 days in the refrigerator, wait closer to 5 days.

Instructions for Creating Every Shape of Bread

Shaping a boule

❧ On a well-floured surface, flatten the dough into a disk, then pull the edges toward the center of the disk and secure the edges together by pressing them between your thumb and forefinger.

❧ Turn the dough over so that the gathered edges are on the bottom and cup your whole hands around the dough, to coax it into a round shape.

❧ Rotate the dough in a circular motion with cupped hands, to perfect the shape.

Shaping small round rolls

❧ On a well-floured surface, flatten the dough into a disk, then pull the edges toward the center of the disk and secure the edges together by pressing them between your thumb and forefinger.

❧ Turn the dough over so that the gathered edges are on the bottom and cup your whole hands around the dough, to coax it into a round shape.

❧ Place the round of dough on a lightly floured surface and cup only one palm around the dough with the side of your hand resting on the counter (the side of your hand nearest your pinkie). Maintaining contact between the side of your hand and the surface, begin to move your hand in a circular motion while gently coaxing the edges of the dough upward (toward the top of the round) with the tips of your fingers.

❧ Slash the dough with a sharp knife or lame held at a 45 degree angle to the dough.

Shaping batards

❧ On a well-floured surface, flatten the dough into a disk, then pull the edges toward the center of the disk and secure the edges together by pressing them between your thumb and forefinger.

❧ Turn the dough over so that the gathered edges are on the bottom and cup your whole hands around the dough, to coax it into a round shape.

❧ Pull the dough gently at opposite ends with your whole hands, in opposite directions, to create an oblong shape.

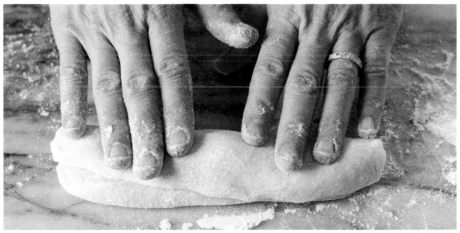

Shaping baguettes and hoagie rolls

❧ On a well-floured surface, pat the dough into a rectangle about ½ inch thick. For a baguette, the rectangle should be about 12 inches long. For a hoagie roll, the rectangle should be about 5 inches long.

❧ Fold the rectangle along the length from bottom and top, each fold halfway up the width of the rectangle. Fold the now smaller rectangle in half, each side just folded over one another.

❧ Roll the dough back and forth on the lightly floured surface to seal the edges and to elongate it slightly until the dough is nearly 16 inches long for baguettes, and about 7 inches long for hoagie rolls.

❧ Baguettes may be set to rise in a couche, as they are made with a lean

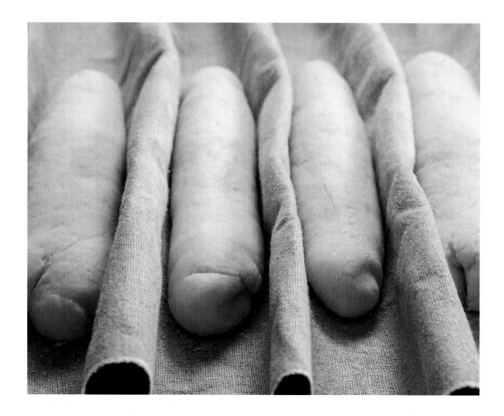

dough. Flour the couche generously and place one baguette on it length-wise. Pleat the fabric on each side of the baguette, all along the length of the couche, to create a wall on either side of the baguette taller than the baguette will ultimately rise. This will coax the baguette to rise up instead of out, and to maintain its shape. Cover the couche with plastic wrap (it should not need to be oiled as it will only touch the tops of the pleats in the couche, not the bread itself) as the baguettes rise. Once the baguettes have completed their rise, slide them gently off the couche and onto a pizza peel before slashing and sliding into a hot oven.

Shaping sandwich bread

❧ On a well-floured surface, pat the dough into a rectangle about 7 inches long by 5 inches wide.

❧ Fold both 7-inch sides of the dough about 2 inches in toward the center, and then roll up the dough from one 5-inch side toward the other until the dough is completely coiled.

✤ Roll the dough gently back and forth on the lightly floured surface, to seal the edges. Tuck the short ends slightly under the loaf, if necessary to fit the loaf in the loaf pan. Lift the shaped loaf carefully into the loaf pan, seam side down.

Shaping bagels

✤ Bagels can be shaped either by coiling a rope of dough into a circular shape, or by poking a hole in the center of a round of dough. For either method, begin with a well-floured surface.

✤ To shape a bagel with a rope of dough, roll a piece of dough (pressing down and out with your palms) into a rope about 8 inches long. Shape it into a bagel by joining the ends of the rope together, one overlapping the other by about 1 inch. Press to seal together. This is the method pictured on page 39.

✤ To shape a bagel by poking a hole in the center of a round of dough, follow the directions for shaping a small round roll, and then poke a hole with a well-floured finger vertically into the center of the round. Move your finger in a circular motion to widen the hole so that it does not close during proofing.

✤ Before placing a bagel on a parchment-lined baking sheet to rise after shaping, either flour the parchment paper generously or spray it with cooking oil. The flour or the cooking oil on the paper will keep the bagel from sticking to the paper as it rises, and allow you to lift it off the baking sheet cleanly before boiling it (see Plain [or Seeded] Bagels, page 123).

Rolling out pizza dough

✤ Place the dough onto a well-floured piece of unbleached parchment paper and dust it with flour. Pat it into a disk with your fingers.

✤ With a floured French rolling pin, roll the dough flat into a round until it is about ¼ inch thicker than what you would like it to be, sprinkling lightly with flour if the dough gets sticky. Shift the dough around frequently as you work.

✤ To create a raised edge around the perimeter of the dough that will serve as a crust, place gentle but firm pressure with well-floured hands from the center of the dough out toward the edges. Flatten the dough from the center out, stopping about 1 inch short of the perimeter.

Braiding bread

❧ Regardless of how many strands you are braiding, flour a sheet of unbleached parchment paper and place 10-inch-long strands of dough lengthwise on the paper. The strands of dough should be smooth and sprinkled with flour. Pinch all the strands together at one end. Once the bread dough is shaped, you will slide the parchment, along with the dough, onto a baking surface.

❧ To braid a three-strand bread, beginning as close to the sealed edge as possible, cross one outside strand over the center strand. That strand becomes the new center strand. Cross the other outside strand over the new center strand. Repeat the process, alternating sides, until you reach the end of the strands and pinch the ends together, and press both ends toward the center so that the loaf is thicker in the center.

❧ To braid a four-strand bread, such as that pictured here, first mentally assign numbers 1, 2, 3, and 4 to the four positions the strands occupy on the surface (not to the strands themselves). Beginning as close to the sealed edge as possible, cross the strands over one another in the following pattern (remember that numbers refer to position, and not actual strands). Repeat the pattern until you reach the end, then pinch the ends together and press both ends toward the center so the loaf is thicker toward the center:

strand 4 over strand 2

strand 1 over strand 3

strand 2 over strand 3

4 LOAVES OF BREAD

EVERYTHING FROM LEAN CRUSTY WHITE AND WHOLE-GRAIN BREADS TO ENRICHED CINNAMON SWIRL AND CHEESE BREADS

LEAN CRUSTY WHITE SANDWICH BREAD
MAKES 1 LOAF

T HIS IS THE BREAD RECIPE THAT STARTED IT ALL. WELL, ACTUALLY
this is the bread recipe that I had imagined in my mind's eye long before
it ever came into being. This recipe is good clean gluten-free fun to make,
and pure joy to eat. Beginning with a starter makes an enormous difference.
So does a long, slow first rise in the refrigerator. Follow the recipe, dutifully
weighing your ingredients and faithfully keeping pace with the technique,
and you shall be rewarded with a simple, lean (no eggs, no butter, no other enrichments), crusty and intensely flavorful loaf of gluten-free bread. And dare I
say it? You'll never go back to the bread you were eating before. It would simply be either depressing or terrifying to go back. You might even be tempted
to draw a line in the sand at the baking and eating of this bread, and allow it
to come to define your life as "before" and "after." Okay, I'll stop.

STARTER
1¼ cups (175 g) Gluten-Free Bread Flour (page 8)
2 teaspoons (6 g) instant yeast
1½ tablespoons (18 g) sugar
1 cup warm water (about 95°F)

DOUGH
2¼ cups (315 g) Gluten-Free Bread Flour (page 8), plus more for sprinkling
½ teaspoon cream of tartar
2 teaspoons (12 g) kosher salt
1 tablespoon honey
¼ cup plus 2 tablespoons water, at room temperature
Starter

To make the starter, place all the starter ingredients in a medium-size bowl,
and whisk until well combined. The mixture will be thick and shapeless.
Cover and set the bowl aside in a warm, draft-free location to rise until doubled (about 40 minutes).

Once the starter has finished rising, make the dough. Place the flour,
cream of tartar, and salt in the bowl of your stand mixer, and use a handheld

whisk to combine well. Add the honey, water, and risen starter to the bowl, and mix on low speed with the dough hook until combined. Raise the mixer speed to medium and knead for about 5 minutes. The dough will be quite sticky but should be smooth and stretchy. Spray a silicone spatula lightly with cooking oil spray, and scrape down the sides of the bowl. Transfer the dough to a lightly oiled bowl or proofing bucket large enough for the dough to rise to double its size, and cover with an oiled piece of plastic wrap (or the oiled top to your proofing bucket). Place the dough in the refrigerator for at least 12 hours and up to 5 days.

On baking day, grease an 8½ by 4½-inch loaf pan and set it aside. Remove the dough from the refrigerator and turn it out onto a lightly floured surface. Sprinkle the dough with additional bread flour and, using a lightly oiled bench scraper, turn the dough over on itself until it begins to become smoother, sprinkling with flour when the dough becomes sticky (about 5 minutes).

To shape the dough, follow the instructions on page 36 for shaping sandwich bread. Carefully lift the shaped dough into the prepared loaf pan, seam side down. Sprinkle the top of the dough with a thin layer of flour to form a cloak that the dough will rise into. Cover the loaf pan with a piece of lightly oiled plastic wrap, and place in a warm, draft-free location until nearly doubled in size (about 1½ hours).

Once the dough has finished rising, remove the plastic wrap and sprinkle the top of the loaf lightly with flour once more. Slash down the center of the loaf at a 45-degree angle and about ¼ inch deep, using a lame or very sharp knife. Place the pan in the center of a cold oven, and turn the heat to 350°F. Bake for 30 minutes before removing the loaf from the loaf pan, placing it on a rimmed baking sheet, and placing it back in the oven. Continue to bake until the loaf is lightly golden brown, sounds hollow when thumped on the underside, and the internal temperature reaches about 195°F on an instant-read thermometer (about 10 minutes more).

Remove from the oven and place the loaf on a wire rack to cool for at least 20 minutes before slicing and serving.

SOFT WHITE SANDWICH BREAD
MAKES 1 LOAF

THIS BREAD IS THE HOME-BAKED EQUIVALENT OF WONDER BREAD. But did you know that Wonder Bread comes presliced because it would be too soft to slice into otherwise? Well, this loaf is then, obviously, better than Wonder Bread. It is soft and enriched in all the right ways, but you can slice it however you like—whenever you like.

INGREDIENTS

3¾ cups (525 g) Gluten-Free Bread Flour (page 8), plus more for sprinkling

40 grams nonfat dry milk, ground finely in a blender or food processor

1⅔ teaspoons (5 g) instant yeast

2 tablespoons honey

½ cup plus 2 tablespoons plain whole-milk yogurt (not Greek), at room temperature

¾ cup plus 1½ teaspoons warm water (about 95°F)

5 tablespoons (70 g) unsalted butter, at room temperature

2 teaspoons (12 g) kosher salt

In the bowl of your stand mixer, place the flour, dry milk, and yeast, and use a handheld whisk to combine well. Add the honey, yogurt, water, butter, and salt, and mix on low speed with the dough hook until combined. Raise the mixer speed to medium and knead for about 5 minutes. It will still be quite sticky and the dough will begin to climb up the dough hook, but it should be smooth and stretchy. Spray a silicone spatula lightly with cooking oil spray, and scrape down the sides of the bowl. Transfer the dough to a lightly oiled bowl or proofing bucket large enough for the dough to rise to double its size, spray the top of the dough with cooking oil spray, and cover with an oiled piece of plastic wrap (or the oiled top to your proofing bucket). Place the dough in the refrigerator for at least 12 hours and up to 3 days. After 3 days, the flavor of the enriched dough begins to change.

On baking day, grease an 8½ by 4½-inch loaf pan and set it aside. Remove the dough from the refrigerator and turn it out onto a lightly floured surface. Knead until smoother as described in the General Shaping Tips in Chapter 3.

To shape the dough, follow the instructions on page 36 for shaping

sandwich bread. Carefully lift the shaped dough into the prepared loaf pan, seam side down. Sprinkle the top of the dough with a thin layer of flour to form a cloak that the dough will rise into. Cover the loaf pan with a piece of lightly oiled plastic wrap, and place in a warm, draft-free location until nearly doubled in size (about 1 hour).

Once the dough has finished rising, remove the plastic wrap and sprinkle the top of the loaf lightly with flour once more. Slash down the center of the loaf at a 45-degree angle and about ¼ inch deep, using a lame or very sharp knife. Place the pan in the center of a cold oven, and turn the heat to 350°F. Bake for 30 minutes before removing the loaf from the loaf pan, placing it on a rimmed baking sheet, and placing it back in the oven. Continue to bake until the loaf is golden brown, sounds hollow when thumped on the underside, and the internal temperature reaches about 195°F on an instant-read thermometer (about 15 minutes more). The crust will be dark and will soften as the bread cools.

Remove from the oven and place the loaf on a wire rack to cool for at least 20 minutes before slicing and serving.

CINNAMON SWIRL BREAD
MAKES 1 LOAF

CINNAMON SWIRL BREAD IS THE STUFF OF SUNDAY MORNING dreams. It's perfect with a melting pat of butter and makes the most delectable French toast. The trick to getting it right is to knead the cinnamon-sugar filling into ⅓ of the dough, and then roll it together with the plain dough into a swirl. Pay careful attention to the directions that show you how to shape the dough and how to get it into the pan seamlessly.

STARTER
1¼ cups (175 g) Gluten-Free Bread Flour (page 8)
2 teaspoons (6 g) instant yeast
1½ tablespoons (18 g) sugar
1 cup warm water (about 95°F)

DOUGH
2¼ cups (315 g) Gluten-Free Bread Flour (page 8), plus more for sprinkling
½ teaspoon cream of tartar
2 teaspoons (12 g) kosher salt
1 tablespoon honey
¼ cup plus 2 tablespoons warm water (about 95°F)
Starter

FILLING
3 tablespoons (36 g) granulated sugar
3 tablespoons (41 g) packed light brown sugar
2 teaspoons ground cinnamon

To make the starter, place all the starter ingredients in a medium-size bowl, and whisk until well combined. The mixture will be thick and shapeless. Cover and set the bowl aside in a warm, draft-free location to rise until doubled (about 40 minutes). Once the starter has finished rising, make the dough. Place the flour, cream of tartar, and salt in the bowl of your stand mixer, and use a handheld whisk to combine well. Add the honey, water, and risen starter to the bowl, and mix on low speed with the dough hook until combined. Raise the mixer speed to medium and knead for about 5 minutes. The dough will be quite sticky, but should be smooth and stretchy. Spray a silicone spatula lightly with cooking oil spray, and scrape down the sides of the bowl. Transfer the dough to a lightly oiled bowl or proofing bucket large enough for the dough to rise to double its size, and cover with an oiled piece of plastic wrap (or the oiled top to your proofing bucket). Place the dough in the refrigerator for at least 12 hours and up to 5 days.

On baking day, grease an 8½ by 4½-inch loaf pan and set it aside. Place all the filling ingredients in a small bowl, mix well, and set aside. Remove the dough from the refrigerator and turn it out onto a lightly floured surface. Knead until smoother as described in the General Shaping Tips in Chapter 3.

To shape the dough, with floured hands, pull off about ⅓ of the dough. On a well-floured surface, knead in the cinnamon-sugar filling into the dough until well incorporated. Dusting with flour when sticky, roll the cinnamon-sugared dough out into a 7- by 12-inch rectangle. Spray a piece of unbleached parchment paper with cooking oil spray, place the remaining ⅔ of the plain dough on it, and shape and roll the plain dough into a 7 by 12 inch rectangle. Place the cinnamon-sugared rectangle on top of the plain dough rectangle, and match up the corners. Starting on a short side and using the oiled parchment paper to guide the dough, roll it tightly away from your body, pressing the seam to seal as you go, finishing with the seam side down. Place a greased 8½ by 4½-inch loaf pan on top of the loaf and flip the loaf pan over with the loaf of bread inside, using the parchment paper to guide the loaf into the pan. Dust the top of the loaf with flour and cover the pan with a lightly greased piece of plastic wrap. Place in a warm, draft-free location until doubled in size (about 1½ hours).

Once the dough has finished rising, remove the plastic wrap and sprinkle the top of the loaf lightly with flour once more. Slash down the center of the loaf at a 45-degree angle and about ¼ inch deep, using a lame or very sharp knife. Place the pan in the center of a cold oven, and turn the heat to 350°F. Bake for 30 minutes before removing the loaf from the loaf pan, placing it on a rimmed baking sheet, and placing it back in the oven. Continue to bake until the loaf is golden brown, sounds hollow when thumped on the underside, and the internal temperature reaches about 195°F on an instant-read thermometer (about 20 minutes more). Remove from the oven and place the loaf on a wire rack to cool for at least 20 minutes before slicing and serving.

BRIOCHE BREAD
MAKES 1 LOAF

BRIOCHE IS THE ULTIMATE IN ENRICHED BREADS. RICH WITH BUT-ter and eggs, it rises heartily and is one of the most fragrant breads in this book. Try adding some finely grated lemon zest to the dough after adding the starter, for an even more fragrant, flavorful loaf.

STARTER
1 cup (140 g) Gluten-Free Bread Flour (page 8)
2⅔ teaspoons (8 g) instant yeast
1 tablespoon (12 g) sugar
½ cup warm milk (about 95°F) (not nonfat)
¼ cup plus 2 tablespoons warm water (about 95°F)

DOUGH
3 cups (420 g) Gluten-Free Bread Flour (page 8), plus more for sprinkling
1 teaspoon (6 g) kosher salt
1½ tablespoons honey
3 large eggs, at room temperature, beaten
11 tablespoons (154 g) unsalted butter, at room temperature
Starter

To make the starter, place all the starter ingredients in a medium-size bowl, and whisk until well combined. The mixture will be thick and shapeless. Cover and set the bowl aside in a warm, draft-free location to rise until doubled (about 30 minutes).

Once the starter has finished rising, make the dough. Place the flour and salt in the bowl of your stand mixer, and use a handheld whisk to combine well. Add the honey, eggs, butter, and risen starter to the bowl, and mix on low speed with the dough hook until combined. Raise the mixer speed to medium and knead for about 5 minutes. The dough will be quite sticky but should be smooth and stretchy. Spray a silicone spatula lightly with cooking oil spray, and scrape down the sides of the bowl. Transfer the dough to a lightly oiled bowl or proofing bucket large enough for the dough to rise to double its size, and cover with an oiled piece of plastic wrap (or the oiled top to your proofing bucket). Place the dough in the refrigerator for at least 12 hours and up to 3 days. After 3 days, the flavor of this highly enriched dough begins to change.

On baking day, grease an 8½ by 4½-inch loaf pan and set it aside. Remove the dough from the refrigerator and turn it out onto a lightly floured surface. Knead until smoother as described in the General Shaping Tips in Chapter 3.

To shape the dough, follow the instructions on pages 36–37 for shaping sandwich bread. Carefully lift the shaped dough into the prepared loaf pan, seam side down. Sprinkle the top of the dough with a thin layer of flour to form a cloak that the dough will rise into. Cover the loaf pan with a piece of lightly oiled plastic wrap, and place in a warm, draft-free location until nearly doubled in size (about 1 hour).

Once the dough has finished rising, remove the plastic wrap and sprinkle the top of the loaf lightly with flour once more. Slash down the center of the loaf at a 45-degree angle and about ¼ inch deep, using a lame or very sharp knife. Place the pan in the center of a cold oven, and turn the heat to 350°F. Bake for 30 minutes before removing the loaf from the loaf pan, placing it on a rimmed baking sheet, and placing it back in the oven. Continue to bake until the loaf is lightly golden brown, sounds hollow when thumped on the underside, and the internal temperature reaches about 195°F on an instant-read thermometer (about 15 minutes more).

Remove from the oven and place the loaf on a wire rack to cool for at least 20 minutes before slicing and serving.

CHEESE BREAD
MAKES 1 LARGE ROUND LOAF

YOU CAN SEE FOR YOURSELF WHAT AN EMBARRASSMENT OF RICHES this bread is. It needs absolutely no extra adornments to be enjoyed. Instead of slicing it in the traditional way, by cross section, I simply cut off hunks of this bread. Whoever gets the piece with the most melted cheese on top feels like the birthday girl with the biggest slice of cake (and the most frosting).

INGREDIENTS

3½ cups (490 g) Gluten-Free Bread Flour (page 8), plus more for sprinkling

40 grams (about ⅔ cup) nonfat dry milk, ground finely in a blender or food processor

2⅓ teaspoons (7 g) instant yeast

1⅓ teaspoons (9 g) kosher salt

2 tablespoons honey

2½ tablespoons (35 g) unsalted butter, melted and cooled

1⅓ cups warm water (about 95°F)

6 ounces Cheddar cheese, shredded

In the bowl of your stand mixer, place the flour, dry milk, and yeast, and use a handheld whisk to combine well. Add the salt, and whisk to combine. Add the honey, butter, and water, and mix on low speed with the dough hook until combined. Raise the mixer speed to medium and knead for about 5 minutes. It will still be quite sticky and the dough will begin to climb up the dough hook, but it should be smooth and stretchy. Spray a silicone spatula lightly with cooking oil spray, and scrape down the sides of the bowl. Transfer the dough to a lightly oiled bowl or proofing bucket large enough for the dough to rise to double its size, spray the top of the dough with cooking oil spray, and cover with an oiled piece of plastic wrap (or the oiled top to your proofing bucket). Place the dough in the refrigerator for at least 12 hours and up to 3 days. Enriched dough like this should not be refrigerated raw for more than 3 days.

On baking day, sprinkle an 8-inch round banetton or proofing basket liberally with flour and set it aside. Line a rimmed baking sheet with unbleached

parchment paper and set it aside. Remove the dough from the refrigerator and turn it out onto a lightly floured surface. Knead until smoother as described in the General Shaping Tips in Chapter 3. Gently fold and knead in 5 ounces of the cheese, sprinkling with flour again if the dough becomes sticky. Follow the instructions on page 32 for shaping a boule on a flat, well-floured surface and place, seam side up, in the prepared proofing basket. Place the banetton in a plastic bag and loosely secure the end. Place in a warm, draft-free location until the dough has doubled in size.

Once the bread is fully risen, working carefully so as not to deflate it, invert the dough onto the prepared baking sheet, seam side down. Sprinkle the top of the dough lightly with flour and, using a lame or sharp knife at a 45-degree angle, slash a crisscross pattern of four slashes, each ¼ inch deep. Scatter the remaining 1 ounce of cheese in the slashes.

Place the baking sheet in a cold oven and turn the heat to 350°F. Bake until the internal temperature of the loaf is 185°F on an instant-read thermometer (about 45 minutes). Tent the loaf with foil if it begins to brown too quickly. Turn off the oven, prop open the oven door, and allow the bread to sit in the oven as it cools. This will help the bread maintain its shape, as it is a very moist loaf. Remove the bread after 15 minutes, or once the oven temperature reaches 150°F.

Place the loaf on a wire rack to cool for at least 20 minutes before slicing and serving.

LEAN CRUSTY WHOLE-GRAIN BREAD
MAKES 1 LOAF BREAD

I F I COULD, I WOULD CALL THIS BREAD "WHOLE WHEAT" BREAD. BUT that would just be confusing. Adding this particular blend of teff flour and sweet white sorghum flour really gives this lean bread that satisfying wheat-like bite—and all the extra nutrition that goes along with it.

STARTER
¾ cup (105 g) Gluten-Free Bread Flour (page 8)
¾ cup (105 g) Whole-Grain Gluten-Free Flour (page 10)
2 teaspoons (6 g) instant yeast
1½ tablespoons (18 g) sugar
1 cup warm water (about 95°F)

DOUGH
2 cups (280 g) Gluten-Free Bread Flour (page 8), plus more for sprinkling
½ teaspoon cream of tartar
2 teaspoons (12 g) kosher salt
1 tablespoon honey
3 tablespoons (42 g) unsalted butter, at room temperature
Starter

To make the starter, place all the starter ingredients in a medium-size bowl, and whisk until well combined. The mixture will be thick and shapeless. Cover and set the bowl aside in a warm, draft-free location to rise until doubled (about 40 minutes).

Once the starter has finished rising, make the dough. Place the flour, cream of tartar, and salt in the bowl of your stand mixer, and use a hand-held whisk to combine well. Add the honey, butter, and the risen starter to the bowl, and mix on low speed with the dough hook until combined. Raise the mixer speed to medium and knead for about 5 minutes. The dough will be quite sticky, but should be smooth and stretchy. Spray a silicone spatula lightly with cooking oil spray, and scrape down the sides of the bowl. Transfer the dough to a lightly oiled bowl or proofing bucket large enough for the dough to rise to double its size, and cover with an oiled piece of plastic wrap (or the oiled top to your proofing bucket). Place the dough in the refrigerator for at least 12 hours and up to 5 days.

On baking day, grease an 8½ by 4½-inch loaf pan and set it aside. Remove the dough from the refrigerator and turn it out onto a lightly floured surface. Knead until smoother as described in the General Shaping Tips in Chapter 3.

To shape the dough, follow the instructions on page 36 for shaping sandwich bread. Carefully lift the shaped dough into the prepared loaf pan, seam side down. Sprinkle the top of the dough with a thin layer of flour to form a cloak into which the dough will rise. Cover the loaf pan with a piece of lightly oiled plastic wrap, and place in a warm, draft-free location until nearly doubled in size (about 1½ hours).

Once the dough has finished rising, remove the plastic wrap and sprinkle the top of the loaf lightly with flour once more. Slash down the center of the loaf at a 45-degree angle and about ¼ inch deep, using a lame or very sharp knife. Place the pan in the center of a cold oven, and turn the heat to 350°F. Bake for 30 minutes before removing the loaf from the loaf pan, placing it on a rimmed baking sheet, and placing it back in the oven. Continue to bake until the loaf is lightly golden brown, sounds hollow when thumped on the underside, and the internal temperature reaches about 195°F on an instant-read thermometer (about 10 minutes more).

Remove from the oven and place the loaf on a wire rack to cool for at least 20 minutes before slicing and serving.

POTATO BREAD
MAKES 1 LOAF

I HAVE NEVER IN MY LIFE MADE A LOAF OF POTATO BREAD, GLUTEN-free or otherwise, for which I cooked a separate batch of mashed potatoes. I simply add about a half-dozen small potatoes to the batch when I am already boiling a whole bunch, and then set the extras aside, earmarked for another day soon. Then, when I'm ready to make this dough, I'm already halfway there. The boiled and mashed potatoes in this bread make the dough a bit stickier by nature than the standard recipe for lean bread, but they yield a more toothsome and moist result. Well worth it, no doubt.

STARTER
9 tablespoons (80 g) Gluten-Free Bread Flour (page 8)
1 teaspoon (3 g) instant yeast
¾ cup warm water (about 95°F)

DOUGH
3 cups (420 g) Gluten-Free Bread Flour (page 8), plus more for sprinkling
1⅔ teaspoons (5 g) instant yeast
2 teaspoons (12 g) kosher salt
1 tablespoon honey
1 cup boiled and mashed potatoes (about 6 small potatoes)
½ cup water, at room temperature
Starter

To make the starter, place all the starter ingredients in a medium-size bowl, and whisk until well combined. The mixture will be thick and shapeless. Cover and set the bowl aside in a warm, draft-free location to rise until doubled (about 30 minutes).

Once the starter has finished rising, make the dough. Place the flour and yeast in the bowl of your stand mixer, and use a handheld whisk to combine well. Add the salt, and whisk to combine. Add the honey, potatoes, water, and risen starter to the bowl, and mix on low speed with the dough hook until combined. Raise the mixer speed to medium and mix for about 5 minutes. The dough will be quite sticky, but should be mostly smooth and stretchy. Spray a silicone spatula lightly with cooking oil spray, and scrape down the sides of the bowl. Transfer the dough to a lightly oiled bowl or proofing bucket large enough for the dough to rise to double its size, and cover with an oiled piece of plastic wrap (or the oiled top to your proofing bucket). Place the dough in the refrigerator for at least 12 hours and up to 5 days.

On baking day, grease an 8½ by 4½-inch loaf pan and set it aside. Remove the dough from the refrigerator and turn it out onto a lightly floured surface. Knead until smoother as described in the General Shaping Tips in Chapter 3. This dough will be stickier by nature than other lean dough (e.g., Lean Crusty White Sandwich Bread, page 43).

To shape the dough, follow the instructions on page 36 for shaping sandwich bread. Carefully lift the shaped dough into the prepared loaf pan, seam side down. Sprinkle the top of the dough with a thin layer of flour to form a cloak that the dough will rise into. Cover the loaf pan with a piece of lightly oiled plastic wrap, and place in a warm, draft-free location until nearly doubled in size (about 1½ hours).

Once the dough has finished rising, remove the plastic wrap and sprinkle the top of the loaf lightly with flour once more. Slash down the center of the loaf at a 45-degree angle and about ¼ inch deep, using a lame or very sharp knife. Place the pan in the center of a cold oven, and turn the heat to 350°F. Bake for 30 minutes before removing the loaf from the loaf pan, placing it on a rimmed baking sheet, and placing it back in the oven. Continue to bake until the loaf is lightly golden brown, sounds hollow when thumped on the underside, and the internal temperature reaches about 195°F on an instant-read thermometer (about 15 minutes more).

Remove from the oven and place the loaf on a wire rack to cool for at least 20 minutes before slicing and serving.

JAPANESE MILK BREAD
MAKES 1 LOAF

THIS IS THE FIRST OF A NUMBER OF RECIPES IN THIS BOOK THAT begin with a water roux, which is just a cooked mixture of flour and water in about a 1:4 ratio. Using this magic mixture not only makes for a very soft bread with very little enrichment, it helps keep the bread fresher longer. The recipe will work just as well without going through the moment's extra work of dividing the dough in three parts, but the folds of this bread really make the otherwise somewhat ordinary loaf of bread seem truly extraordinary.

WATER ROUX
3 tablespoons (25 g) Gluten-Free Bread Flour (page 8)
½ cup water, at room temperature

DOUGH
3 cups (420 g) Gluten-Free Bread Flour (page 8), plus more for sprinkling
¼ teaspoon cream of tartar
¼ cup (50 g) sugar
1⅔ teaspoons (7 g) instant yeast
½ teaspoon (3 g) kosher salt
1 large egg, at room temperature
3 tablespoons (42 g) unsalted butter, at room temperature
Water Roux
¾ cup milk, at room temperature

To make the water roux, whisk together the flour and water in a small sauce-pan. Cook over medium-high heat, whisking constantly, until thickened. It is ready when the whisk leaves a visible trail as it moves through the roux (as pictured on page 60). Remove from the heat and allow to cool until no longer hot to the touch.

To make the dough, place the flour, cream of tartar, sugar, and yeast in the bowl of a stand mixer, and use a handheld whisk to combine well. Add the salt, and whisk to combine. Add the egg, butter, roux, and milk, and mix on low speed with the dough hook until the dry ingredients are incorporated into the wet. Raise the mixer speed to medium and mix for about 5 minutes.

The dough will be quite sticky but should be smooth and stretchy. Spray a silicone spatula lightly with cooking oil spray, and scrape down the sides of the bowl. Transfer the dough to a lightly oiled bowl or proofing bucket large enough for the dough to rise to double its size, and cover with an oiled piece of plastic wrap (or the oiled top to your proofing bucket). Place the dough in the refrigerator for at least 12 hours and up to 5 days.

On baking day, turn the dough out onto a lightly floured surface and divide it into three equal pieces. Dust each piece with flour, shape into a round, and then pat into a rectangle about ¾ inch thick. Fold each piece of dough in half. Place the folded pieces of dough side by side, seam side down, in the prepared pan. Sprinkle the top of the dough with a thin layer of flour to form a cloak that the dough will rise into. Cover the loaf pan with a piece of lightly oiled plastic wrap, and place in a warm, draft-free location until nearly doubled in size (about 1½ hours).

Once the dough has finished rising, remove the plastic wrap. Place the pan in the center of a cold oven, and turn the heat to 350°F. Bake for 25 minutes before removing the loaf from the loaf pan, placing it on a rimmed baking sheet, and placing it back in the oven. Turn down the oven temperature to 325°F and bake until the internal temperature is 185°F on an instant-read thermometer (another 15 to 20 minutes).

Remove from the oven and place the loaf on a wire rack to cool for at least 20 minutes before slicing and serving.

BRAIDED CHALLAH BREAD
MAKES 1 LARGE LOAF

I TRIED MAKING BRAIDED CHALLAH BREAD EVERY WHICH WAY, AND this was one of the last recipes in the book that I felt comfortable making final. A water roux became essential to making a braided and enriched bread that is both beautiful and moist. This recipe strikes the right balance. Too many eggs have the paradoxical effect of making bread dry, as the egg white has a tendency to remove moisture from the dough. The bread is dairy, so keep that tidbit in mind if you are hosting an observant kosher meat meal. For best results with this recipe, build your Gluten-Free Bread Flour (page 8) using the Make-It-Simpler All-Purpose Gluten-Free Flour (page 9).

WATER ROUX
3 tablespoons (25 g) Gluten-Free Bread Flour (page 8)
½ cup water, at room temperature

DOUGH
3 cups (420 g) Gluten-Free Bread Flour (page 8), plus more for sprinkling
¼ teaspoon cream of tartar
3 tablespoons (36 g) sugar
1⅔ teaspoons (7 g) instant yeast 2.7 teaspoons
1 teaspoon (6 g) kosher salt
2 large eggs plus 1 large egg yolk at room temperature, beaten
5 tablespoons (70 g) unsalted butter, at room temperature
½ cup milk, at room temperature
Water roux
Egg wash (1 large egg, at room temperature, beaten with 1 tablespoon water)
1 tablespoon toasted sesame seeds
1 tablespoon poppy seeds

To make the water roux, whisk together the flour and water in a small saucepan. Cook over medium-high heat, whisking constantly, until thickened. It is ready when the whisk leaves a visible trail as it moves through the roux. Remove from the heat and allow to cool until no longer hot to the touch.

To make the dough, place the flour, cream of tartar, sugar, and yeast in the bowl of a stand mixer, and use a handheld whisk to combine well. Add the salt, and whisk to combine. Add the eggs, butter, milk, and roux, and mix on low speed with the dough hook until the dry ingredients are incorporated into the wet. Raise the mixer speed to high and mix again for about 5 minutes. The dough will be quite sticky but should be smooth and stretchy. Spray a silicone spatula lightly with cooking oil spray, and scrape down the sides of the bowl. Transfer the dough to a lightly oiled bowl or proofing bucket large enough for the dough to rise to double its size, and cover with an oiled piece of plastic wrap (or the oiled top to your proofing bucket). Place the dough in the refrigerator for at least 12 hours and up to 5 days.

On baking day, line a rimmed baking sheet with unbleached parchment paper and set it aside. Remove the dough from the refrigerator and turn it out onto a lightly floured surface. Knead until smoother as described in the General Shaping Tips in Chapter 3.

To make braided bread, follow the directions for braiding bread on page 40. Once it is braided, carefully transfer the braided dough, already on parchment paper, to a rimmed baking sheet. Next brush the top of the dough carefully but liberally with the egg wash. Cover the braided bread with oiled plastic wrap and allow to rise in a warm, draft-free location for 40 minutes. Brush again with egg wash, sprinkle with the sesame and poppy seeds, and allow to continue to rise uncovered until nearly doubled in size (about another 20 minutes).

Place the bread in the center of a cold oven, and turn the heat to 350°F. Bake for 20 minutes, then turn down the oven temperature to 325°F and bake until the internal temperature of the bread is 185°F on an instant-read thermometer, about another 15 minutes. Allow the bread to cool briefly before serving.

CHOCOLATE BREAD

MAKES 1 LOAF

CHOCOLATE BREAD SOUNDS LIKE A DESSERT. I KNOW. BUT I PROMise you this bread is only very mildly sweet with exactly the right amount of rich, chocolate flavor. It almost tastes like pumpernickel. That is, until you have had the "Pumpernickel" Bread (page 105), and you remember what pumpernickel bread really tastes like. It is then, if not before, that you know the beauty that is this sweet and savory, cocoa-flavored bread. It is as well suited to a savory sandwich as it is to a Sunday morning, with a generous schmear of cream cheese.

INGREDIENTS

4 tablespoons (56 g) unsalted butter, at room temperature

3 ounces semisweet chocolate, chopped coarsely

3½ cups (490 g) Gluten-Free Bread Flour (page 8), plus more for sprinkling

½ cup (100 g) sugar

2 teaspoons (6 g) instant yeast

6 tablespoons (30 g) Dutch-processed cocoa powder

½ teaspoon ground cinnamon

½ teaspoon cream of tartar

1 teaspoon (6 g) kosher salt

1 tablespoon vegetable oil

1 teaspoon gluten-free vanilla extract

1½ cups warm milk (about 95°F) (not nonfat)

In a medium-size microwave-safe bowl, place the butter and chocolate. Microwave on high at 30-second intervals, stirring in between, until the chocolate and butter are smooth and shiny. Set the bowl aside to cool briefly.

In the bowl of a stand mixer, place the flour, sugar, yeast, cocoa powder, cinnamon, and cream of tartar, and use a handheld whisk to combine well. Add the salt, and whisk to combine. Add the melted chocolate mixture, oil, vanilla, and milk to the flour mixture, and mix on low speed with the dough hook until the dry ingredients are just moistened. Once the dough has come together, raise the mixer speed to medium and mix for about 5 minutes. The dough will be quite sticky but should be smooth and stretchy. Spray a silicone spatula lightly with cooking oil spray, and scrape down the sides of the bowl. Transfer the dough to a lightly oiled bowl or proofing bucket large enough for the dough to rise to double its size, and cover with an oiled piece of plastic wrap (or the oiled top to your proofing bucket). Place the dough in the refrigerator for at least 12 hours and up to 5 days.

On baking day, grease an 8½ by 4½-inch loaf pan and set it aside. Remove the dough from the refrigerator and turn it out onto a lightly floured surface. Knead until smoother as described in the General Shaping Tips in Chapter 3.

To shape the dough, follow the instructions on page 36 for shaping sandwich bread. Carefully lift the shaped dough into the prepared loaf pan, seam side down. Sprinkle the top of the dough with a thin layer of flour to form a cloak that the dough will rise into. Cover the loaf pan with a piece of lightly oiled plastic wrap, and place in a warm, draft-free location until nearly doubled in size (about 1 hour).

Once the dough has finished rising, remove the plastic wrap and sprinkle the top of the loaf lightly with flour once more. Slash down the center of the loaf at a 45-degree angle and about ¼ inch deep, using a lame or very sharp knife. Place the pan in the center of a cold oven, and turn the heat to 350°F. Bake for 30 minutes before removing the loaf from the loaf pan, placing it on a rimmed baking sheet, and placing it back in the oven. Continue to bake until the loaf is dark brown, sounds hollow when thumped on the underside, and the internal temperature reaches about 195°F on an instant-read thermometer (about 15 minutes more). The crust will be dark and will soften as the bread cools.

Remove from the oven and place the loaf on a wire rack to cool for at least 20 minutes before slicing and serving.

OATMEAL BREAD
MAKES 1 LOAF

B E PREPARED. THIS HEARTY OATMEAL LOAF IS GOING TO BECOME A fast favorite. Soft but not delicate, this tender and moist bread might just be the one your family, like mine, begs you to make again and again. Well, my family begs me to make it. They don't know you (although I'm sure if they did, they'd be quite fond of you).

INGREDIENTS

3 cups (420 g) Gluten-Free Bread Flour (page 8), plus more for sprinkling
40 grams (about ⅔ cup) nonfat dry milk, ground finely in a blender or
    food processor
2½ tablespoons (19 g) certified gluten-free oat flour
2 teaspoons (6 g) instant yeast
1½ teaspoons (9 g) kosher salt
1 cup (100 g) certified gluten-free old-fashioned rolled oats
3 tablespoons honey
2 tablespoons (28 g) unsalted butter, at room temperature
1¼ cups plus 3 tablespoons water, at room temperature

In the bowl of your stand mixer, place the flour, dry milk, oat flour, and yeast, and use a handheld whisk to combine well. Add the salt, and whisk to combine. Add the rolled oats and stir to combine. Add the honey, butter, and water, and mix on low speed with the dough hook until the dry ingredients are absorbed into the wet. Raise the mixer speed to medium and knead for about 5 minutes, or until the dough is smooth except for the oats. It will still be quite sticky but should not be shaggy. Spray a silicone spatula lightly with cooking oil spray, and scrape down the sides of the bowl. Transfer the dough to a lightly oiled bowl or proofing bucket large enough for the dough to rise to double its size, spray the top of the dough with cooking oil spray, and cover with an oiled piece of plastic wrap (or the oiled top to your proofing bucket). Place the dough in the refrigerator for at least 12 hours and up to 5 days.

On baking day, grease an 8½ by 4½-inch loaf pan and set it aside. Remove the dough from the refrigerator and turn it out onto a lightly floured surface. Knead until smoother as described in the General Shaping Tips in Chapter 3.

To shape the dough, follow the instructions on page 36 for shaping sandwich bread. Carefully lift the shaped dough into the prepared loaf pan, seam side down. Sprinkle the top of the dough with a thin layer of flour to form a cloak that the dough will rise into. Cover the loaf pan with a piece of lightly oiled plastic wrap, and place in a warm, draft-free location until nearly doubled in size (about 1 hour).

Once the dough has finished rising, remove the plastic wrap and sprinkle the top of the loaf lightly with flour once more. Slash down the center of the loaf at a 45-degree angle and about ¼ inch deep, using a lame or very sharp knife. Place the pan in the center of a cold oven, and turn the heat to 350°F. Bake for 30 minutes before removing the loaf from the loaf pan, placing it on a rimmed baking sheet, and placing it back in the oven. Continue to bake until the loaf is golden brown, sounds hollow when thumped on the underside, and the internal temperature reaches about 185°F on an instant-read thermometer (about 10 minutes more).

Remove from the oven and place the loaf on a wire rack to cool for at least 20 minutes before slicing and serving.

RICOTTA BREAD

MAKES 1 LOAF

DO ME A FAVOR. MAKE THIS RICOTTA BREAD FIRST WITH THE CINnamon (no more or less than a teaspoon), then decide whether you need it. I made it first without the cinnamon and I thought it was a great, tender loaf of bread. But then I made it with cinnamon, and I knew it had reached new heights of flavor. My kids associate cinnamon with sugar and so they think they're getting some sort of dessert bread, which this most certainly is not. Everybody wins!

STARTER

9 tablespoons (80 g) Gluten-Free Bread Flour (page 8)
1 teaspoon (3 g) instant yeast
¾ cup warm water (about 95°F)

DOUGH

3 cups (420 g) Gluten-Free Bread Flour (page 8), plus more for sprinkling
1⅓ teaspoons (4 g) instant yeast
1 teaspoon ground cinnamon
2 teaspoons (12 g) kosher salt
1 tablespoon honey
1 cup (8 ounces) ricotta cheese, at room temperature
2 tablespoons (28 g) unsalted butter, at room temperature
½ cup water, at room temperature
Starter

To make the starter, place all the starter ingredients in a medium-size bowl, and whisk until well combined. The mixture will be thick and shapeless. Cover and set the bowl aside in a warm, draft-free location to rise until doubled (about 30 minutes).

Once the starter has finished rising, make the dough. Place the flour and yeast in the bowl of your stand mixer, and use a handheld whisk to combine well. Add the cinnamon and salt, and whisk to combine. Add the honey, ricotta cheese, butter, water, and risen starter to the bowl, and mix on low speed with the dough hook until the dry ingredients are absorbed into the wet. Raise the mixer speed to medium and mix for about 5 minutes, then raise the mixer speed to medium-high speed and beat for at least 5 minutes, or until smooth. The dough will be heavy, will pull away from the mixing bowl a bit as it is kneaded, and will fall easily off an ungreased spatula. Transfer the dough to a lightly oiled bowl or proofing bucket large enough for the dough to rise to double its size, and cover with an oiled piece of plastic wrap (or the oiled top to your proofing bucket). Place the dough in the refrigerator for at least 12 hours and up to 5 days.

On baking day, grease an 8½ by 4½-inch loaf pan and set it aside. Remove the dough from the refrigerator and turn it out onto a lightly floured surface. Knead until smoother as described in the General Shaping Tips in Chapter 3. This dough will be stickier by nature than other lean dough (e.g., Crusty White Sandwich Bread, page 43).

To shape the dough, follow the instructions on page 36 for shaping sandwich bread. Carefully lift the shaped dough into the prepared loaf pan, seam side down. Sprinkle the top of the dough with a thin layer of flour to form a cloak that the dough will rise into. Cover the loaf pan with a piece of lightly oiled plastic wrap, and place in a warm, draft-free location until nearly doubled in size (about 1½ hours). About 25 minutes before the dough has finished rising, preheat your oven to 350°F.

Once the dough has finished rising, remove the plastic wrap and sprinkle the top of the loaf lightly with flour once more. Slash down the center of the loaf at a 45-degree angle and about ¼ inch deep, using a lame or very sharp knife. Place the pan in the center of the preheated oven. Bake for 40 minutes before removing the loaf from the loaf pan, placing it on a rimmed baking sheet, and placing it back in the oven. Continue to bake until the loaf is lightly golden brown, sounds hollow when thumped on the underside, and the internal temperature reaches about 195°F on an instant-read thermometer (about 15 minutes more). This bread will take a bit longer to reach the proper internal temperature than, for example, the Potato Bread (page 57) as it is a very moist dough.

Remove from the oven and place the loaf on a wire rack to cool for at least 20 minutes before slicing and serving.

SWEET POTATO BREAD
MAKES 1 LOAF

S WEET POTATOES SEEM TO ME TO BE SO VASTLY DIFFERENT THAN, say Yukon Golds or red-skinned potatoes as to barely be related. In the Potato Bread (page 57), the instructions say to boil and then mash the potatoes. But since sweet potatoes are so different, they must be treated accordingly. Roasting the sweet potatoes before peeling and mashing them brings out their natural sweetness, as well as deepens their color. The result is a beautifully strawberry-blond, fragrant loaf of bread.

STARTER

9 tablespoons (80 g) Gluten-Free Bread Flour (page 8)
1 teaspoon (3 g) instant yeast
¾ cup warm water (about 95°F)

DOUGH

3 cups (420 g) Gluten-Free Bread Flour (page 8), plus more for sprinkling
1⅓ teaspoons (4 g) instant yeast
2 teaspoons (12 g) kosher salt
1 tablespoon honey
1 cup (7 ounces) sweet potatoes, roasted until soft, then peeled and mashed
2 tablespoons (28 g) unsalted butter, at room temperature
½ cup water, at room temperature
Starter

To make the starter, place all the starter ingredients in a medium-size bowl, and whisk until well combined. The mixture will be thick and shapeless. Cover and set the bowl aside in a warm, draft-free location to rise until doubled (about 30 minutes).

Once the starter has finished rising, make the dough. Place the flour and yeast in the bowl of your stand mixer, and use a handheld whisk to combine well. Add the salt, and whisk to combine. Add the honey, sweet potatoes, butter, water, and risen starter to the bowl, and mix on low speed with the dough hook until combined. Raise the mixer speed to medium and mix for about 5 minutes. The dough will be quite sticky, but should be mostly smooth and stretchy. Spray a silicone spatula lightly with cooking oil spray, and scrape down the sides of the bowl. Transfer the dough to a lightly oiled bowl or proofing bucket large enough for the dough to rise to double its size, and cover with an oiled piece of plastic wrap (or the oiled top to your proofing bucket). Place the dough in the refrigerator for at least 12 hours and up to 5 days.

On baking day, grease an 8½ by 4½-inch loaf pan and set it aside. Remove the dough from the refrigerator and turn it out onto a lightly floured surface. Knead until smoother as described in the General Shaping Tips in Chapter 3. This dough will be stickier by nature than other lean dough (e.g., Lean Crusty White Sandwich Bread, page 43).

To shape the dough, follow the instructions on page 36 for shaping sandwich bread. Carefully lift the shaped dough into the prepared loaf pan, seam side down. Sprinkle the top of the dough with a thin layer of flour to form a cloak that the dough will rise into. Cover the loaf pan with a piece of lightly oiled plastic wrap, and place in a warm, draft-free location until nearly doubled in size (about 1½ hours).

Once the dough has finished rising, remove the plastic wrap and sprinkle the top of the loaf lightly with flour once more. Slash down the center of the loaf at a 45-degree angle and about ¼ inch deep, using a lame or very sharp knife. Place the pan in the center of a cold oven, and turn the heat to 350°F. Bake for 30 minutes before removing the loaf from the loaf pan, placing it on a rimmed baking sheet, and placing it back in the oven. Continue to bake until the loaf is lightly golden brown, sounds hollow when thumped on the underside, and the internal temperature reaches about 195°F on an instant-read thermometer (about 15 minutes more).

Remove from the oven and place the loaf on a wire rack to cool for at least 20 minutes before slicing and serving.

ENGLISH MUFFIN BREAD

MAKES 1 LOAF

I F YOU HAVE SOME PREVIOUS EXPERIENCE BAKING GLUTEN-FREE
bread and recall how wet the dough generally is (and how its texture could
fairly be compared to—gasp!—cookie dough), the dough for this English
Muffin Bread might just bring back some memories. Rest assured that we
have, indeed, turned a corner in the baking of gluten-free bread. But English
Muffin Bread, like the English Muffins (page 118), has an extremely high hydration ratio. So gluten-free or not, it is a very, very wet dough. But because it
is, in fact, so wet, this dough rises very quickly and makes a very fluffy, pleas-
ingly simple loaf of bread. And unlike most of the other bread in this book, it
doesn't benefit from a long, slow refrigerator rise before baking. Near-instant
gratification!

INGREDIENTS

3 cups (420 g) Gluten-Free Bread Flour (page 8), plus more for sprinkling

1⅔ teaspoons (5 g) instant yeast

1 tablespoon (12 g) sugar

1½ teaspoons (9 g) kosher salt

1⅔ cups hot milk (110°F)

Coarsely ground gluten-free cornmeal, for sprinkling

In the bowl of your stand mixer, place the flour, yeast, and sugar, and use a
handheld whisk to combine well. Add the salt, and whisk to combine. Add the
milk and mix with the paddle attachment until the dough is smooth. It will be
very wet. Cover the bowl with oiled plastic wrap and set in a warm, draft-free
location to rise until nearly doubled in size (about 40 minutes).

Preheat your oven to 350°F. Grease well an 8½ by 4½-inch loaf pan and
sprinkle the bottom and sides with cornmeal. Once the dough has doubled,
stir it down to deflate it a bit. Scrape the dough into the prepared loaf pan,
smooth the top with a wet spatula, and sprinkle the top with flour to create
a cloak. Cover with oiled plastic wrap and place in a warm, draft-free location to rise until the dough is about ½ inch above the sides of the pan (about 1
hour). Remove the plastic wrap from the loaf pan and slash down the center
of the loaf at a 45 degree angle and about ¼ inch deep with a sharp knife or

lame. Sprinkle the top of the loaf lightly with cornmeal, and place it in the center of the preheated oven. Bake until the loaf is lightly golden brown, registers 185°F in the center on an instant-read thermometer, and sounds hollow when thumped on the bottom (about 35 minutes).

Remove from the oven and allow to cool in the loaf pan for about 10 minutes before transferring to a wire rack to cool completely. This bread in particular must be completely cool before slicing as it is very tender.

PANETTONE BREAD

MAKES 1 LARGE LOAF

I F YOU CELEBRATE CHRISTMAS, OR EVEN IF YOU ARE JUST CONSCIOUS during the Christmas season, you're going to find yourself face to face with quite a lot of panettone bread. It's as inevitable as fruitcake (but much more pleasant). Now, you can make your own. This is a fast-rising bread, mostly because the dough has plenty of enrichments that lead to high hydration. And because it has so much flavor-enhancement from lemon, butter, and dried fruit, it only needs a single rise.

INGREDIENTS

2½ cups (350 g) Gluten-Free Bread Flour (page 8)

½ cup (100 g) sugar

2 teaspoons (6 g) instant yeast

1 teaspoon cream of tartar

¾ teaspoon (5 g) kosher salt

Grated zest and juice of 1 medium-size lemon

1 teaspoon gluten-free vanilla extract

¾ cup warm milk (about 95°F) (not nonfat)

3 large eggs, at room temperature, beaten

8 tablespoons (112 g) unsalted butter, at room temperature

6 ounces dried currants

Grease and lightly flour a panettone or brioche mold (a 9 by 5-inch loaf pan will work with perhaps a bit of overflow), and set it aside.

In the bowl of a stand mixer, place the flour, sugar, yeast, and cream of tartar, and use a handheld whisk to combine well. Add the salt and lemon zest, and whisk to combine well. Secure the bowl. Add the lemon juice, vanilla, milk, eggs, and butter to the bowl, one ingredient at a time, and mix on low speed with the paddle attachment to combine after each addition. Once the final ingredient has been added, switch to the dough hook, raise the mixer speed to medium-high and knead for about 6 minutes uninterrupted. Add the currants and mix until evenly distributed throughout. The dough will be very soft and smooth. Scrape the dough into the prepared pan until it is a bit more than half-full, and smooth the top with wet hands. If you have extra dough, grease and flour another small pan and scrape the remaining dough into that pan. Cover the pan(s) with oiled plastic wrap and place in a warm and humid, draft-free location to rise until the dough has doubled in size (about an hour).

While the dough is rising, preheat your oven to 375°F. Once the dough has finished rising, place the pan(s) in the center of the preheated oven and lower the heat to 350°F. Bake for 25 minutes, or until the top is deep brown (check after 15 minutes; the small pan will be done first). Remove the pan(s) from the oven, cover the top of the bread tightly with a piece of foil, and return the bread to the center of the oven. Bake for another 20 minutes (10 to 15 minutes for the smaller pan), or until the internal temperature of the bread is about 210°F and/or it sounds hollow when thumped with a finger.

Remove the bread from the oven and allow to cool in the pan(s) for about 10 minutes. Remove from the pan(s) and serve immediately.

BUCKWHEAT BREAD

MAKES 1 LOAF

I USED TO AVOID DEVELOPING RECIPES THAT CALLED FOR BUCK-
wheat, as it was inexcusably difficult to find an affordable source of reliably
gluten-free buckwheat flour. But now King Arthur Flour carries it! If you have
never tried it, buckwheat is a cult favorite for a reason: This fruit seed is high
in fiber, contains all eight essential amino acids (they're essential!), and has
a really earthy, nutty taste. This bread dough is lightly enriched with a bit of
honey and butter, which help mellow the hearty flavor of buckwheat and keep
the bread from being too heavy. The texture of the bread itself is similar to
the Lean Crusty Whole-Grain Bread (page 55), but with even more earthiness.

STARTER

¾ cup (105 g) Gluten-Free Bread Flour (page 8)
⅞ cup (105 g) gluten-free buckwheat flour
1 teaspoon (3 g) instant yeast
1½ tablespoons (18 g) sugar
1 cup warm water (about 95°F)

DOUGH

2 cups (280 g) Gluten-Free Bread Flour (page 8), plus more for sprinkling
40 grams (about ⅔ cup) nonfat dry milk, ground finely in a blender or
    food processor
1 teaspoon (3 g) instant yeast
⅓ cup (40 g) gluten-free buckwheat flour
1½ teaspoons (9 g) kosher salt
2 tablespoons honey
2 tablespoons (28 g) unsalted butter, at room temperature
¼ cup plus 3 tablespoons water, at room temperature
Starter

To make the starter, place all the starter ingredients in a medium-size bowl,
and whisk until well combined. The mixture will be thick and shapeless.
Cover and set the bowl aside in a warm, draft-free location to rise until doubled (about 40 minutes).

Once the starter has finished rising, make the dough. Place the flour, dry milk, yeast, and buckwheat flour in the bowl of your stand mixer, and use a handheld whisk to combine well. Add the salt and whisk to combine well. Add the honey, butter, water, and risen starter to the bowl, and mix on low speed with the dough hook until combined. Raise the mixer speed to medium and knead for about 5 minutes. The dough will be quite sticky but should be smooth and stretchy. Spray a silicone spatula lightly with cooking oil spray, and scrape down the sides of the bowl. Transfer the dough to a lightly oiled bowl or proofing bucket large enough for the dough to rise to double its size, and cover with an oiled piece of plastic wrap (or the oiled top to your proofing bucket). Place the dough in the refrigerator for at least 12 hours and up to 5 days.

On baking day, grease an 8½ by 4½-inch loaf pan and set it aside. Remove the dough from the refrigerator and turn it out onto a lightly floured surface. Knead until smoother as described in the General Shaping Tips in Chapter 3.

To shape the dough, follow the instructions on page 36 for shaping sandwich bread. Carefully lift the shaped dough into the prepared loaf pan, seam side down. Sprinkle the top of the dough with a thin layer of flour to form a cloak that the dough will rise into. Cover the loaf pan with a piece of lightly oiled plastic wrap, and place in a warm, draft-free location until nearly doubled in size (about 1½ hours).

Once the dough has finished rising, remove the plastic wrap and sprinkle the top of the loaf lightly with flour once more. Slash down the center of the loaf at a 45-degree angle and about ¼ inch deep, using a lame or very sharp knife. Place the pan in the center of a cold oven, and turn the heat to 350°F. Bake for 30 minutes before removing the loaf from the loaf pan, placing it on a rimmed baking sheet, and placing it back in the oven. Continue to bake until the loaf is lightly golden brown, sounds hollow when thumped on the underside, and the internal temperature reaches about 195°F on an instant-read thermometer (about 15 minutes more).

Remove from the oven and place the loaf on a wire rack to cool for at least 20 minutes before slicing and serving.

OLIVE BREAD
MAKES 1 ROUND LOAF

I LIKE TO SERVE OLIVE BREAD AS AN APPETIZER, EITHER ALONE OR with a light balsamic vinaigrette for dipping. It has a beautiful crisp crust, and a quick glance at the ingredient list is all you need to know how fragrant and flavorful it is (rosemary and olives!).

INGREDIENTS

3½ cups (490 g) Gluten-Free Bread Flour (page 8)

40 grams (about ⅔ cup) nonfat dry milk, ground finely in a blender or
  food processor

2⅓ teaspoons (7 g) instant yeast

1½ teaspoons (9 g) kosher salt

2 tablespoons honey

2½ tablespoons (35 g) unsalted butter, melted and cooled

1⅓ cups warm water (about 95°F)

1 cup kalamata olives, pitted and halved

1 tablespoon fresh rosemary, chopped finely

In the bowl of your stand mixer, place the flour, dry milk, and yeast, and use a handheld whisk to combine well. Add the salt, and whisk to combine. Add the honey, butter, and water, and mix on low speed with the dough hook until combined. Raise the mixer speed to medium and knead for about 5 minutes. It will still be quite sticky and the dough will begin to climb up the dough hook, but it should be smooth and stretchy. Spray a silicone spatula lightly with cooking oil spray, and scrape down the sides of the bowl. Transfer the dough to a lightly oiled bowl or proofing bucket large enough for the dough to rise to double its size, spray the top of the dough with cooking oil spray, and cover with an oiled piece of plastic wrap (or the oiled top to your proofing bucket). Place the dough in the refrigerator for at least 12 hours and up to 3 days.

On baking day, sprinkle an 8-inch round banetton or proofing basket liberally with flour and set it aside. Line a rimmed baking sheet with unbleached parchment paper and set it aside. Remove the dough from the refrigerator and turn it out onto a lightly floured surface. Knead until smoother as described in the General Shaping Tips in Chapter 3. Lightly fold and knead in the olives and rosemary, sprinkling with flour again if the dough becomes sticky. Follow the instructions for shaping a boule on a flat, well-floured surface (see page 32) and place, seam side up, in the prepared proofing basket. Place the banetton in a plastic bag and loosely secure the end. Place in a warm, draft-free location until the dough has doubled in size.

Once the bread is fully risen, working carefully so as not to deflate the dough, invert the dough onto the prepared baking sheet, seam side down. Sprinkle the top of the dough lightly with flour and, using a lame or sharp knife at a 45-degree angle, slash a crisscross pattern of four slashes, each ¼ inch deep.

Place the bread on the baking sheet, place in a cold oven, and turn the heat to 350°F. Bake until the internal temperature of the loaf is 185°F on an instant-read thermometer (about 45 minutes). Tent the loaf with foil if it begins to brown too much. Turn off the oven, prop open the oven door, and allow the bread to sit in the oven as it cools, to help the bread maintain its shape, as it is a very moist loaf. Remove the bread after 15 minutes, or once the oven temperature reaches 150°F.

Remove from the oven and place the loaf on a wire rack to cool for at least 20 minutes before slicing and serving.

5 PURE SOURDOUGH BREADS

BREAD MADE WITH A WILD YEAST STARTER AND NO COMMERCIAL YEAST

Wild Yeast Starter: How It All Begins

OMMERCIAL YEAST, SUCH AS THE INSTANT YEAST THAT IS CALLED for in the yeast bread recipes in other chapters of this book, is a single, isolated strain of yeast. But yeast is all around us. To create a wild yeast starter, we must create an environment conducive to the growth of this naturally occurring yeast. We do this with gluten-free flours, water, and warmth. There are a few wild yeast starter principles to keep in mind:

🌿 Simply stated, the key to the entire process is patience. If the instructions say to wait until the Mother Starter or the Bread Starter has doubled, it must double. If it hasn't, wait longer!

🌿 Never use a metal utensil to store or stir a starter, especially before it is fully active.

🌿 Always clean utensils and containers meticulously when getting started, including drying them very well after washing them with tap water. Tap water is chlorinated, and chlorine will kill wild yeast.

❧ For the same reason, when making, refreshing, or rebuilding a starter, avoid using tap water as an ingredient in favor of bottled or distilled water.

❧ Through Step 4, continue to work through the process specified in the steps, regardless of how the mixture seems to be behaving.

❧ Volume measurements are simply insufficient here. A basic digital food scale is essential. All measurements here are in grams, including water.

❧ A "warm, draft-free environment" is of particular importance. You will need a bread proofer set to 78°F, or a heating pad on its lowest setting with two thick towels. See page 14 for a more thorough discussion of this equipment.

Here's how to get that starter started, one step at a time. I find that it is easiest to understand the process if it is made as concrete as possible, which is why I've listed everything, step by step. At the start of each day's instructions, I have also indicated how much flour and how much liquid, total, is necessary to complete that step. But I recommend reading through all of the steps before you begin. The general concept is to create an environment in which the wild yeast that is present in flours, and to a smaller extent in the air around us, thrives. Think of the flours as the nutrient-rich soil in which flowers grow.

Step 1

❧ Day 1 (note the time you begin)

❧ Requires 100 grams of sweet white sorghum ("sorghum") flour, 100 grams of teff flour, and 200 grams of bottled water, at room temperature

❧ Make a note of the weight of the empty large glass jar you intend to use to create the starter, without the lid. You will need that measurement in a few days.

❧ In a large glass jar, combine the sorghum flour and teff flour with the bottled water. Mix with a clean wooden spoon or silicone spatula until well combined. Cover loosely and allow to sit for 24 hours in a warm, draft-free location. Stir once or twice during these 24 hours to aerate the mixture, if possible.

Step 2

❧ Day 2 (around the same time of day)

❧ Requires 100 grams of sorghum flour, 100 grams of Basic Gum-Free

Gluten-Free Flour Blend (page 9), and 200 grams of bottled water, at room temperature

❧ The mixture will not yet be active, but because of the teff flour it will likely have a relatively strong smell. Don't worry—we won't be using teff flour again. Discard approximately three-quarters of the existing mixture (no need to weigh; eyeball it) and add the sorghum flour, Basic Gum-Free Gluten-Free Flour, and bottled water. Mix with a clean wooden spoon or silicone spatula until well combined. Cover loosely and allow to sit for 24 hours in a warm, draft-free location. Stir once or twice during these 24 hours to aerate the mixture, if possible.

Step 3

❧ Day 3 (around the same time of day)

❧ Requires 50 grams of sorghum flour, 50 grams of Basic Gum-Free Gluten-Free Flour Blend (page 9), and 100 grams of bottled water, at room temperature

❧ Discard approximately half of the existing mixture (no need to weigh; eyeball it) and add the sorghum flour, Basic Gum-Free Gluten-Free Flour, and bottled water. Mix with a clean wooden spoon or silicone spatula until well combined. Cover loosely and allow to sit for 24 hours in a warm, draft-free location. Stir once or twice during these 24 hours to aerate the mixture, if possible. The mixture should smell more sour, and will likely have become at least somewhat active by now. Using a glass jar is helpful as it allows you to see the bubbles as they develop.

Step 4

❧ Day 4 (around the same time of day)

❧ Requires 100 grams of Basic Gum-Free Gluten-Free Flour Blend (page 9) and 100 grams of bottled water, at room temperature

❧ The mixture should be active at this point. If it is not, don't panic! It just needs more time, and perhaps a warmer environment. If possible, place in the warmest spot in your home. I use my proofer, which works a treat, but if you don't have one, just set up an electric heating pad set to low heat, lined with towels, to keep the starter warm. Whether it is active or not, discard approximately half of the existing mixture (no need to weigh; eyeball it), and add the Basic Gum-Free Gluten-Free Flour and bottled water. Mix with a clean wooden spoon or silicone spatula until well combined. Cover loosely and allow to sit for 12 hours in a warm, draft-free location. Stir once or twice during these 12 hours to aerate the mixture, if possible.

Step 5

- Day 4, 12 hours later (the same day as Step 4)
- Requires 100 grams of Basic Gum-Free Gluten-Free Flour (page 9) and 100 grams of bottled water, at room temperature
- The mixture should be fully active by now. If not, repeat Step 4 every 12 hours until the starter is fully active. Once it is fully active, discard all but 200 grams of the mixture. Here's where the weight of your empty glass jar is essential—just weigh the entire mixture in the jar and discard the mixture a bit at a time until the weight of the jar plus the mixture is the weight of your empty jar plus 200 grams. So if your jar weighs 476 grams like mine does, discard the mixture until the total weight of the jar plus the mixture is 476 grams plus 200 grams, or 676 grams.

- To the 200 grams of starter mixture, add the Basic Gum-Free Gluten-Free Flour and bottled water. Mix with a clean wooden spoon or silicone spatula until well combined. Cover loosely. Continue to the next steps immediately.

Next Steps

The next step is to make the Mother Starter, also referred to sometimes as a stiff starter. It has a doughlike consistency (instead of being a liquid, as it is now) and is what we will use in the bread recipes in this chapter. I find it to be much easier to maintain than a liquid starter. It's more stable and takes up less space in your refrigerator than a liquid starter would. Plus, it's simple to reconstitute the Mother Starter as directed in each recipe, when you are ready to use it.

Converting Liquid Starter to Mother Starter

MAKES 700 GRAMS MOTHER STARTER

MOTHER STARTER

128 grams liquid starter, at room temperature (page 83)
160 grams bottled water, at room temperature
350 grams Gluten-Free Bread Flour (page 8)

Place all the ingredients in the bowl of your stand mixer fitted with the dough hook. Mix on low speed until the wet ingredients are absorbed into the dry ingredients. Raise the mixer speed to medium and knead for about 3 minutes. The dough will be almost buoyant. With lightly floured hands, knead the ball on a flat, lightly floured surface until fairly smooth and integrated (about 1 minute or so). Place the Mother Starter in a lightly oiled, nonreactive (non-metal) bowl, turn to coat the Mother Starter in the oil, and cover with plastic wrap or loosely with a lid. Leave at room temperature until the Mother Starter is doubled in size (about 6 hours). Deflate the raised starter, knead back into a ball, and either use it immediately, or cover tightly and refrigerate until ready to use. The starter is ripe and ready to use anytime during the next 7 days. A brand-new Mother Starter is considered ripe at this point. However, it will "mature" over time as it ages and is refreshed and rebuilt, becoming more complex in flavor and generally more active and effective in creating rise. In other words, it will work right away but will improve with age.

Rebuilding the Mother Starter

When the Mother Starter gets very low or begins to dry out or to break down, it needs to be rebuilt. Rebuilding the Mother Starter to a full size is done in two simple stages, designed to rebuild it slowly and prevent it from losing any of its potency. The first step creates 140 grams of ripe Mother Starter, which can be used immediately in recipes in this chapter. If you would like to rebuild the ripe Mother Starter to its full size, continue to the next step.

First, rebuild the starter to 140 grams:

28 grams Mother Starter, chilled or at room temperature (discard rest, if any) (page 87)

35 grams bottled water, at room temperature

77 grams Gluten-Free Bread Flour

Tear the 28 grams of the Mother Starter into five pieces and place all five pieces in the bowl of a stand mixer fitted with the paddle attachment. Add the water, and mix on low speed until the mixture looks like a liquid slurry (about 2 minutes). Add the bread flour, and mix on low speed until the flour is incorporated into the liquid. Switch to the dough hook, and knead on medium speed for 2 minutes. The dough will be stretchy and smooth. Transfer the Mother Starter to a lightly oiled bowl or proofing bucket large enough for the dough to rise to double its size, spray the top of the dough with cooking spray, and cover with an oiled piece of plastic wrap (or the oiled top to your proofing bucket). Allow it to rise in a warm, draft-free location until doubled in size (6 to 8 hours).

The Mother Starter is now rebuilt to 140 grams and can be used immediately or any time during the next 7 days in the recipes in this chapter that call for a ripe Mother Starter. If you would like to rebuild the ripe Mother Starter to its full size, combine the following in the same manner as indicated in the first stage above:

140 grams Mother Starter, chilled or at room temperature (entire amount from above)

175 grams bottled water, at room temperature

385 grams Gluten-Free Bread Flour (page 8)

The Mother Starter is now rebuilt to a full 700 grams. It is ready to use (ripe) from the refrigerator any time during the next 7 days.

Refreshing the Mother Starter

If you have had the Mother Starter sitting in the refrigerator unused for 7 days, it should be refreshed so that it continues to stay active. That said, I have left it alone in the refrigerator, untended, for 14 days before refreshing it, and once very mature it has been fine. However, if you are at all unsure of how mature your Mother Starter is and whether it will be truly viable, refresh it. Refreshing is very similar to rebuilding but begins with a larger piece of the original Mother Starter, as it is done with a viable ripe Mother Starter and is designed to prolong its life. Rebuilding is done with a Mother Starter that has become very small or has begun to dry out, and begins as described in rebuilding, just with a much smaller piece of the Mother Starter.

MAKES 200 GRAMS REFRESHED MOTHER STARTER

60 grams original Mother Starter, chilled or at room temperature (discard rest) (page 87)

60 grams bottled water, at room temperature

110 grams Gluten-Free Bread Flour (page 8)

Tear the 60 grams of Mother Starter into five pieces and place all five pieces in the bowl of a stand mixer fitted with the paddle attachment. Add the water, and mix on low speed until the mixture looks like a liquid slurry (about 2 minutes). Add the bread flour, and mix on low speed until the flour is incorporated into the liquid. Switch to the dough hook, and knead on medium speed for 2 minutes. The dough will be stretchy and smooth. Transfer the Mother Starter to a lightly oiled bowl or proofing bucket large enough for the dough to rise to double its size, spray the top of the dough with cooking spray, and cover with an oiled piece of plastic wrap (or the oiled top to your proofing

bucket). Allow it to rise in a warm, draft-free location until doubled in size (about 6 to 8 hours).

The Mother Starter is now refreshed and is ready to use (ripe) from the refrigerator at any time during the next 7 days. It can also be rebuilt larger at this stage by combining 140 grams of the 200 grams of refreshed ripe Mother Starter with 175 grams bottled water, at room temperature and then 385 grams Gluten-Free Bread Flour (page 8) in the same manner as indicated on the previous page for refreshing the Mother Starter.

PAIN AU LEVAIN
(BASIC SOURDOUGH BREAD)
MAKES 1 LOAF

THIS RECIPE IS FOR A BASIC SOURDOUGH LOAF. IT ABSOLUTELY works best with a mature Mother Starter, by which I only mean to say that it will rise highest and most proud once the starter is no longer brand new. It will also have more flavor. Although a ripe Mother Starter is one that has been converted from a ready liquid starter to a Mother Starter as directed on page 87, a "mature" Mother Starter is one that has been refreshed and rebuilt over time. Maturity in wild yeast starters is much the same as maturity in people. It tends to increase with age (although presumably, a Mother Starter is more of a sure thing!). But even when your ripe Mother is new, she will still rise. Go, Mom!

BREAD STARTER
80 grams ripe Mother Starter, chilled or at room temperature (page 87)
½ cup plus 3 tablespoons bottled water, at room temperature
1 cup plus 10 tablespoons (225 g) Gluten-Free Bread Flour (page 8)

DOUGH
Bread Starter
1¼ cups plus 3 scant tablespoons warm bottled water (about 95°F)
3 cups plus 7 tablespoons (480 g) Gluten-Free Bread Flour, plus more for
    sprinkling
1 tablespoon (18 g) kosher salt

To make the bread starter, tear the ripe Mother Starter into five pieces and place all of them in the bowl of a stand mixer fitted with the paddle attachment. Add the water and mix on low speed until it looks like a liquid slurry (about 2 minutes). Add the bread flour and mix on low speed until combined. Switch to the dough hook and knead on medium speed until stretchy and smooth. Transfer the bread starter to a lightly oiled bowl or proofing bucket large enough for the dough to rise to double its size, spray the top of the dough with cooking oil spray, and cover with an oiled piece of plastic wrap (or the oiled top to your proofing bucket). Allow to rise in a warm, draft-free location until doubled in size (6 to 8 hours). Do not proceed until the bread starter has doubled fully.

Once the bread starter has doubled in size, use it to make the bread dough. Place the bread starter in the bowl of your stand mixer, add the water, and mix with the paddle attachment on low speed to soften the bread starter (about 1 minute). Add the bread flour and switch to the dough hook. Turn the mixer on low speed and knead for about 2 minutes, until the dough is once again stretchy and smooth. Add the salt to the bowl, raise the mixer speed to medium and knead for 3 minutes. Transfer the dough to a lightly oiled bowl or proofing bucket large enough for the dough to rise to double its size, and cover with an oiled piece of plastic wrap (or the oiled top to your proofing bucket). Place the dough in the refrigerator for at least 12 hours and up to 2 days. After 2 days, the dough has a tendency to become too active and can overproof after being shaped.

On baking day, grease an 8½ by 4½-inch loaf pan and set it aside. Remove the dough from the refrigerator and turn it out onto a lightly floured surface. Knead until smoother as described in the General Shaping Tips in Chapter 3.

To shape the dough, follow the instructions on page 36 for shaping sandwich bread. Carefully lift the shaped dough into the prepared loaf pan, seam side down. Sprinkle the top of the dough with a thin layer of flour to form a cloak that the dough will rise into. Cover the loaf pan with a piece of lightly oiled plastic wrap, and place in a warm, draft-free location until nearly doubled in size (about 1½ hours).

Once the dough has finished rising, remove the plastic wrap and sprinkle the top of the loaf lightly with flour once more. Slash down the center of the loaf at a 45-degree angle and about ¼ inch deep, using a lame or very sharp knife. Place the pan in the center of a cold oven and turn the heat to 375°F. Bake for 10 minutes, and then lower the heat to 350°F. Continue to bake for another 20 minutes, then remove the loaf from the loaf pan, place it on a rimmed baking sheet, and place it back in the oven. Continue to bake until the loaf is lightly golden brown, sounds hollow when thumped on the underside, and the internal temperature reaches about 195°F on an instant-read thermometer (about 10 minutes more).

Remove from the oven and place the loaf on a wire rack to cool for at least 20 minutes before slicing and serving.

CRUNCHY LEVAIN BREADSTICKS
MAKES 15 TO 18 BREADSTICKS

THIS DOUGH IS STRONG ENOUGH THAT YOU CAN ROLL IT OUT, SLICE it into strips, and then twist those strips at both ends. That fact alone is something to write home about, especially if you compare it with any past gluten-free bread dough experience you may have had. But to just talk about the strength of this dough would not do it justice. If you've been wishing upon a star for crunchy and snappy breadsticks, the kind you might see standing up in a jar in a cute little Italian bistro, breadsticks that are the perfect munchy snack as you decide what you'd like to do with the rest of your day, then you've come to the right place.

BREAD STARTER
40 grams ripe Mother Starter, chilled or at room temperature (page 87)
¼ cup plus 1½ tablespoons bottled water, at room temperature
13 tablespoons (115 g) Gluten-Free Bread Flour (page 8)

DOUGH
Bread Starter
¾ cup plus 2 tablespoons warm bottled water (about 95°F)
3½ tablespoons extra-virgin olive oil
2½ cups (350 g) Gluten-Free Bread Flour (page 8), plus more for sprinkling
1 tablespoon (18 g) kosher salt
Egg wash (1 large egg, at room temperature, beaten with 1 teaspoon water)
2 teaspoons dried oregano
1 teaspoon poppy seeds
1 teaspoon toasted sesame seeds

To make the bread starter, tear the ripe Mother Starter into five pieces and place all of them in the bowl of a stand mixer fitted with the paddle attachment. Add the water and mix on low speed until the mixture looks like a liquid slurry (about 2 minutes). Add the bread flour and mix on low speed until the flour is incorporated into the liquid. Switch to the dough hook and knead on medium speed for 2 minutes. The dough will be stretchy and smooth. Transfer the bread starter to a lightly oiled bowl or proofing bucket large enough for the dough to rise to double its size, spray the top of the dough with cooking oil spray, and cover with an oiled piece of plastic wrap (or the oiled top of your proofing bucket). Allow to rise in a warm, draft-free location until doubled in size (about 6 to 8 hours). Do not proceed until the bread starter has doubled fully.

Once the bread starter has doubled in size, use it to make the breadsticks dough. Place the bread starter in the bowl of your stand mixer, add the water and olive oil, and mix with the paddle attachment on low speed to soften the bread starter (about 1 minute). Add the bread flour and salt and switch to the dough hook. Turn the mixer on low speed and knead for about 2 minutes, until the dough is once again stretchy and smooth. Raise the mixer speed to medium, and knead for 3 minutes. Transfer the dough to a lightly oiled bowl or proofing bucket large enough for the dough to rise to double its size, and cover with an oiled piece of plastic wrap (or the oiled top to your proofing bucket). Place the dough in the refrigerator for 12 to 18 hours (no more).

Preheat your oven to 350°F. Line a large, rimmed baking sheet with unbleached parchment paper and set it aside. Remove the dough from the refrigerator and, on a lightly floured surface, roll the dough into a 4- by 12-inch rectangle. With a pastry wheel or sharp knife, cut it into fifteen to eighteen strips along the 12-inch width, each about ¾ inch wide. Place the strips on the prepared baking sheet about 1 inch apart from one another. Stretch the strips of dough to about 14 inches long and twist each strip at both ends in opposite directions to form a spiral shape. Brush each of the strips fully but carefully with the egg wash (if beaten egg pools around the breadsticks, it will burn during baking). Crush the dried oregano with your fingers on your palm to release its oils. Sprinkle the breadsticks evenly with the crushed oregano, poppy seeds, and sesame seeds. Press the oregano and seeds gently onto the surface of the breadsticks to secure them.

Place the baking sheet in the center of the preheated oven and bake for about 20 minutes, or until the breadsticks are golden brown and firm to the touch. Remove the breadsticks from the oven and allow them cool for 5 minutes on the baking sheet before transferring them to a wire rack to cool completely. They will continue to crisp as they cool.

LEVAIN DINNER ROLLS
MAKES 16 DINNER ROLLS

THESE LIGHTLY SOUR DINNER ROLLS ARE ENRICHED WITH JUST enough butter and egg to make them a bit more tender than would be, say, the Pain au Levain (page 91) if you shaped it into rolls instead of a loaf. Try serving them with just a pat of unsalted butter and some coarse salt.

BREAD STARTER
80 grams ripe Mother Starter, chilled or at room temperature (page 87)
½ cup plus 3 tablespoons bottled water, at room temperature
1 cup plus 10 tablespoons (225 g) Gluten-Free Bread Flour (page 8)

DOUGH
Bread Starter
1¼ cups warm milk (about 95°F) (not nonfat)
4 cups (560 g) Gluten-Free Bread Flour (page 8), plus more for sprinkling
2 tablespoons (24 g) sugar
4 tablespoons (56 g) unsalted butter, at room temperature
1 tablespoon (18 g) kosher salt
1 large egg plus 1 large egg yolk, at room temperature

To make the bread starter, tear the ripe Mother Starter into five pieces and place all of them in the bowl of a stand mixer fitted with the paddle attachment. Add the water and mix on low speed until the mixture looks like a liquid slurry (about 2 minutes). Add the bread flour and mix on low speed until the flour is incorporated into the liquid. Switch to the dough hook and knead on medium speed for 2 minutes. The dough will be stretchy and smooth. Transfer the bread starter to a lightly oiled bowl or proofing bucket large enough for the dough to rise to double its size, spray the top of the dough with cooking oil spray, and cover with an oiled piece of plastic wrap (or the oiled top to your proofing bucket). Allow the dough to rise in a warm, draft-free location until doubled in size (6 to 8 hours). Do not proceed until the bread starter has doubled fully.

Once the bread starter has doubled in size, use it to make the bread dough. Place the bread starter in the bowl of your stand mixer, add the warm milk, and mix with the paddle attachment on low speed to soften the bread starter (about 1 minute). Add the bread flour and sugar and switch to the dough hook. Turn the mixer on low speed and knead for about 2 minutes, until the dough is once again stretchy and smooth. Add the butter, salt, and eggs, raise the mixer speed to medium, and knead for 3 minutes. Transfer the dough to a lightly oiled bowl or proofing bucket large enough for the dough to rise to double its size, and cover with an oiled piece of plastic wrap (or the oiled top to your proofing bucket). Place the dough in the refrigerator for at least 12 hours and up to 2 days. After 2 days, the dough has a tendency to become too active and will easily overproof after being shaped.

On baking day, preheat your oven to 350°F. Line a small, rimmed baking sheet with unbleached parchment paper and set it aside. Remove the dough from the refrigerator and turn it out onto a lightly floured surface. Knead until smoother as described in the General Shaping Tips in Chapter 3. Divide the dough into fifteen pieces of equal size and follow the instructions on page 32 for shaping small, round rolls. Place the rounds less than 1 inch apart on the prepared baking sheet, in rows. Cover the baking sheet with oiled plastic wrap and allow to rise in a warm, draft-free location until nearly doubled in size (about 1½ hours). With a sharp knife or lame, slash each roll with an X on the top, each line of the X at a 45-degree angle to the bread (see page 34).

Place the rolls in the center of the preheated oven and bake for about 20 minutes, or until the rolls are lightly golden brown and register 185°F on an instant-read thermometer. Remove from the oven and serve warm.

LEVAIN BOULE BREAD
MAKES 2 SMALL ROUND LOAVES

MADE WITH THE SAME LIGHTLY ENRICHED DOUGH AS THE LEVAIN Dinner Rolls (page 97), this boule bread is great for sandwiches or just for tearing into soon after it comes out of the oven.

BREAD STARTER
80 grams ripe Mother Starter, chilled or at room temperature (page 87)
½ cup plus 3 tablespoons bottled water, at room temperature
1 cup plus 10 tablespoons (225 g) Gluten-Free Bread Flour (page 8)

DOUGH
Bread Starter
1¼ cups warm milk (about 95°F) (not nonfat)
4 cups (560 g) Gluten-Free Bread Flour (page 8), plus more for sprinkling
2 tablespoons (24 g) sugar
4 tablespoons (56 g) unsalted butter, at room temperature
1 tablespoon (18 g) kosher salt
1 large egg plus 1 large egg yolk, at room temperature

To make the bread starter, tear the ripe Mother Starter into five pieces and place all of them in the bowl of a stand mixer fitted with the paddle attachment. Add the water and mix on low speed until the mixture looks like a liquid slurry (about 2 minutes). Add the bread flour and mix on low speed until the flour is incorporated into the liquid. Switch to the dough hook and knead on medium speed for 2 minutes. The dough will be stretchy and smooth. Transfer the bread starter to a lightly oiled bowl or proofing bucket large enough for the dough to rise to double its size, spray the top of the dough with cooking oil spray, and cover with an oiled piece of plastic wrap (or the oiled top to your proofing bucket). Allow to rise in a warm, draft-free location until doubled in size (6 to 8 hours). Do not proceed until the bread starter has doubled fully.

Once the bread starter has doubled in size, use it to make the bread dough. Place the bread starter in the bowl of your stand mixer, add the milk, and mix with the paddle attachment on low speed to soften the bread starter (about 1 minute). Add the bread flour and sugar and switch to the dough hook. Turn the mixer on low speed and knead for about 2 minutes, until the dough is once again stretchy and smooth. Add the butter, salt, and eggs, raise the mixer speed to medium, and knead for 3 minutes. Transfer the dough to a lightly oiled bowl or proofing bucket large enough for the dough to rise to double its size, and cover with an oiled piece of plastic wrap (or the oiled top to your proofing bucket). Place the dough in the refrigerator for at least 12 hours and up to 2 days. After 2 days, the dough has a tendency to become too active and will easily overproof after being shaped.

On baking day, line a rimmed baking sheet with unbleached parchment paper and set it aside. Remove the dough from the refrigerator and turn it out onto a lightly floured surface. Knead until smoother as described in the General Shaping Tips in Chapter 3. Divide the dough into two equally weighted pieces. To shape the first loaf (covering the other with a moist tea towel so that it doesn't dry out), follow the instructions on page 34 for shaping a *boule*. Place the shaped dough onto the prepared baking sheet, seam side down, and dust with more flour. Repeat the process with the other piece of dough. Cover both loaves with oiled plastic wrap and set to rise in a warm, draft-free location until doubled in size (about 1 hour).

About 25 minutes before the dough has finished rising, preheat your oven to 350°F. Once the dough has finished rising, remove the plastic wrap, dust both loaves with more flour, and carefully slash each risen loaf horizontally near the base with a sharp knife or lame at a 45 degree angle and ¼ inch deep. Place the bread in the center of the preheated oven, quickly throw a few ice cubes into the bottom of the oven to create steam, and quickly close the oven door. Bake until lightly golden brown, and each loaf reads about 190°F in the center on an instant-read thermometer (about 40 minutes). Remove from the oven, transfer to a wire rack, and allow to cool for about 20 minutes before slicing and serving.

NO-RYE "RYE" BREAD
MAKES 1 LARGE ROUND LOAF

EVERYBODY WHO KNOWS ANYTHING ABOUT A GLUTEN-FREE DIET knows that we can't have rye bread. It's rye bread! And wheat, barley, and rye are the most common sources of gluten. But now, thanks to the complex flavor of our wild yeast starter, the right mix of Gluten-Free Bread Flour, plus the sorghum flour and teff flour in our Whole-Grain Gluten-Free Flour, we can mimic the taste of rye bread. Add some molasses, honey, and, of course, caraway seeds, and we can have the taste and the smell of real rye bread. No lie, this is your no-rye rye.

BREAD STARTER
80 grams ripe Mother Starter, chilled or at room temperature (page 87)
½ cup plus 3 tablespoons bottled water, at room temperature
1 cup plus 10 tablespoons (225 g) Gluten-Free Bread Flour (page 8)

DOUGH
Bread Starter
1¼ cups plus 2 tablespoons warm bottled water (about 95°F)
3¼ cups (455 g) Gluten-Free Bread Flour (page 8), plus more for sprinkling
½ cup (70 g) Whole-Grain Gluten-Free Flour (page 10)
1 tablespoon (18 g) kosher salt
1 tablespoon unsulfured molasses
1 tablespoon honey
1½ tablespoons caraway seeds

To make the bread starter, tear the ripe Mother Starter into five pieces and place all of them in the bowl of a stand mixer fitted with the paddle attachment. Add the water and mix on low speed until the mixture looks like a liquid slurry (about 2 minutes). Add the bread flour and mix on low speed until the flour is incorporated into the liquid. Switch to the dough hook and knead on medium speed for 2 minutes. The dough will be stretchy and smooth. Transfer the bread starter to a lightly oiled bowl or proofing bucket large enough for the dough to rise to double its size, spray the top of the dough with cooking oil spray, and cover with an oiled piece of plastic wrap (or the oiled top to your proofing bucket). Allow to rise in a warm, draft-free location until doubled in size (6 to 8 hours). Do not proceed until the bread starter has doubled fully.

Once the bread starter has doubled in size, use it to make the bread dough. Place the bread starter in the bowl of your stand mixer, add the water, and mix with the paddle attachment on low speed to soften it (about 1 minute). Add the bread flour and the whole-grain flour and switch to the dough hook. Turn the mixer on low speed and knead, until the dough is stretchy and smooth. Add the salt, molasses, and honey, raise the mixer speed to medium, and knead for 3 minutes. Add the caraway seeds and mix again until the seeds are incorporated throughout the dough. Transfer the dough to a lightly oiled bowl or proofing bucket large enough for the dough to rise to double its size, and cover with an oiled piece of plastic wrap (or the oiled top to your proofing bucket). Place the dough in the refrigerator for at least 12 hours and up to 2 days.

On baking day, flour a 9-inch banetton (or proofing basket) and set it aside. Remove the dough from the refrigerator and turn it out onto a lightly floured surface. With well-floured hands and a bench scraper, gently shape and pat the dough into a round, sprinkling the dough very lightly with flour if it gets very sticky. Place the dough into the banetton, seam side up. Sprinkle the top of the dough with flour and cover loosely with a plastic bag. Place in a warm, draft-free location until nearly doubled in size (about 2 hours).

About 25 minutes before the dough is ready to bake, preheat your oven to 450°F. Grease a 4- to 6-quart covered Dutch oven with vegetable shortening or ghee (ghee is pure butterfat and is more heat-stable than butter). Turn the dough out of the proofing basket and into the prepared Dutch oven, seam side down, taking care not to deflate the dough. Reach in to the pan and slash the raised bread horizontally near the base carefully with a sharp knife or lame at a 45 degree angle and ¼ inch deep. Cover and place in the center of the preheated oven. Bake for 30 minutes. Uncover the pot and continue to bake until the loaf is deep golden brown, the center of the loaf reads about 195°F on an instant-read thermometer, and sounds hollow when thumped on the side (about 15 to 20 minutes).

Remove from the oven and turn the bread out of the Dutch oven onto a wire rack to cool for 20 minutes before slicing and serving.

"PUMPERNICKEL" BREAD

MAKES 2 LARGE LOAVES

W ELL, IF WE CAN HAVE NO-RYE "RYE" BREAD (PAGE 101), IT SEEMS
reasonable to expect that we can have pumpernickel. And I am nothing if not reasonable. Like in our No-Rye "Rye" Bread, we rely upon the right
blend of Gluten-Free Bread Flour and our Whole-Grain Gluten-Free Flour,
plus molasses and honey. But here we add Dutch-processed cocoa powder for
depth of flavor and color, plus coarsely ground cornmeal for added bite. The
moment you taste it, you'll "get" it.

BREAD STARTER

80 grams ripe Mother Starter, chilled or at room temperature (page 87)
½ cup plus 3 tablespoons bottled water, at room temperature
1 cup plus 10 tablespoons (225 g) Gluten-Free Bread Flour (page 8)

DOUGH

Bread Starter
1 cup plus 1 tablespoon bottled water, at room temperature
2½ cups (350 g) Gluten-Free Bread Flour (page 8), plus more for sprinkling
½ cup (70 g) Whole-Grain Gluten-Free Flour (page 10)
1½ teaspoons kosher salt
¼ cup (33 g) coarsely ground gluten-free cornmeal
2 tablespoons (10 g) Dutch-processed cocoa powder
2 tablespoons unsulfured molasses
2 tablespoons honey
2 tablespoons vegetable oil

To make the bread starter, tear the ripe Mother Starter into five pieces and
place all of them in the bowl of a stand mixer fitted with the paddle attachment. Add the water and mix on low speed until the mixture looks like a liquid
slurry (about 2 minutes). Add the bread flour and mix on low speed until the
flour is incorporated into the liquid. Switch to the dough hook and knead on
medium speed for 2 minutes. The dough will be stretchy and smooth. Transfer the bread starter to a lightly oiled bowl or proofing bucket large enough
for the dough to rise to double its size, spray the top of the dough with cooking

oil spray, and cover with an oiled piece of plastic wrap (or the oiled top to your proofing bucket). Allow to rise in a warm, draft-free location until doubled in size (6 to 8 hours). Do not proceed until the bread starter has doubled fully.

Once the bread starter has doubled in size, use it to make the bread dough. Place the bread starter in the bowl of your stand mixer, add the water, and mix with the paddle attachment on low speed to soften the bread starter (about 1 minute). Add the bread flour and the whole-grain blend and switch to the dough hook. Turn the mixer on low speed and knead for about 2 minutes, until the dough is once again stretchy and smooth. Add the salt, cornmeal, cocoa powder, molasses, honey, and oil, raise the mixer speed to medium, and knead for 3 minutes. Transfer the dough to a lightly oiled bowl or proofing bucket large enough for the dough to rise to double its size, and cover with an oiled piece of plastic wrap (or the oiled top to your proofing bucket). Place the dough in the refrigerator for at least 12 hours and up to 2 days. After 2 days, the dough has a tendency to become too active and will easily overproof after being shaped.

On baking day, remove the dough from the refrigerator and turn it out onto a lightly floured surface. With well-floured hands and a bench scraper, gently shape and pat the dough into a round, sprinkling the dough very lightly with flour if it gets very sticky. Pull into a *batard* shape as directed on page 34 and place it on a parchment-lined baking sheet. Sprinkle the top of the dough with flour, and cover with lightly oiled plastic wrap and slash the raised bread a few times on top with a sharp knife or lame about ¼ inch deep. Place the loaf in a warm, draft-free location until nearly doubled in size (about 2 hours).

About 20 minutes before the dough has finished rising, preheat your oven to 375°F. Once the dough has finished rising, remove the plastic wrap, place in the center of the oven, and bake until it is dark brown, sounds hollow when thumped on the side, and the center of the loaf reads about 195°F on an instant-read thermometer (about 40 minutes). Remove from the oven and transfer onto a wire rack to cool for 20 minutes before slicing and serving.

SOURDOUGH SOFT PRETZELS
MAKES 12 PRETZELS

E VEN THOUGH YOU COULD CONCEIVABLY SHAPE MANY OF THE
doughs in this book into soft pretzels, boil them in a baking soda bath,
and then bake them, these sourdough ones are my favorite. Because this is
such a simple recipe, with only a few tablespoons of butter as an enrichment,
the flavor of the sourdough starter really shines through. Truly authentic
pretzels are soaked in a water bath with food-grade lye, but working with lye
is dangerous and requires rubber gloves and eye protection! The most common way to mimic the effect of soaking homemade pretzels in a lye bath is to
soak them in a boiling baking soda bath.

BREAD STARTER
40 grams ripe Mother Starter, chilled or at room temperature (page 87)
¼ cup plus 1½ tablespoons bottled water, at room temperature
13 tablespoons (115 g) Gluten-Free Bread Flour (page 8)

DOUGH
Bread Starter
1 cup plus 2 tablespoons warm bottled water (about 95°F)
3 tablespoons (42 g) unsalted butter, at room temperature
3 cups (420 g) Gluten-Free Bread Flour (page 8), plus more for sprinkling
2 teaspoons (12 g) kosher salt
Baking soda bath, for boiling (6 cups water plus 1 tablespoon baking soda plus
   1 teaspoon kosher salt)
Coarse salt, for sprinkling

To make the bread starter, tear the ripe Mother Starter into five pieces and
place all of them in the bowl of a stand mixer fitted with the paddle attachment. Add the water and mix on low speed until the mixture looks like a liquid
slurry (about 2 minutes). Add the bread flour and mix on low speed until the
flour is incorporated into the liquid. Switch to the dough hook and knead on
medium speed for 2 minutes. The dough will be stretchy and smooth. Transfer the bread starter to a lightly oiled bowl or proofing bucket large enough
for the dough to rise to double its size, spray the top of the dough with cooking

oil spray, and cover with an oiled piece of plastic wrap (or the oiled top to your proofing bucket). Allow to rise in a warm, draft-free location until doubled in size (6 to 8 hours). Do not proceed until the bread starter has doubled fully.

Once the bread starter has doubled in size, use it to make the pretzel dough. Place the bread starter in the bowl of your stand mixer, add the warm water and butter, and mix with the paddle attachment on low speed to soften the bread starter (about 1 minute). Add the bread flour and kosher salt, and switch to the dough hook. Turn the mixer on low speed and knead until the dough is stretchy and smooth. Transfer the dough to a lightly oiled bowl or proofing bucket large enough for the dough to rise to double its size, and cover with an oiled piece of plastic wrap (or the oiled top to your proofing bucket). Place the dough in the refrigerator for 12 to 18 hours.

On baking day, line a large, rimmed baking sheet with unbleached parchment paper, grease lightly with cooking oil, and set it aside. Remove the dough from the refrigerator. Turn the dough out onto a lightly floured surface and knead until smoother as described in the General Shaping Tips in Chapter 3. Divide the dough into twelve parts, each about 2 ounces. Flouring the surface as necessary to keep the dough from sticking, roll each piece of dough (pressing down and out with your palms) into a rope about 8 inches long. Shape into a pretzel by turning both ends of the rope inward toward one another, crossing one end over the other in an X. Place each piece of shaped dough on the prepared baking sheet, 2 inches apart from one another. Cover with lightly oiled plastic wrap, and set in a warm, draft-free location to rise until nearly doubled in size (about 1 hour).

As the dough nears the end of its rise, preheat your oven to 375°F. In a large pot, make a baking soda bath by dissolving 1 tablespoon of baking soda in 6 cups of water (approximate measurements are fine here), with 1 teaspoon of kosher salt added for flavor. Simply bring the mixture to a boil over medium-high to high heat. Once the dough has finished rising, place the pretzels a few at a time into the boiling baking soda bath for just under a minute per side. Remove the pretzels with a strainer and return them to the baking sheet. Sprinkle with coarse salt. Place the pretzels in the center of the preheated oven and bake until golden brown all over (about 20 minutes). Allow to cool on the pan briefly before serving.

"RYE" BAGELS
MAKES 6 BAGELS

MAKING GLUTEN-FREE "RYE" BAGELS IS ITS OWN SORT OF VIC-tory. Almost everyone has to live without a good rye bagel. They are just so inexplicably hard to come by! In fact, I predict that, if you're not terribly careful, you will have your gluten-full friends putting in orders for these bagels if they catch wind of your making these. So let's just keep it between us. If you're looking for more traditional plain and whole-grain bagels, you'll find just what you're looking for in Chapter 6.

BREAD STARTER
40 grams ripe Mother Starter, chilled or at room temperature (page 87)
¼ cup plus 1½ tablespoons bottled water, at room temperature
13 tablespoons (115 g) Gluten-Free Bread Flour (page 8)

DOUGH
Bread Starter
½ cup plus 3 tablespoons bottled water, at room temperature
1 cup plus 10 tablespoons (228 g) Gluten-Free Bread Flour (page 8), plus more
    for sprinkling
¼ cup (35 g) Whole-Grain Gluten-Free Flour (page 10)
1½ teaspoons (9 g) kosher salt
1½ teaspoons unsulfured molasses
1½ teaspoons honey
1 tablespoon caraway seeds, plus more for sprinkling
Molasses bath, for boiling (6 cups water plus 1 tablespoon molasses plus
    1 teaspoon kosher salt)
Egg wash (1 large egg, at room temperature, beaten with 1 tablespoon water)

To make the bread starter, tear the ripe Mother Starter into five pieces and place all of them in the bowl of a stand mixer fitted with the paddle attachment. Add the water and mix on low speed until the mixture looks like a liquid slurry (about 2 minutes). Add the bread flour and mix on low speed until the flour is incorporated into the liquid. Switch to the dough hook and knead on medium speed for 2 minutes. The dough will be stretchy and smooth.

Transfer the bread starter to a lightly oiled bowl or proofing bucket large enough for the dough to rise to double its size, spray the top of the dough with cooking oil spray, and cover with an oiled piece of plastic wrap (or the oiled top to your proofing bucket). Allow to rise in a warm, draft-free location until doubled in size (6 to 8 hours). Do not proceed until the bread starter has doubled fully.

Once the bread starter has doubled in size, use it to make the bread dough. Place the bread starter in the bowl of your stand mixer, add the water, and mix with the paddle attachment on low speed to soften the bread starter (about 1 minute). Add the bread flour and the whole-grain flour and switch to the dough hook. Turn the mixer on low speed and knead until the dough is stretchy and smooth. Add the salt, molasses, and honey, raise the mixer speed to medium, and knead for 3 minutes. Add the caraway seeds, and mix again until the seeds are incorporated throughout the dough. Transfer the dough to a lightly oiled bowl or proofing bucket large enough for the dough to rise to double its size, and cover with an oiled piece of plastic wrap (or the oiled top to your proofing bucket). Place the dough in the refrigerator for 12 to 18 hours.

On baking day, line a large, rimmed baking sheet with unbleached parchment paper, grease lightly with cooking oil, and set it aside. Remove the dough from the refrigerator, turn it out onto a lightly floured surface and knead until smooth. Divide the dough into six parts. To shape each piece of dough, follow the instructions on page 38 for shaping bagels. Place each piece of bagel-shaped dough on the prepared baking sheet, 2 inches apart from one another. Cover with lightly oiled plastic wrap, and set in a warm, draft-free location to rise until nearly doubled in size (about 1 hour). About 25 minutes before the dough has finished rising, preheat your oven to 375°F.

As the dough nears the end of its rise, make the molasses bath by dissolving 1 tablespoon of molasses and 1 teaspoon of kosher salt in 6 cups of water (approximate measurements are fine here). Bring the mixture to a boil over medium-high to high heat. Once the dough has finished rising, place the shaped bagels, a few at a time, into the boiling bath for just less than a minute per side. Remove the bagels with a strainer and return them to the baking sheet. Brush the boiled bagels with the egg wash and sprinkle with caraway seeds. Repeat with the remaining bagels. Place them in the center of the preheated oven and bake until the bagels are golden brown all over (about 20 minutes). Allow to cool on the pan briefly before serving.

"PUMPERNICKEL" BAGELS
MAKES 6 BAGELS

I N THESE BAGELS, AS IN THE "PUMPERNICKEL" BREAD (PAGE 105), WE marry whole-grain flours, cocoa powder, and coarsely ground cornmeal to match the color, flavor, and even the texture of traditional pumpernickel. I've always thought that pumpernickel bagels were best enjoyed lightly toasted, with nothing more than a warm pat of salted butter.

BREAD STARTER
40 grams ripe Mother Starter, chilled or at room temperature (page 87)
¼ cup plus 1½ tablespoons bottled water, at room temperature
13 tablespoons (115 g) Gluten-Free Bread Flour (page 8)

DOUGH
Bread Starter
½ cup plus 1 tablespoon bottled water, at room temperature
1¼ cups (175 g) Gluten-Free Bread Flour (page 8), plus more for sprinkling
¼ cup (35 g) Whole-Grain Gluten-Free Flour (page 10)
2 tablespoons (17 g) coarsely ground gluten-free cornmeal
1 tablespoon (5 g) Dutch-processed cocoa powder
1 teaspoon (6 g) kosher salt
1 tablespoon unsulfured molasses
1 tablespoon honey
1 tablespoon canola oil
Molasses bath, for boiling (6 cups water plus 1 tablespoon molasses plus
    1 teaspoon kosher salt)
Egg wash (1 large egg, at room temperature, beaten with 1 tablespoon water)

To make the bread starter, tear the ripe Mother Starter into five pieces and place all of them in the bowl of a stand mixer fitted with the paddle attachment. Add the water and mix on low speed until the mixture looks like a liquid slurry (about 2 minutes). Add the bread flour and mix on low speed until the flour is incorporated into the liquid. Switch to the dough hook and knead on medium speed for 2 minutes. The dough will be stretchy and smooth. Transfer the bread starter to a lightly oiled bowl or proofing bucket large enough for the dough to rise to double its size, spray the top of the dough with cooking oil spray, and cover with an oiled piece of plastic wrap (or the oiled top to your proofing bucket). Allow to rise in a warm, draft-free location until doubled in size (6 to 8 hours). Do not proceed until the bread starter has doubled fully.

Once the bread starter has doubled in size, use it to make the bread dough. Place the bread starter in the bowl of your stand mixer, add the water, and mix with the paddle attachment on low speed to soften the bread starter (about 1 minute). Add the bread flour and the whole-grain blend and switch to the dough hook. Turn the mixer on low speed and knead for about 2 minutes, until the dough is once again stretchy and smooth. Add the cornmeal, cocoa powder, salt, molasses, honey, and oil, raise the mixer speed to medium, and knead for 3 minutes. Transfer the dough to a lightly oiled bowl or proofing bucket large enough for the dough to rise to double its size, and cover with an oiled piece of plastic wrap (or the oiled top to your proofing bucket). Place the dough in the refrigerator for 12 to 18 hours.

On baking day, line a large, rimmed baking sheet with unbleached parchment paper, grease lightly with cooking oil, and set it aside. Remove the dough from the refrigerator, turn out the dough onto a lightly floured surface, and knead until smooth. Divide the dough into six parts. To shape each piece of dough, follow the instructions on page 38 for shaping bagels. Place each piece of bagel-shaped dough on the prepared baking sheet, each 2 inches apart from one another. Cover with lightly oiled plastic wrap, and set in a warm, draft-free location to rise until nearly doubled in size (about 1 hour). About 25 minutes before the dough has finished rising, preheat your oven to 375°F.

As the dough nears the end of its rise, make the molasses bath by dissolving 1 tablespoon of molasses and 1 teaspoon of kosher salt in 6 cups of water (approximate measurements are fine here). Bring the mixture to a boil over medium-high to high heat. Once the dough has finished rising, place the bagels a few at a time into the boiling bath for just less than a minute per side. Remove the bagels with a strainer and return them to the baking sheet. Brush the boiled bagels with the egg wash. Repeat with the remaining bagels. Place them in the center of the preheated oven and bake until the bagels are dark brown all over (about 20 minutes). Allow to cool on the pan briefly before serving.

PLAIN SOURDOUGH BAGELS
MAKES 6 BAGELS

EVEN MOST CONVENTIONAL, GLUTEN-CONTAINING SOURDOUGH bagels aren't really sourdough. They're really just plain bagels that some-one who thought he was clever stuck in the basket that says "sourdough" at the bagel place. This recipe makes real, sour sourdough bagels, using the wild yeast starter (pages 83–90), which is unique in its ability to lend that truly organic tang of pure sourdough. The dough has relatively low hydration, as any real bagel does, and the use of the starter gives rise to a less brown, more golden color that plain bagels simply do not achieve.

BREAD STARTER
80 grams ripe Mother Starter (page 87)
½ cup plus 3 tablespoons bottled water, at room temperature
1 cup plus 10 tablespoons (225 g) Gluten-Free Bread Flour (page 8)

DOUGH
Bread Starter
½ cup plus 2 tablespoons warm bottled water (about 95°F)
2¼ cups (315 g) Gluten-Free Bread Flour (page 8), plus more for sprinkling
2 teaspoons (12 g) kosher salt
Molasses bath, for boiling (6 cups water plus 1 tablespoon molasses plus
    1 teaspoon kosher salt)
Egg wash (1 large egg, at room temperature, beaten with 1 tablespoon water)

To make the bread starter, tear the ripe Mother Starter into five pieces and place all of them in the bowl of a stand mixer fitted with the paddle attach-ment. Add the water and mix on low speed until the mixture looks like a liquid slurry (about 2 minutes). Add the bread flour and mix on low speed until the flour is incorporated into the liquid. Switch to the dough hook and knead on medium speed for 2 minutes. The dough will be stretchy and smooth. Transfer the bread starter to a lightly oiled bowl or proofing bucket large enough for the dough to rise to double its size, spray the top of the dough with cooking oil spray, and cover with an oiled piece of plastic wrap (or the oiled top to your proofing bucket). Allow to rise in a warm, draft-free location until doubled in size (6 to 8 hours). Do not proceed until the bread starter has doubled fully.

Once the bread starter has doubled in size, use it to make the bagel dough. Place the bread starter in the bowl of your stand mixer, add the warm water, and mix with the paddle attachment on low speed to soften the bread starter (about 1 minute). Add the bread flour and salt and switch to the dough hook. Turn the mixer on low speed and knead until the dough is stretchy and smooth. Transfer the dough to a lightly oiled bowl or proofing bucket large enough for the dough to rise to double its size, and cover with an oiled piece of plastic wrap (or the oiled top to your proofing bucket). Place the dough in the refrigerator for 12 to 18 hours.

On baking day, line a large, rimmed baking sheet with unbleached parchment paper, grease lightly with cooking oil, and set it aside. Remove the dough from the refrigerator, turn out onto a lightly floured surface, and knead until smooth. Divide the dough into six parts. To shape each piece of dough, follow the instructions on page 38 for shaping bagels. Place each piece of bagel-shaped dough on the prepared baking sheet, 2 inches from one another. Cover with lightly oiled plastic wrap, and set in a warm, draft-free location to rise until nearly doubled in size (about 1 hour). About 25 minutes before the dough has finished rising, preheat your oven to 375°F.

As the dough nears the end of its rise, make the molasses bath by dissolving 1 tablespoon of molasses and 1 teaspoon of kosher salt in 6 cups of water (approximate measurements are fine here). Bring the mixture to a boil over medium-high to high heat. Once the dough has finished rising, place the bagel-shaped dough, a few at a time, into the boiling bath, for less than a minute per side. Remove the bagels with a strainer and return them to the baking sheet. Brush the boiled bagels with the egg wash. Repeat with the remaining bagels. Place them in the center of the preheated oven and bake until the bagels are golden brown all over (about 20 minutes). Allow to cool on the pan briefly before serving.

SOURDOUGH PANCAKES
MAKES 16 PANCAKES

WITH JUST A LITTLE ADVANCE PLANNING, SOURDOUGH PANCAKES are just as easy to make as regular pancakes but, of course, way more special. The tang of the starter gives these light and fluffy pancakes enough depth of flavor that I like them best plain, or maybe with a few fresh berries on top.

INGREDIENTS

80 grams ripe Mother Starter (page 87)

½ cup plus 3 tablespoons bottled water, at room temperature

2 cups (280 g) Gluten-Free Bread Flour (page 8)

2 tablespoons (24 g) sugar

1 teaspoon (6 g) kosher salt

1 cup plus 1 tablespoon milk, at room temperature (not nonfat, plus more if necessary)

3 tablespoons (42 g) unsalted butter, melted and cooled, plus more for greasing the skillet

2 large eggs, at room temperature, beaten

½ teaspoon baking soda

Tear the ripe Mother Starter into five pieces and place all of them in the bowl of a stand mixer fitted with the paddle attachment. Add the water and mix on low speed until the mixture looks like a liquid slurry (about 2 minutes). Add the flour, sugar, and salt to the bowl, then 1 cup of the milk, then the butter, and mix with the paddle attachment first on low speed, and then on medium speed until the batter is smooth (about 3 minutes). Cover the bowl (or transfer to another bowl large enough to allow the starter to double in size), and leave it out at room temperature overnight. The batter will nearly double.

When you are ready to cook the pancakes, line a rimmed baking sheet with parchment paper and set it aside. Preheat your oven to 200°F, as you'll use the oven to keep the first batches of pancakes warm while you make the rest. Heat a large (ideally, cast-iron) skillet over medium heat and brush with a thin layer of unsalted butter. Immediately before cooking the pancakes, stir down the pancake batter, add the beaten eggs and baking soda, and mix to combine well. The batter will be relatively thick, but should be very thickly pourable. Add more milk by the teaspoon as necessary to achieve the proper consistency. It will never be a thin batter that is as pourable as traditional pancake batter. Ladle the pancake batter into the hot skillet in rounds, smoothing them out to about 5 inches in diameter and about ¼ inch thick. As the pancakes cook on the underside, bubbles will form but few will break through the surface. Once the pancakes are mostly set (about 1½ minutes), carefully flip them over and press down on the cooked side with a wide spatula to sear the other side. The pancakes should have nearly cooked all the way through before you flip them, but finish on the second side for at least 30 seconds or until set.

Transfer the cooked pancakes from the skillet to the prepared baking sheet. Place the baking sheet in the preheated oven to stay warm until you have finished with all of the pancake batter. Brush the skillet lightly with more unsalted butter, and repeat with the remaining batter. Serve the pancakes warm.

6 ROLLS AND OTHER SHAPED BREADS

SMALLER BREADS SHAPED INTO BAGELS, ROLLS, ENGLISH MUFFINS, KNOTS, AND HOAGIES

ENGLISH MUFFINS
MAKES 8 MUFFINS

THE KEYS TO THE KINGDOM OF THE PROPER NOOKS AND CRANNIES in real English muffins are a very high-rising bread (check), which is then fork-split to reveal all those yeasty holes in irregular fashion (check). Searing them first in a hot, dry cast-iron skillet before finishing them in the oven ensures a lightly crisp outside, and muffin rings coax the relatively shapeless dough into a tall, round muffin. If you don't have special muffin rings, you can order them online, or try using large round cookie cutters or even cutting 1-inch-tall rings out of an empty and sanitized aluminum can. Because this dough has very high hydration, it requires only one, exceedingly short, rise. And a last-minute addition of baking soda to the dough supercharges the muffins' oven-spring.

INGREDIENTS
2½ cups (350 g) Gluten-Free Bread Flour (page 8)

1 tablespoon (12 g) sugar

2 teaspoons (6 g) instant yeast

1 teaspoon (6 g) kosher salt

2 tablespoons (28 g) unsalted butter, at room temperature

1½ cups warm water (about 95°F)

Coarsely ground gluten-free cornmeal, for sprinkling

1 teaspoon baking soda

Place the flour, sugar, and yeast in a large bowl and whisk to combine well. Add the salt, then the butter and water, whisking to combine well after each addition. The dough will be very wet. Cover with oiled plastic wrap and set aside in a warm, draft-free location to rise for 30 minutes.

Line two small, rimmed baking sheets with unbleached parchment paper and set them aside. Preheat your oven to 325°F.

Place a 10-inch cast-iron skillet over medium-high heat. While the pan is heating, grease four metal English muffin rings and place them in the hot pan. Sprinkle a little bit of cornmeal inside each ring. Uncover the bowl of dough and scrape half of the dough into a separate bowl. Mix ½ teaspoon of the baking soda into one bowl, and then fill the rings in the pan about three-quarters of the way full with the bread dough. Sprinkle a bit more cornmeal on top of each muffin, cover the pan, and cook for 5 minutes. Remove the cover of the pan, flip the rings with the muffins inside (using tongs), cover again, and cook for 5 minutes more. Transfer the muffins in the rings to one of the prepared baking sheets, and place it in the preheated oven to bake until the internal temperature reaches 195°F (7 to 10 minutes).

Add the remaining ½ teaspoon of baking soda to the remaining dough and mix well. Grease four more English muffin rings, place them in the hot pan, and repeat the same process as before to cook both sides of the remaining English muffins. Transfer the muffins in their rings to the remaining prepared baking sheet of the muffins. Place the baking sheet in the preheated oven and bake until the internal temperature of the muffins reaches 195°F on an instant-read thermometer (7 to 10 minutes). Allow to cool very briefly. Split each muffin with a fork by inserting the tines in the center of the muffin along the middle, parallel to the muffin itself, and then gently prying open with your fingers. Serve warm.

CIABATTA BREAD
MAKES 2 CIABATTAS

HYDRATION AND YEAST HAVE AN INVERSE RELATIONSHIP IN BREAD baking. The more moisture you have, typically the less yeast you need. And vice versa. This is a very, very wet dough, and it has less yeast than many of the other breads in this book. It is particularly important to let it rise slowly for days in the refrigerator before shaping and baking it. It not only makes handling the dough possible, but it allows even that comparatively little bit of yeast to develop a truly complex flavor. So although you can bake and shape it after the dough spends a mere 12 hours in the refrigerator, aim for closer to the 5-day mark.

STARTER

1 cup (140 g) Gluten-Free Bread Flour (page 8)
1⅓ teaspoons (4 g) instant yeast
¾ cup water, at room temperature
1 tablespoon honey

DOUGH

2 cups (280 g) Gluten-Free Bread Flour (page 8), plus more for sprinkling
¾ teaspoon cream of tartar
1 (6 g) teaspoon kosher salt
1 tablespoon (12 g) sugar
¾ cup water, at room temperature
Starter

Make the starter. In a medium-size bowl, whisk together the bread flour and yeast. Add the water and honey, and mix with a wooden spoon until smooth. Cover tightly with oiled plastic wrap and set aside until it has more than doubled in size and filled with bubbles (about an hour).

Once the starter has finished rising, make the dough. Place the flour, cream of tartar, salt, and sugar in the bowl of your stand mixer, and use a handheld whisk to combine well. Add the water and risen starter to the bowl, and mix on low speed with the dough hook until combined. Raise the mixer speed to medium and knead for about 5 minutes. When you lift the dough hook, a trail of dough from the hook to the bowl should be intact for at least the count of five. The dough will be quite sticky. Spray a silicone spatula lightly with cooking oil spray, and scrape down the sides of the bowl. Transfer the dough to a lightly oiled bowl or proofing bucket large enough for the dough to rise to double its size, and cover with an oiled piece of plastic wrap (or the oiled top to your proofing bucket). Place the dough in the refrigerator for at least 12 hours and up to 5 days.

On baking day, remove the dough from the refrigerator, scatter a generous amount of flour on a flat surface, and scrape the dough out of the bowl on top of the flour. Turn the dough over on itself with a lightly oiled bench scraper. It will remain very sticky. Divide the dough into two equal pieces, and place both carefully on a parchment-lined half-sheet baking sheet. With lightly oiled hands, press each piece of dough into a rectangle 10 inches long by 4 inches wide and 1 inch high. Dust both pieces of dough with flour, then cover them loosely with greased plastic wrap and let rise until at least doubled in size (about 2 hours).

About 20 minutes before the dough is fully risen, preheat your oven to 400°F and place a pizza stone on the lower rack. Once the dough has finished rising, using a pizza peel, slide the dough, already on parchment paper, on the pizza stone. Throw some ice cubes in the bottom of the oven and quickly close the door. Bake at 400°F for 5 minutes. Lower the heat to 375°F, and bake for another 10 minutes or until the center of each loaf reaches 205°F on an instant-read thermometer. Turn off the heat and prop open the oven door, leaving the bread inside for 5 minutes. Remove from the oven and allow the bread to cool for about 20 minutes before slicing and serving.

PLAIN (OR SEEDED) BAGELS
MAKES 6 BAGELS

A BAGEL IS A SPECIAL THING. IT ISN'T JUST A ROLL WITH AN UN-fortunate hole in the middle. It is a relatively simple, stiff dough, but it is boiled in a molasses bath before being baked to achieve its crispy-on-the-outside, chewy-on-the-inside perfection. Just be sure not to add extra moisture to the dough because you're worried that it's too stiff. Otherwise, the bagels will rise too much and fall apart before you can boil them. I always sprinkle seeds on top of the egg wash right before baking, as bagels are simply much prettier with seeds. But the fact that a plain bagel with butter is one of life's simple pleasures is not lost on me.

STARTER
1¼ cups (175 g) Gluten-Free Bread Flour (page 8)
1 teaspoon (3 g) instant yeast
2½ tablespoons (30 g) sugar
1 cup warm water (about 95°F)

DOUGH
2 cups (280 g) Gluten-Free Bread Flour (page 8), plus more for sprinkling
⅔ teaspoon (2 g) instant yeast
2 teaspoons (12 g) kosher salt
Starter
Molasses bath, for boiling (6 cups water plus 1 tablespoon molasses plus
   1 teaspoon kosher salt)
Egg wash (1 large egg, at room temperature, beaten with 1 tablespoon water)
Sesame and/or poppy seeds, for sprinkling (optional)

To make the starter, place all the starter ingredients in a medium-size bowl, and whisk until well combined. The mixture will be thick and shapeless. Cover and set the bowl aside in a warm, draft-free location to rise until doubled (about 40 minutes).

Once the starter has finished rising, make the dough. Place the flour and yeast in the bowl of your stand mixer, and use a handheld whisk to combine well. Add the salt, and whisk to combine. Add the risen starter to the bowl, and mix on low speed with the dough hook until combined. Raise the mixer speed to medium and knead for about 5 minutes. It will be very sticky dough, and because it is such a stiff dough, it will not trail from the dough hook when you raise the hook out of the bowl. Spray a silicone spatula lightly with cooking oil spray, and scrape down the sides of the bowl. Transfer the dough to a lightly oiled bowl or proofing bucket large enough for the dough to rise to double its size, and cover with an oiled piece of plastic wrap (or the oiled top to your proofing bucket). Place the dough in the refrigerator for at least 12 hours and up to 5 days.

On baking day, line a large, rimmed baking sheet with unbleached parchment paper, grease it lightly with cooking oil, and set it aside. Remove the dough from the refrigerator and, on a lightly floured surface, knead lightly as described in the General Shaping Tips in Chapter 3 until smooth. Divide the dough into six parts. To shape each piece of dough, follow the instructions on page 38 for shaping bagels. Place each piece of bagel-shaped dough on the prepared baking sheet, 2 inches apart from one another. Cover with lightly oiled plastic wrap, and set in a warm, draft-free location to rise until nearly doubled in size (about 1 hour). About 25 minutes before the dough has finished rising, preheat your oven to 375°F.

As the dough nears the end of its rise, make the molasses bath by dissolving 1 tablespoon of molasses and 1 teaspoon of kosher salt in 6 cups of water (approximate measurements are fine here). Bring the mixture to a boil over medium-high to high heat. Once the dough has finished rising, place the shaped bagels a few at a time into the boiling bath for less than a minute per side. Remove the bagels with a strainer and return them to the baking sheet. Brush the boiled bagels with the egg wash, and sprinkle with seeds, if using. Repeat with the remaining bagels. Place the baking sheet in the center of the preheated oven and bake until the bagels are golden brown all over (about 20 minutes). Allow to cool on the pan briefly before serving.

WHOLE-GRAIN BAGELS

MAKES 6 BAGELS

OTHER THAN REPLACING SOME OF THE GLUTEN-FREE BREAD flour with my gluten-free whole-grain blend and adding some butter to the dough, this recipe is very much like our Plain (or Seeded) Bagels (page 126). But it does boast that wheaty bite that a plain bagel simply cannot offer.

STARTER

¾ cup (105 g) Gluten-Free Bread Flour (page 8)
¾ cup (105 g) Whole-Grain Gluten-Free Flour (page 10)
1 teaspoon (3 g) instant yeast
2½ tablespoons (30 g) sugar
1 cup water, at room temperature

DOUGH

2 cups (280 g) Gluten-Free Bread Flour (page 8), plus more for sprinkling
⅔ teaspoon (2 g) instant yeast
2 teaspoons (12 g) kosher salt
Starter
2 tablespoons (28 g) unsalted butter, at room temperature
Molasses bath, for boiling: 3 quarts water plus 1 tablespoon molasses plus 1 teaspoon kosher salt
Egg wash (1 large egg, at room temperature, beaten with 1 tablespoon water)

To make the starter, place all the starter ingredients in a medium-size bowl, and whisk until well combined. The mixture will be thick and shapeless. Cover and set the bowl aside in a warm, draft-free location to rise until doubled (about 40 minutes).

Once the starter has finished rising, make the dough. Place the flour and yeast in the bowl of your stand mixer, and use a handheld whisk to combine well. Add the salt, and whisk to combine. Add risen starter and butter to the bowl, and mix on low speed with the dough hook until combined. Raise the mixer speed to medium and knead for about 5 minutes. It will be very sticky dough, and because it is such a stiff dough, it will not trail from the dough hook when you raise the hook out of the bowl. Spray a silicone spatula lightly with cooking oil spray, and scrape down the sides of the bowl. Transfer the dough to a lightly oiled bowl or proofing bucket large enough for the dough to rise to double its size, and cover with an oiled piece of plastic wrap (or the oiled top to your proofing bucket). Place the dough in the refrigerator for at least 12 hours and up to 5 days.

On baking day, line a large, rimmed baking sheet with unbleached parchment paper, grease it lightly with cooking oil, and set it aside. Remove the dough from the refrigerator and, on a lightly floured surface, knead lightly as described in the General Shaping Tips in Chapter 3 until smooth. Divide the dough into six parts. To shape each piece of dough, follow the instructions on page 38 for shaping bagels. Place each piece of bagel-shaped dough on the prepared baking sheet, 2 inches apart from one another. Cover with lightly oiled plastic wrap, and set in a warm, draft-free location to rise until nearly doubled in size (about 1 hour). About 25 minutes before the dough has finished rising, preheat your oven to 375°F.

As the dough nears the end of its rise, make the molasses bath by dissolving 1 tablespoon of molasses and 1 teaspoon of kosher salt in 6 cups of water (approximate measurements are fine here). Bring the mixture to a boil over medium-high to high heat. Once the dough has finished rising, place the shaped bagels a few at a time into the boiling bath for less than a minute per side. Remove the bagels with a strainer and return them to the baking sheet. Brush the boiled bagels with the egg wash. Repeat with the remaining bagels. Place the baking sheet in the center of the preheated oven and bake until the bagels are golden brown all over (about 20 minutes). Allow to cool on the pan briefly before serving.

GARLIC KNOTS
MAKES 16 KNOTS

THERE IS ONE VERY IMPORTANT THING TO REMEMBER WHEN MAKing garlic knots, or any sort of knot with bread dough. It will rise after you shape it. So you don't want (nor does the dough really allow you to make) a tight knot. Just roll a rope of dough and cross one end over the other, about 1½ inches from the ends. Poke one end through the loop you created, and set the knot to rise. It will plump and swell as it rises.

STARTER
1 cup (140 g) Gluten-Free Bread Flour (page 8)
1⅔ teaspoons (7 g) instant yeast
1½ teaspoons (6 g) sugar
1 cup water, at room temperature

DOUGH
2 cups (280 g) Gluten-Free Bread Flour (page 8), plus more for sprinkling
2 teaspoons (12 g) kosher salt
Starter
Extra-virgin olive oil, for brushing

TOPPING
4 tablespoons (56 g) ghee or unsalted butter
3 cloves garlic, peeled and minced
1 teaspoon (6 g) kosher salt

To make the starter, place all the starter ingredients in a medium-size bowl, and whisk until well combined. The mixture will be thick and shapeless. Cover and set the bowl aside in a warm, draft-free location to rise until doubled (about 40 minutes).

Once the starter has finished rising, make the dough. Place the flour and salt in the bowl of your stand mixer, and use a handheld whisk to combine well. Add the risen starter to the bowl, and mix on low speed with the dough hook until combined. Raise the mixer speed to medium and knead for about 5 minutes. It will be very sticky dough, and because it is such a stiff dough, it will not trail from the dough hook when you raise the hook out of the bowl. Spray a silicone spatula lightly with cooking oil spray, and scrape down the sides of the bowl. Transfer the dough to a lightly oiled bowl or proofing bucket large enough for the dough to rise to double its size, and cover with an oiled piece of plastic wrap (or the oiled top to your proofing bucket). Place the dough in the refrigerator for at least 12 hours and up to 5 days.

On baking day, line a large, rimmed baking sheet with unbleached parchment paper and set it aside. Remove the dough from the refrigerator and, on a lightly floured surface, knead as described in the General Shaping Tips in Chapter 3 until smooth. Divide the dough in half, then each half in half, and finally each fourth into four parts, until you have sixteen pieces of equal size. Flouring the surface as necessary to keep the dough from sticking, roll each piece of dough (pressing down and out with your palms) into a thin rope about 8 inches long. Shape each into a knot by dusting the rope of dough with flour and crossing one end over the other about 1½ inches from the ends. Poke one end through the loop you created and lay that end on top of the knot. Turn the knot on its side and place it on the prepared baking sheet. Repeat with the remaining pieces of dough, placing them 2 inches apart from one another on the prepared baking sheet. Cover with lightly oiled plastic wrap, and set in a warm, draft-free location to rise until nearly doubled in size (about 1 hour). About 25 minutes before the dough has finished rising, preheat your oven to 375°F.

Once the dough has finished rising, uncover the knots and brush them with olive oil. Place the baking sheet in the center of the preheated oven and bake until the knots are just beginning to brown, 10 to 12 minutes.

While the knots are baking, make the topping. Place the ghee, garlic, and salt in a small saucepan and sauté the garlic over medium heat, stirring frequently, until the garlic becomes fragrant (about 2 minutes). Remove the saucepan from the heat and set it aside. Remove the knots from the oven, brush them generously with the garlic topping, and serve warm.

TIGER ROLLS
MAKES 6 ROLLS

HAVE ALWAYS KNOWN THESE AS TIGER ROLLS. YOU MAY KNOW THEM
as Dutch Crunch rolls. We are both talking about the same thing, whatever
its name: yeasted round rolls with a lightly sweet, yeasty, and crunchy rice
flour topping that crackles as the rolls bake.

STARTER
1¼ cups (175 g) Gluten-Free Bread Flour (page 8)

2 teaspoons (6 g) instant yeast

1½ tablespoons (18 g) sugar

1 cup warm water (about 95°F)

DOUGH
2¼ cups (315 g) Gluten-Free Bread Flour (page 8), plus more for sprinkling

½ teaspoon cream of tartar

2 teaspoons (12 g) kosher salt

1 tablespoon honey

¼ cup plus 2 tablespoons water, at room temperature

Starter

TOPPING
¼ cup plus 2 tablespoons water, at room temperature

1½ teaspoons (heavy 5 g) instant yeast

1 tablespoon (12 g) sugar

⅛ teaspoon kosher salt

2 tablespoons (28 g) melted butter

½ cup (80 g) superfine rice flour

To make the starter, place all the starter ingredients in a medium-size bowl,
and whisk until well combined. The mixture will be thick and shapeless.
Cover and set the bowl aside in a warm, draft-free location to rise until doubled (about 40 minutes).

Once the starter has finished rising, make the dough. Place the flour,
cream of tartar, and salt in the bowl of your stand mixer, and use a handheld

whisk to combine well. Add the honey, water, and risen starter to the bowl, and mix on low speed with the dough hook until combined. Raise the mixer speed to medium and knead for about 5 minutes. The dough will be quite sticky, but should be smooth and stretchy. Spray a silicone spatula lightly with cooking oil spray, and scrape down the sides of the bowl. Transfer the dough to a lightly oiled bowl or proofing bucket large enough for the dough to rise to double its size, and cover with an oiled piece of plastic wrap (or the oiled top to your proofing bucket). Place the dough in the refrigerator for at least 12 hours and up to 5 days.

On baking day, line a rimmed baking sheet with unbleached parchment paper and set it aside. Remove the dough from the refrigerator and turn it out onto a lightly floured surface. Knead until smoother as described in the General Shaping Tips in Chapter 3. With a floured bench scraper, divide the dough into six pieces of equal size. To shape each piece of dough, follow the instructions on page 32 for shaping small, round rolls. Place the first shaped roll on the prepared baking sheet. Repeat with the remaining pieces of dough, and place the rolls 3 inches apart from one another on the prepared baking sheet. Cover the baking sheet with oiled plastic wrap and set it aside to rise for 30 minutes.

After the 30-minute rise, make the topping: Whisk together the water and the yeast, then add the remaining ingredients, one at a time, whisking well to combine after each addition. Spread the mixture over the top of each roll as it is rising. Allow the rolls to continue to rise, uncovered, until fully doubled (about another 45 minutes). About 20 minutes before the rolls have completed their final rise, preheat your oven to 375°F.

Once the rolls have finished rising, place the baking sheet on the bottom rack of the preheated oven until the topping is set, lightly browned and crackled, and the rolls are lightly golden brown with an internal temperature of about 190°F on an instant-read thermometer (about 25 minutes). Let cool briefly before serving.

PITA BREAD
MAKES 8 PITAS

PROMISE ME YOU WON'T LET PITA BREAD STRESS YOU OUT. A MOIST dough in a hot oven, on a hot pizza stone should make your pitas "pop," creating a pocket for you to stuff to your heart's content. Sometimes, they just won't "pop." Maybe the oven isn't hot enough, or the air doesn't circulate well enough or the dough just isn't exactly wet enough. No worries. Just slice off an edge of the baked dough, and coax open a pocket with a sharp knife. They'll taste just the same—and will still allow themselves to be stuffed.

STARTER
1¼ cups (175 g) Gluten-Free Bread Flour (page 8)
1 teaspoon (3 g) instant yeast
1 cup warm water (about 95°F)

DOUGH
1¾ cups (245 g) Gluten-Free Bread Flour (page 8), plus more for sprinkling
½ teaspoon cream of tartar
1 teaspoon (3 g) instant yeast
2 teaspoons (12 g) kosher salt
1 tablespoon extra-virgin olive oil
3 tablespoons water, at room temperature
Starter

To make the starter, place all the starter ingredients in a medium-size bowl, and whisk until well combined. The mixture will be thick and shapeless. Cover and set the bowl aside in a warm, draft-free location to rise until doubled (about 40 minutes).

Once the starter has finished rising, make the dough. Place the flour, cream of tartar, and yeast in the bowl of your stand mixer, and use a handheld whisk to combine well. Add the salt, and whisk to combine. Add the olive oil, water, and risen starter to the bowl, and mix on low speed with the dough hook until combined. Raise the mixer speed to medium and knead for about 5 minutes. The dough will be quite sticky, but should be smooth and stretchy. Spray a silicone spatula lightly with cooking oil spray, and scrape down the sides of the bowl. Transfer the dough to a lightly oiled bowl or proofing bucket large enough for the dough to rise to double its size, and cover with an oiled piece of plastic wrap (or the oiled top to your proofing bucket). Place the dough in the refrigerator for at least 24 hours and up to 5 days.

On baking day, preheat your oven to 400°F about 25 minutes before baking. Place a pizza stone on the bottom rack of your oven during heating. Remove the dough from the refrigerator and turn it out onto a lightly floured surface. Sprinkle the dough with additional bread flour, and, using a lightly oiled bench scraper, knead lightly, as described in the General Shaping Tips in Chapter 3, until smoother. With a floured bench scraper, divide the dough in half, and then each resulting portion in half again and again until you have eight pieces of equal size. Shape each piece into a ball, then roll into a disk 6 inches in diameter, about ¼ inch thick in the center, and thinner as you work toward the edge.

Place the pitas, three at a time, directly on the hot pizza stone and bake for 3 to 4 minutes, or until puffed but not very brown. Wrap the pitas in a tea towel to keep them soft and warm until you are ready to serve them.

HOAGIE ROLLS

MAKES 8 ROLLS

THIS IS A VERY IMPORTANT ROLL . . . WITH A VERY UNCERTAIN name. Hoagies, grinders, subs, heros. They're all roughly the same, when it comes to sandwich making. When I say "hoagie roll," I mean a soft tubular roll with a light crust on the outside. A roll by any other name would be as versatile. Would it not?

STARTER
1¼ cups (175 g) Gluten-Free Bread Flour (page 8)
1 tablespoon (12 g) sugar
1⅔ teaspoons (5 g) instant yeast
1 cup warm water (about 95°F)

DOUGH
3½ cups (490 g) Gluten-Free Bread Flour (page 8), plus more for sprinkling
1½ teaspoons (18 g) kosher salt
1½ teaspoons honey
3 tablespoons (42 g) unsalted butter, at room temperature
¾ cup plain whole-milk yogurt, at room temperature
1 large egg, at room temperature
Starter

To make the starter, place all the starter ingredients in a medium-size bowl, and whisk until well combined. The mixture will be thick and shapeless. Cover and set the bowl aside in a warm, draft-free location to rise until doubled (about 40 minutes).

Once the starter has finished rising, make the dough. Place the flour and salt in the bowl of your stand mixer, and use a handheld whisk to combine well. Add the honey, butter, yogurt, egg, and risen starter to the bowl, and mix on low speed with the dough hook until combined. Raise the mixer speed to medium and knead for about 5 minutes. The dough will be quite sticky, but should be smooth and stretchy. Spray a silicone spatula lightly with cooking oil spray, and scrape down the sides of the bowl. Transfer the dough to a lightly oiled bowl or proofing bucket large enough for the dough to rise to double its size, and cover with an oiled piece of plastic wrap (or the oiled top to your proofing bucket). Place the dough in the refrigerator for at least 12 hours and up to 5 days.

On baking day, line a rimmed baking sheet with unbleached parchment paper and set it aside. Remove the dough from the refrigerator and turn it out onto a lightly floured surface. Knead until smoother as described in the General Shaping Tips in Chapter 3. With a floured bench scraper, divide the dough in half, and then each resulting portion in half again and again until you have eight pieces of equal size. Shape each piece of dough into a hoagie roll, one at a time. To shape each piece of dough, follow the instructions on page 35 for shaping hoagie rolls. Place the first shaped roll on the prepared baking sheet. Repeat with the remaining pieces of dough, and place the rolls 3 inches apart from one another on the prepared baking sheet. Dust the rolls with flour, then cover the baking sheet with oiled plastic wrap and set it aside to rise for about 45 minutes or until the rolls are just a bit more than 150 percent of their original size (do not overproof). Dust with flour again, slash down the center of each roll at a 45-degree angle, just less than ¼ inch deep. Place in a cold oven , turn on the oven to 350°F, and bake for 20 minutes, or until the rolls are golden brown all over and the internal temperature reaches 185°F on an instant-read thermometer. Allow to cool for 10 minutes before slicing and serving.

SOFT HAMBURGER BUNS

MAKES 6 BUNS

THESE HAMBURGER BUNS ARE MADE BY ROLLING OUT A SOFT, EN-riched dough, and then cutting out rounds. This technique ensures that the buns will rise up much more than they will rise out. As written, the instructions call for a 4-inch biscuit or cookie cutter, but there isn't a reason in the world that you can't cut these into 2½-inch rounds and make slider buns. When in doubt, err on the side of slightly underbaking rather than overbaking these rolls. That way, they'll stay soft and almost squishy when you bite into them.

WATER ROUX

3 tablespoons (25 g) Gluten-Free Bread Flour (page 8)
½ cup water, at room temperature

DOUGH

3 cups (420 g) Gluten-Free Bread Flour (page 8), plus more for sprinkling
¼ teaspoon cream of tartar
¼ cup (48 g) sugar
2 teaspoons (6 g) instant yeast
2 teaspoons (12 g) kosher salt
2 tablespoons (28 g) unsalted butter, at room temperature
½ cup plain whole-milk yogurt, at room temperature
⅔ cup milk, at room temperature (not nonfat)
Water roux
Unsalted butter, for brushing tops of buns
Toasted sesame seeds, for sprinkling (optional)

To make the water roux, whisk together the flour and water in a small saucepan. Cook over medium-high heat, whisking constantly, until thickened. It is ready when the whisk leaves a visible trail as it moves through the roux. Remove from the heat and allow to cool until no longer hot to the touch.

To make the dough, place the flour, cream of tartar, sugar, and yeast in the bowl of a stand mixer, and use a handheld whisk to combine well. Add the salt, and whisk to combine. Add the butter, yogurt, milk, and water roux, then attach the dough hook to the stand mixer, and mix on low speed until combined. Raise the mixer speed to medium and mix for about 5 minutes. The dough will be quite sticky, but should be smooth and stretchy. Spray a silicone spatula lightly with cooking oil spray, and scrape down the sides of the bowl. Transfer the dough to a lightly oiled bowl or proofing bucket large enough for the dough to rise to double its size, and cover with an oiled piece of plastic wrap (or the oiled top to your proofing bucket). Place the dough in the refrigerator for at least 12 hours and up to 5 days.

On baking day, line a rimmed baking sheet with unbleached parchment paper and set it aside. Remove the dough from the refrigerator and turn it out onto a lightly floured surface. Knead until smoother as described in the General Shaping Tips in Chapter 3. Place the dough on a lightly oiled piece of unbleached parchment paper and sprinkle the top with flour. Roll out the dough ½ inch thick, and with a floured 4-inch biscuit or cookie cutter, cut out rounds. Place the rounds on the prepared baking sheet, about 3 inches apart from one another. Gather and reroll the remaining scraps of dough, and cut out the rest of the rounds. Place the rounds on the baking sheet and sprinkle the tops of the rounds lightly with flour. Cover the baking sheet with lightly oiled plastic wrap, and place in a warm, draft-free location until nearly doubled in size (about 1½ hours).

About 25 minutes before the buns have finished rising, preheat your oven to 350°F. Once the dough has finished rising, remove the plastic wrap, place the baking sheet in the preheated oven, and bake for about 10 minutes. Turn the heat down to 325°F, remove the buns from the oven, brush the tops of the rolls with the melted butter, and sprinkle with sesame seeds, if using. Return the baking sheet to the oven and bake until the internal temperature of the buns reaches about 185°F (another 5 to 10 minutes, no more, so the buns stay soft). Allow the buns to cool for about 10 minutes before slicing and serving.

SOFT HOT-DOG BUNS
MAKES 6 BUNS

THESE BUNS ARE SHAPED MUCH LIKE A HOAGIE ROLL (SEE PAGE 35), but when they are slashed before baking, you go a little deeper into the dough. That way, they open, or "bloom," more deeply during baking and magically transform themselves into hot-dog buns. If they don't bloom quite enough during baking, just deepen the slash as they come out of the oven.

WATER ROUX
3 tablespoons (25 g) Gluten-Free Bread Flour (page 8)
½ cup water, at room temperature

DOUGH
3 cups (420 g) Gluten-Free Bread Flour (page 8), plus more for sprinkling
¼ teaspoon cream of tartar
¼ cup (48 g) sugar
2 teaspoons (6 g) instant yeast
2 teaspoons (12 g) kosher salt
2 tablespoons (28 g) unsalted butter, at room temperature
½ cup plain whole-milk yogurt, at room temperature
⅔ cup milk, at room temperature (not nonfat)
Water roux
Unsalted butter, for brushing tops of buns

To make the water roux, whisk together the flour and water in a small sauce-pan. Cook over medium-high heat, whisking constantly, until thickened. It is ready when the whisk leaves a visible trail as it moves through the roux. Remove from heat and allow to cool until no longer hot to the touch.

To make the dough, place the flour, cream of tartar, sugar, and yeast in the bowl of a stand mixer, and use a handheld whisk to combine well. Add the salt, and whisk to combine. Add the butter, yogurt, milk, and water roux, then attach the dough hook to the stand mixer, and mix on low speed until combined. Raise the mixer speed to medium and mix for about 5 minutes. The dough will be quite sticky, but should be smooth and stretchy. Spray a silicone spatula lightly with cooking oil spray, and scrape down the sides of the bowl. Transfer the dough to a lightly oiled bowl or proofing bucket large enough for the dough to rise to double its size, and cover with an oiled piece of plastic wrap (or the oiled top to your proofing bucket). Place the dough in the refrigerator for at least 12 hours and up to 5 days.

On baking day, line a rimmed baking sheet with unbleached parchment paper and set it aside. Remove the dough from the refrigerator and turn it out onto a lightly floured surface. Knead until smoother as described in the General Shaping Tips in Chapter 3. With a floured bench scraper, divide the dough into six pieces of equal size. Shape each piece of dough into a hot-dog bun, one at a time. To shape the first bun, follow the instructions on page 35 for shaping hoagie rolls. Place the shaped bun on the prepared baking sheet. Repeat with the remaining pieces of dough, and place the buns 3 inches apart from one another on the prepared baking sheet. Dust the loaves with flour, then cover the baking sheet with oiled plastic wrap and set it aside to rise for about 45 minutes, or until they are just a bit more than 150 percent of their original size (do not overproof).

About 25 minutes before the buns have finished rising, preheat your oven to 350°F. Once the dough has finished rising, remove the plastic wrap, dust the top of the buns with flour, and slash down the center of each bun at a 45-degree angle, just less than ½ inch deep (deeper than a hoagie roll). Place the baking sheet in the preheated oven and bake for about 10 minutes. Turn the oven temperature down to 325°F, remove the buns from the oven, and brush the tops with the melted butter. Return the baking sheet to the oven and bake until the internal temperature of the buns is about 185°F (another 5 to 10 minutes, no more, so they stay soft). If necessary to create a split deep enough to fit a hot dog, slice into the slash to deepen it and scrape out some of the soft center of the bread. Allow to cool for about 10 minutes before serving.

MONKEY BREAD
SERVES 6 TO 8

THIS DOUGH IS A DREAM TO SHAPE. THERE IS ENOUGH BUTTER IN it to make it smooth and supple without becoming dry during baking. If you don't think you can commit to a whole 5 cups of gluten-free bread flour (and an entire tube pan of monkey bread), just halve the recipe right down the middle. It will work beautifully, and if you bake it in a 9-inch round spring form pan, it will still make a lovely presentation.

DOUGH

5 cups (700 g) Gluten-Free Bread Flour (page 8), plus more for sprinkling
½ teaspoon cream of tartar
6 tablespoons (72 g) sugar
3⅓ teaspoons (10 g) instant yeast
1 teaspoon (6 g) kosher salt
6 tablespoons (84 g) unsalted butter, at room temperature
2 cups warm milk (about 95°F) (not nonfat)

TOPPING

6 tablespoons (84 g) unsalted butter, melted
1 cup (218 g) packed light brown sugar
1 tablespoon ground cinnamon

Place the flour, cream of tartar, sugar, and yeast in the bowl of your stand mixer, and use a handheld whisk to combine well. Add the salt, and whisk to combine. Add the butter and milk, and mix on low speed with the dough hook until combined. Raise the mixer speed to medium and knead for about 5 minutes. The dough should be somewhat sticky, but smooth and supple. Spray a silicone spatula lightly with cooking oil spray, and scrape down the sides of the bowl. Transfer the dough to a lightly oiled bowl or proofing bucket large enough for the dough to rise to double its size, and cover with an oiled piece of plastic wrap (or the oiled top to your proofing bucket). Place the dough in the refrigerator for at least 12 hours and up to 5 days.

On baking day, preheat your oven to 400°F about 25 minutes before baking. Grease well a Bundt or tube pan and set it aside. Place the melted butter for the topping in a small bowl. Place the brown sugar and cinnamon for the topping in a separate small bowl and whisk to combine. Set both bowls aside.

Remove the dough from the refrigerator and turn it out onto a lightly floured surface. Sprinkle the dough with additional bread flour and, using a lightly oiled bench scraper, knead lightly as described in the General Shaping Tips in Chapter 3 until smoother. With a floured bench scraper, divide the

dough into about fifty pieces, each about 1 ounce. With well-floured hands, roll each piece of dough into a ball between your floured palms. Dip each ball in the melted butter from the topping, and then in the cinnamon sugar. Stack and stagger the balls of dough in concentric circles in the prepared pan (as pictured). Sprinkle any remaining cinnamon sugar on the top of the dough. Cover the pan with oiled plastic wrap and set in a warm, draft-free location to rise until doubled in size (about 1 hour). About 20 minutes before the end of the rise, preheat your oven to 350°F.

If using a tube pan with a removable bottom, wrap the bottom in foil, as cinnamon and sugar will leak out during baking. Place the pan in the center of the preheated oven and bake until the sugar has begun to caramelize and the bread is lightly golden brown (about 30 minutes).

Let cool in the pan for about 5 minutes, then run a toothpick along the sides of the pan to make sure that nothing is stuck. If your tube pan has a removable bottom, unmold the bottom and invert onto a serving platter. If not, invert the pan over the neck of a glass bottle until the bread begins to fall out of the pan. Remove the bottle and turn out the bread onto a serving platter. Serve warm.

HOT CROSS BUNS
MAKES 12 BUNS

L IKE PANETTONE BREAD (PAGE 76) IN DECEMBER, HOT CROSS BUNS are nearly everywhere in the spring. They have more than a couple of spices, but if you are leaning toward leaving out any of them, don't let it be the cardamom! Cardamom is the telltale spice of the hot cross bun. Make sure they are fully cooled before adding the icing cross, or it will melt right into the warm buns.

DOUGH

3¼ cups (455 g) Gluten-Free Bread Flour (page 8), plus more for sprinkling
½ cup (100 g) sugar
2 teaspoons (6 g) instant yeast
½ teaspoon cream of tartar
½ teaspoon ground cardamom
¼ teaspoon ground cinnamon
¼ teaspoon ground allspice
¾ teaspoon (about 5 g) kosher salt
Zest of 1 medium-size lemon (about 1 teaspoon)
Zest of 1 small orange (about 1 teaspoon)
1 teaspoon gluten-free vanilla extract
1 cup warm milk (about 95°F) (not nonfat)
6 tablespoons (84 g) unsalted butter, melted and cooled
2 large eggs, at room temperature, beaten
6 ounces dried currants

GLAZE

1 large egg, at room temperature, beaten
¼ cup (29 g) confectioners' sugar

ICING FOR CROSS

1 cup (115 g) confectioners' sugar
2 tablespoons milk

Place the flour, sugar, yeast, cream of tartar, cardamom, cinnamon, allspice, and salt in the bowl of your stand mixer, and use a handheld whisk to combine well. Add the lemon and orange zest, and whisk to combine well, working to break up any clumps in the citrus zest. Add the vanilla, milk, butter, and eggs, and mix on low speed with the dough hook until combined. Raise the mixer speed to medium and knead for about 5 minutes. The dough will be quite sticky, but should be smooth and stretchy. Add the currants and turn the mixer on low speed to knead the dough until the currants are evenly distributed throughout. Spray a silicone spatula lightly with cooking oil spray, and scrape down the sides of the bowl. Transfer the dough to a lightly oiled bowl or proofing bucket large enough for the dough to rise to double its size, and cover with an oiled piece of plastic wrap (or the oiled top to your proofing bucket). Place the dough in the refrigerator for at least 12 hours and up to 5 days.

On baking day, line a rimmed baking sheet with unbleached parchment paper and set it aside. Remove the dough from the refrigerator and turn it out onto a lightly floured surface. Knead until smoother as described in the General Shaping Tips in Chapter 3. With a floured bench scraper, divide the dough into twelve pieces of equal size (each just over 3 ounces). To shape each piece of dough, follow the instructions on page 32 for shaping small, round rolls. Place the first shaped bun on the prepared baking sheet. Repeat with the remaining pieces of dough, and place the buns 3 inches apart from one another on the prepared baking sheet. Cover the baking sheet with oiled plastic wrap and set it in a warm, draft-free location to rise for 40 minutes or until doubled in size. Slash a cross or X in each bun with a sharp knife or lame at a 45-degree angle, about ¼ inch deep. It is into these slashes that you will pipe an icing cross on the baked and cooled buns.

Make the glaze by beating the egg with the confectioners' sugar until smooth. Uncover the mostly risen buns and brush them generously with the glaze, but not so generously that the glaze pools on the baking sheet or it will burn during baking. Allow the buns to finish rising, uncovered, until fully doubled in size (about 20 minutes more).

While the buns are completing their rise, preheat your oven to 350°F. Place the fully risen and glazed buns on the lower rack of your preheated oven and bake until lightly golden brown and the inside of the buns registers about 185°F on an instant-read thermometer (about 30 minutes).

Allow the buns to cool for 10 minutes on the baking sheet, then transfer them to a wire rack to cool completely. Next, make the icing for the cross. In a small bowl, place the confectioners' sugar and then the milk. Mix well. The icing should be very thick. Place the icing in a pastry bag fitted with a #10 plain piping tip. Pipe the icing in a cross or X pattern on the top of each cooled bun. Remember to be sure that the buns are completely cool before icing them, or the icing will melt into the buns and not be visible.

GLAZED YEAST-RAISED DONUTS
MAKES 10 DONUTS

AS CARDAMOM IS TO HOT CROSS BUNS (PAGE 147), FRESHLY GRATED nutmeg is to donuts. So whatever you do, don't leave it out of these tender and beautiful bakery-style yeasted donuts. Be sure to keep a close eye on that thermometer while you're frying these, as they tend to blacken if the frying oil gets above 325°F. And as much as we all wish we could make homemade donuts one day and eat them the next, they're really at their best when eaten the very same day. Not a particularly big problem.

DOUGH

3 cups (420 g) Gluten-Free Bread Flour (page 8), plus more for sprinkling
¼ teaspoon cream of tartar
2 teaspoons (6 g) instant yeast
½ cup (100 g) sugar
½ teaspoon (3 g) kosher salt
½ teaspoon freshly finely grated nutmeg
¾ cup plus 2 tablespoons warm milk (about 95°F) (not nonfat)
1 large egg, at room temperature, beaten
4 tablespoons (56 g) unsalted butter, melted and cooled
A mixture of equal parts canola oil and vegetable shortening, for frying

GLAZE

1 cup (115 g) confectioners' sugar
2 tablespoons Lyle's golden syrup or honey
2 to 4 tablespoons water

In the bowl of your stand mixer, place the flour, cream of tartar, yeast, and sugar, and use a handheld whisk to combine well. Add the salt and nutmeg, and whisk to combine well. Add the milk, egg, and butter, and mix on low speed with the dough hook until combined. Raise the mixer speed to medium and knead for about 5 minutes. This is a lovely, smooth, and supple enriched dough. It climbs up the dough hook during kneading but remains intact and smooth. Spray a silicone spatula lightly with cooking oil spray, and scrape down the sides of the bowl. Transfer the dough to a lightly oiled bowl or proofing bucket large enough for it to rise to double its size, spray the top of the dough with cooking oil spray, and cover with an oiled piece of plastic wrap (or the oiled top to your proofing bucket). Place the dough in the refrigerator for at least 12 hours and up to 3 days.

On baking day, line a rimmed baking sheet with unbleached parchment paper, grease it lightly with cooking oil, and set it aside. Turn the dough out onto a lightly floured surface, sprinkle with flour, and knead lightly until smoother as described in the General Shaping Tips in Chapter 3. Roll the dough out into a rectangle about ½ inch thick, sprinkling lightly with flour as necessary to prevent sticking. With a floured 3½-inch biscuit or cookie cutter, cut out rounds of the dough. Next, cut about 1-inch holes in the centers with a small floured cookie cutter or the wide end of a large, plain piping tip. Place the donuts and the holes on the prepared baking sheet, about 2 inches apart from one another. Cover the baking sheet with lightly oiled plastic wrap, and place in a warm, draft-free location to rise until doubled in size (about 1 hour).

When the donuts are nearly finished rising, place the canola oil and shortening in a large stockpot so that, when the shortening melts, it and the oil reach about 3 inches up the side of the pot. Over medium-high heat, bring the temperature of the oil and shortening mixture to precisely 325°F. Place the risen donuts, two or three at a time, in the hot oil and fry until light golden brown all over (about 1 minute per side). Drain on paper towels. Fry the holes, too (less than 1 minute per side).

As the donuts cool briefly, make the glaze. In a small bowl, place the confectioners' sugar and Lyle's golden syrup, and mix well. Add 2 tablespoons of water to the glaze and mix well. The glaze should be smooth and thickly pourable. Add more water by the teaspoon as necessary, mixing between additions, until you reach the desired consistency. Remember that it is easier to thin than to thicken icing, so proceed cautiously. Dip the top of each donut in the glaze, right the donut, and place on a wire rack to set. Serve immediately.

PRETZEL ROLLS
MAKES 8 ROLLS

To me, pretzel rolls are the perfect sandwich roll. I think of them as a terribly efficient way of enjoying a lunch sandwich—with pretzels. Aren't you always saying how busy you are? This dough can easily be made into soft pretzels. Just shape them as directed for the Sourdough Soft Pretzels (page 107) or even soft pretzel bites by rolling the dough into ropes and cutting it into 1-inch pieces and then proceeding with the rest of the recipe as written.

INGREDIENTS
3¼ cups (455 g) Gluten-Free Bread Flour (page 8), plus more for sprinkling
40 grams (about ⅔ cup) nonfat dry milk, ground finely in a blender or food processor
2 teaspoons (6 g) instant yeast
¼ teaspoon cream of tartar
1 tablespoon (14 g) packed light brown sugar
1 teaspoon (6 g) kosher salt
4 tablespoons (56 g) unsalted butter, at room temperature
1¼ cups plus 2 tablespoons warm water (about 95°F)
Baking soda bath for boiling (6 cups water plus 1 tablespoon baking soda plus 1 teaspoon kosher salt) (see instructions in the final paragraph of the instructions for Sourdough Soft Pretzels, page 108)
Coarse salt, for sprinkling

Place the flour, dry milk, yeast, cream of tartar, and brown sugar in the bowl of your stand mixer, and use a handheld whisk to combine well. Add the salt, and whisk to combine. Add the butter and water, and mix on low speed with the dough hook until combined. Raise the mixer speed to medium and knead for about 5 minutes. The dough will be quite sticky, but should be smooth and stretchy. Spray a silicone spatula lightly with cooking oil spray, and scrape down the sides of the bowl. Transfer the dough to a lightly oiled bowl or proofing bucket large enough for the dough to rise to double its size, and cover with an oiled piece of plastic wrap (or the oiled top to your proofing bucket). Place the dough in the refrigerator for at least 12 hours and up to 5 days.

On baking day, line a rimmed baking sheet with unbleached parchment paper, grease it lightly with cooking oil spray, and set it aside. Remove the dough from the refrigerator and turn it out onto a lightly floured surface. Knead until smoother as described in the General Shaping Tips in Chapter 3. With a floured bench scraper, divide the dough in half, and then each resulting portion in half again and again until you have eight pieces of equal size (each nearly 4 ounces). To shape each piece of dough, follow the instructions on page 32 for shaping small, round rolls. Place the first shaped roll on the prepared baking sheet. Repeat with the remaining pieces of dough, and place the rolls 3 inches apart from one another on the prepared baking sheet. Cover the baking sheet with oiled plastic wrap and set it in a warm, draft free location to rise until doubled (about 1 hour). As the dough nears the end of its rise, preheat your oven to 375°F. In a large pot, dissolve the baking soda and kosher salt in the 6 cups of water and bring to a boil over high heat.

Once the dough has finished rising, place the rolls a few at a time into the boiling baking soda bath for less than a minute per side. Remove the rolls with a strainer and return them to the baking sheet. Score 3 to 4 parallel lines on the top of each roll with a sharp knife or lame at a 45-degree angle, about ¼ inch deep. Sprinkle with coarse salt to taste. Place the baking sheet in the center of the preheated oven and bake the rolls until golden brown all over (about 35 minutes). Allow to cool on the baking sheet for 10 minutes before serving.

ONION BIALYS
MAKES 6 BIALYS

IT HAS COME TO MY ATTENTION THAT BIALYS ARE A NEW YORK PHE-nomenon. Or, at the very least, a northeastern US phenomenon. For the un-initiated, they are essentially bagel-shaped—and made with the same dough as the Plain (or Seeded) Bagels (page 123)—but instead of a hole they have a divot filled with sautéed onions. And instead of being boiled and then baked, they are straight-up baked, which means that they are soft but not chewy. And they are best eaten the day they are made. They may sound like terribly fussy wannabe bagels, but really they're their own thing and they just smell like, well, Sunday to me. And Sunday is my favorite day of the week, if that's any indication of how I feel about these bialys.

STARTER
1¼ cups (175 g) Gluten-Free Bread Flour (page 8)
1 teaspoon (3 g) instant yeast
2½ tablespoons (30 g) sugar
1 cup warm water (about 95°F)

DOUGH
2 cups (280 g) Gluten-Free Bread Flour (page 8), plus more for sprinkling
⅔ teaspoon (2 g) instant yeast
2 teaspoons (12 g) kosher salt
Starter

FILLING
2 shallots, peeled and diced
¼ teaspoon kosher salt
2 tablespoons (28 g) ghee or unsalted butter

To make the starter, place all the starter ingredients in a medium-size bowl, and whisk until well combined. The mixture will be thick and shapeless. Cover and set the bowl aside in a warm, draft-free location to rise until dou-bled (about 40 minutes).

Once the starter has finished rising, make the dough. Place the flour and yeast in the bowl of your stand mixer, and use a handheld whisk to combine well. Add the salt, and whisk to combine. Add the risen starter to the bowl, and mix on low speed with the dough hook until combined. Raise the mixer speed to medium and knead for about 5 minutes. It will be very sticky dough, and because it is such a stiff dough, it will not trail from the dough hook when you raise the hook out of the bowl. Spray a silicone spatula lightly with cooking oil spray, and scrape down the sides of the bowl. Transfer the dough to a lightly oiled bowl or proofing bucket large enough for the dough to rise to double its size, and cover with an oiled piece of plastic wrap (or the oiled top to your proofing bucket). Place the dough in the refrigerator for at least 12 hours and up to 5 days.

On baking day, line a rimmed baking sheet with unbleached parchment paper and set it aside. Next, make the filling. In a small skillet, sauté the shallots and salt in the ghee over medium heat until the shallots are translucent and have begun to caramelize. Remove from the heat and let cool.

Turn the dough out onto a lightly floured surface, sprinkle with flour, and knead lightly as described in the General Shaping Tips in Chapter 3 until smooth. Divide the dough into six pieces of equal size. To shape each piece of dough, follow the instructions on page 32 for shaping small, round rolls. Then, place the first bialy on the prepared baking sheet. Repeat to shape the other bialys and place them about 3 inches apart on the prepared baking sheet. Press down on the center of each round of dough, and press out toward the edges, creating a flat center that gradually rises toward the edge of the dough. Sprinkle the bialys lightly with more flour, cover with lightly oiled plastic wrap, and place in a warm, draft-free location until doubled in size (about 45 minutes). During the last 25 minutes of rising, preheat your oven to 400°F.

Once the dough has finished rising, remove the plastic wrap and spoon about 1 teaspoon of cooled filling into the flat center of each bialy. Place the baking sheet in the oven and bake for 5 minutes. Turn down the oven temperature to 350°F and bake for about 7 minutes more, or until the bialys are lightly golden brown on the edges. Remove from the oven and transfer to a wire rack until not too hot to handle. Serve warm.

CLOVERLEAF ROLLS
MAKES 13 ROLLS

CLOVERLEAF ROLLS SIMPLY AREN'T POSSIBLE WITHOUT A ROBUSTLY-rising, enriched dough. Luckily, we already had that in our Hoagie Rolls (page 135). Start with the same recipe, switch up the technique, and you have cloverleaf rolls. Well, you'll have to brush them with butter to make them cloverleaf rolls. Twice. You'll have to.

STARTER
1¼ cups (175 g) Gluten-Free Bread Flour (page 8)
1 tablespoon (12 g) sugar
1⅔ teaspoons (5 g) instant yeast
1 cup warm water (about 95°F)

DOUGH
3½ cups (490 g) Gluten-Free Bread Flour (page 8), plus more for sprinkling
1 tablespoon (18 g) kosher salt
1½ teaspoons honey
¾ cup plain whole-milk yogurt, at room temperature
1 large egg, at room temperature
3 tablespoons (42 g) unsalted butter, at room temperature
Starter
2 tablespoons (28 g) unsalted butter, melted (for brushing)

To make the starter, place all the starter ingredients in a medium-size bowl, and whisk until well combined. The mixture will be thick and shapeless. Cover and set the bowl aside in a warm, draft-free location to rise until doubled (about 40 minutes).

Once the starter has finished rising, make the dough. Place the flour and salt in the bowl of your stand mixer, and use a handheld whisk to combine well. Add the honey, yogurt, egg, room-temperature butter, and risen starter to the bowl, and mix on low with the dough hook until combined. Raise the mixer speed to medium and knead for about 5 minutes. The dough will be quite sticky, but should be smooth and stretchy. Spray a silicone spatula lightly with cooking oil spray, and scrape down the sides of the bowl. Transfer the dough to a lightly oiled bowl or proofing bucket large enough for the dough to rise to double its size, and cover with an oiled piece of plastic wrap (or the oiled top to your proofing bucket). Place the dough in the refrigerator for at least 12 hours and up to 5 days.

On baking day, grease the wells of a standard 12-cup muffin tin and set it aside. Turn the dough out onto a lightly floured surface. Knead until smoother as described in the General Shaping Tips in Chapter 3. Divide the dough into thirty-nine pieces, each about 1 ounce. Roll each piece of dough into a ball between your floured palms, keeping all of the dough that you are not working with at the moment lightly covered in a moist towel to prevent it from drying out. Place three balls of dough together in a triangular shape into one cup of the prepared muffin tin. Repeat with the remaining pieces of dough. Cover the muffin tin with a lightly oiled piece of plastic wrap and place in a warm, draft-free location until doubled in size (about 1 hour).

About 15 minutes before the end of the second rise, preheat your oven to 350°F. Once the rolls have finished rising, brush the entire exposed tops generously with melted butter. Place the muffin tin in the center of the preheated oven and bake until the rolls are just browned (10 to 12 minutes). Remove from the oven and brush again with more melted butter. Serve warm.

PARKER HOUSE ROLLS
MAKES 15 ROLLS

THESE BUTTERY PARKER HOUSE ROLLS OWE THEIR NAME TO BOS-ton's Parker House Hotel. I don't know the whole story, but clearly they were impressive enough to give the hotel a place in history and to convince generations hence to butter up some tender bread dough and fold it over just so before baking it. I like to position the rolls next to one another so they can lend each other support as they rise, as it seems cozy. Too much togetherness? Set them to rise on their sides on a rimmed baking sheet, a couple of inches apart from one another.

STARTER
1¼ cups (175 g) Gluten-Free Bread Flour (page 8)
1 tablespoon (12 g) sugar
1⅔ teaspoons (5 g) instant yeast
1 cup warm water (about 95°F)

DOUGH
3½ cups (490 g) Gluten-Free Bread Flour (page 8), plus more for sprinkling
1 tablespoon (18 g) kosher salt
1½ teaspoons honey
¾ cup plain whole-milk yogurt, at room temperature
1 large egg, at room temperature
3 tablespoons (42 g) unsalted butter, at room temperature
Starter
4 tablespoons (28 g) unsalted butter, melted (for brushing)

To make the starter, place all the starter ingredients in a medium-size bowl, and whisk until well combined. The mixture will be thick and shapeless. Cover and set the bowl aside in a warm, draft-free location to rise until doubled (about 40 minutes).

Once the starter has finished rising, make the dough. Place the flour and salt in the bowl of your stand mixer, and use a handheld whisk to combine well. Add the honey, yogurt, egg, room-temperature butter, and risen starter to the bowl, and mix on low speed with the dough hook until combined. Raise the mixer speed to medium and knead for about 5 minutes. The dough will be quite sticky, but should be smooth and stretchy. Spray a silicone spatula lightly with cooking oil spray, and scrape down the sides of the bowl. Transfer the dough to a lightly oiled bowl or proofing bucket large enough for the dough to rise to double its size, and cover with an oiled piece of plastic wrap (or the oiled top to your proofing bucket). Place the dough in the refrigerator for at least 12 hours and up to 5 days.

On baking day, grease an 8-inch square pan and set it aside. Turn the dough out onto a lightly floured surface. Knead until smoother as described in the General Shaping Tips in Chapter 3. Divide the dough into fifteen pieces, each between 2½ and 3 ounces. Roll each piece of dough into a ball between your floured palms, keeping all of the dough that you are not working with at the moment lightly covered in a moist towel to prevent it from drying out. Roll or pat out each ball of dough into an oval shape, brush the surface with melted butter, fold the oval over on itself until the ends meet, and place it on its folded end, with the opening of the fold facing up, in the prepared pan. Repeat with the remaining pieces of dough, and place each roll right next to the others, so they support one another as they rise. Cover the baking dish with a lightly oiled piece of plastic wrap and place in a warm, draft-free location until doubled in size (about 1 hour).

About 15 minutes before the end of the second rise, preheat your oven to 350°F. Once the rolls have finished rising, brush the entire exposed tops generously with melted butter. Place the pan in the center of the preheated oven and bake until the rolls are just browned (10 to 12 minutes). Remove from the oven, brush again with more melted butter. Serve warm.

CRESCENT ROLLS
MAKES 18 ROLLS

BECAUSE YOU ALREADY KNOW ABOUT THE CRESCENT ROLLS IN THE refrigerated section of every single grocery store in every single town in America, you may know how versatile this dough is. This buttery, rolled dough can be rolled up all by itself and baked, as in the instructions below, but it can also be wrapped around cocktail franks or rolled up with deli meats and baked up into roll-ups. The appetizer ideas are endless!

STARTER
1¼ cups (175 g) Gluten-Free Bread Flour (page 8)
1 tablespoon (12 g) sugar
1⅔ teaspoons (5 g) instant yeast
1 cup warm water (about 95°F)

DOUGH
3½ cups (490 g) Gluten-Free Bread Flour (page 8), plus more for sprinkling
1 tablespoon (18 g) kosher salt
1½ teaspoons honey
¾ cup plain whole-milk yogurt, at room temperature
1 large egg, at room temperature
3 tablespoons (42 g) unsalted butter, at room temperature
Starter
4 tablespoons (28 g) unsalted butter, melted (for brushing)

To make the starter, place all the starter ingredients in a medium-size bowl, and whisk until well combined. The mixture will be thick and shapeless. Cover and set the bowl aside in a warm, draft-free location to rise until doubled (about 40 minutes).

Once the starter has finished rising, make the dough. Place the flour and salt in the bowl of your stand mixer, and use a handheld whisk to combine well. Add the honey, yogurt, egg, room-temperature butter, and risen starter to the bowl, and mix on low speed with the dough hook until combined. Raise the mixer speed to medium and knead for about 5 minutes. The dough will be quite sticky, but should be smooth and stretchy. Spray a silicone spatula lightly with cooking oil spray, and scrape down the sides of the bowl. Transfer the dough to a lightly oiled bowl or proofing bucket large enough for the dough to rise to double its size, and cover with an oiled piece of plastic wrap (or the oiled top to your proofing bucket). Place the dough in the refrigerator for at least 12 hours and up to 5 days.

On baking day, line a rimmed baking sheet with unbleached parchment paper and set it aside. Turn the dough out onto a lightly floured surface. Knead until smoother as described in the General Shaping Tips in Chapter 3. Sprinkle with more flour and knead lightly until smooth. Roll out the dough into a 16-inch circle. With a pastry wheel or sharp knife, slice the round of dough into quarters, then slice each quarter into thirds, making twelve triangles total. Before separating the triangles, brush the dough with 2 tablespoons of the melted butter. Allow the dough to sit for about 5 minutes while the butter sets, to make it less messy for shaping. Once the butter has begun to set, separate one triangle from the circle, and roll it gently but securely from the base to the tip. Place the roll on the prepared baking sheet, with the tip of the triangle secured on the bottom. Repeat with the remaining triangles, spacing the rolls about 2 inches apart on the prepared baking sheet.

Cover the baking sheet with lightly oiled plastic wrap and place it in a warm, draft-free location to rise until it is 150 percent of its original size (about 45 minutes). Do not overproof.

About 15 minutes before the end of the second rise, preheat your oven to 350°F. Once the rolls have finished rising, brush the tops generously with melted butter. Place the baking sheet in the center of the preheated oven and bake until the rolls are just browned (10 to 12 minutes). Remove from the oven, and serve warm.

CINNAMON STICKY BUNS
MAKES 9 BUNS

STICKY BUNS ARE SO-NAMED BECAUSE OF THE CARAMELIZED BOT-tom that becomes the topping for the buns when you turn them out onto a serving platter. Rather than making a caramel sauce on the stovetop, I let the oven do the work for me by adding the caramel ingredients to the bottom of the baking dish before baking. These buns are sticky, gooey, and . . . heavenly. Wonder what happens if you leave out the bottom-turned-topping? Flip to page 166 to find out.

DOUGH
3 cups (420 g) Gluten-Free Bread Flour (page 8), plus more for sprinkling
¼ teaspoon cream of tartar
2 teaspoons (6 g) instant yeast
½ cup (100 g) sugar
½ teaspoon (3 g) kosher salt
½ teaspoon finely grated nutmeg
¾ cup plus 2 tablespoons warm milk (about 95°F) (not nonfat)
1 large egg, at room temperature, beaten
4 tablespoons (56 g) unsalted butter, melted and cooled

TOPPING
½ cup (100 g) sugar
½ teaspoon (3 g) kosher salt
¼ cup heavy cream, at room temperature
1 tablespoon (14 g) unsalted butter, melted

FILLING
2 tablespoons (28 g) unsalted butter, melted
½ cup (109 g) packed light brown sugar
1 tablespoon ground cinnamon

In the bowl of your stand mixer, place the flour, cream of tartar, yeast, and sugar, and whisk with a handheld whisk until combined well. Add the salt and nutmeg, and whisk to combine well. Add the milk, egg, and butter, and mix on low speed with the dough hook until combined. Raise the mixer speed to medium and knead for about 5 minutes. This is a lovely, smooth, and supple enriched dough. It climbs up the dough hook during kneading but remains intact and smooth. Spray a silicone spatula lightly with cooking oil spray, and scrape down the sides of the bowl. Transfer the dough to a lightly oiled bowl or proofing bucket large enough for the dough to rise to double its size, spray the top of the dough with cooking oil spray, and cover with an oiled piece of plastic wrap (or the oiled top to your proofing bucket). Place the dough in the refrigerator for at least 12 hours and up to 3 days.

On baking day, grease a 9-inch round baking dish and set it aside. Make the topping: In a medium-size bowl, place all of the topping ingredients and mix well. Pour the topping into the prepared baking dish and spread into an even layer. Set the pan aside.

Turn the dough out onto a lightly floured surface. Knead until smoother as described in the General Shaping Tips in Chapter 3. Roll the dough out into a 12- by 15-inch rectangle. Brush the surface of the rectangle with the melted butter and sprinkle evenly with the brown sugar and cinnamon from the filling. Beginning at the 12-inch side of the dough, roll it tightly away from your body until it is a coil. With a sharp knife, slice the roll crosswise into nine pieces, each about 1⅓ inches wide. Place the rolls, one flat side down, on the topping in the bottom of the prepared baking dish, evenly spaced from one another. There should be enough room for the rolls to expand as they rise.

Cover the baking dish with oiled plastic wrap and place in a warm, draft-free location until doubled in size (about 1 hour). Once the rolls have finished rising, remove the plastic wrap and place the baking dish in the center of a cold oven. Turn the oven on to 350°F, and bake until the buns are golden brown and bubbling (about 25 minutes). Do not overbake or the filling (and the rolls) will burn. Remove from the oven and invert the entire baking dish immediately onto a serving platter. Wait for the rolls to fall out in one piece from the baking dish, then remove the dish. Serve warm.

CINNAMON ROLLS

MAKES 9 BUNS

THIS IS WHAT HAPPENS WHEN CINNAMON STICKY BUNS (PAGE 164) are made without the caramelized bottom-turned-topping. These rolls are for when you're not feeling like you can power through both the bun and the caramelized topping. We all have our limits.

DOUGH

3 cups (420 g) Gluten-Free Bread Flour (page 8), plus more for sprinkling

¼ teaspoon cream of tartar

2 teaspoons (6 g) instant yeast

½ cup (100 g) sugar

½ teaspoon kosher salt

½ teaspoon finely grated nutmeg

¾ cup plus 2 tablespoons warm milk (not nonfat)

1 large egg, at room temperature, beaten

4 tablespoons (56 g) unsalted butter, melted and cooled

FILLING

2 tablespoons (28 g) unsalted butter, melted

½ cup (109 g) packed light brown sugar

1 tablespoon ground cinnamon

In the bowl of your stand mixer, place the flour, cream of tartar, instant yeast and sugar, and use a handheld whisk to combine well. Add the salt and nutmeg and whisk to combine well. Add the milk, egg, and butter, and mix on low speed with the dough hook until combined. Raise the mixer speed to medium and knead for about 5 minutes. The dough is a lovely, smooth, enriched dough. It climbs up the dough hook during kneading but remains intact and smooth. Spray a silicone spatula lightly with cooking oil spray, and scrape down the sides of the bowl. Transfer the dough to a lightly oiled bowl or proofing bucket large enough for the dough to rise to double its size, spray the top of the dough with cooking oil spray, and cover with an oiled piece of plastic wrap (or the oiled top to your proofing bucket). Place the dough in the refrigerator for at least 12 hours and up to 3 days.

On baking day, grease a 9-inch round baking dish and set it aside. Turn the dough out onto a lightly floured surface. Knead until smoother as described in the General Shaping Tips in Chapter 3. Roll out the dough into a 12 by 15-inch rectangle. Brush the surface of the rectangle with the melted butter from the filling and sprinkle evenly with the brown sugar and cinnamon. Beginning at the 12-inch side of the dough, roll it tightly away from your body until it is a coil. With a sharp knife, slice the roll crosswise into nine pieces, each about 1⅓ inches wide. Place the rolls, one flat side down, on the prepared baking dish, evenly spaced from one another. There should be enough room for the rolls to expand as they rise.

Cover the baking dish with oiled plastic wrap and place in a warm, draft-free location until doubled in size (about 1 hour). Once the rolls have finished rising, remove the plastic wrap and place the baking dish in the center of a cold oven. Turn the oven on to 350°F, and bake until the rolls are golden brown and bubbling (about 25 minutes). Remove from the oven, and serve warm.

BASIC BAGUETTES
MAKES TWO 16-INCH BAGUETTES

THIS IS HOW I PICTURE YOU: WALKING HOME WITH A SHOPPING bag slung over your shoulder, a hunk of cheese, and an aged salami on the bottom of the bag. And what's that sticking out of the bag? Fresh-cut flowers . . . and two 16-inch baguettes! Go run and get the cheese and charcuterie. I'll meet you back here with the crustiest truly authentic-tasting gluten-free baguettes you've never had (until now)!

STARTER
1¼ cups (175 g) Gluten-Free Bread Flour (page 8)
2 teaspoons (6 g) instant yeast
1½ tablespoons (18 g) sugar
1 cup warm water (about 95°F)

DOUGH
2¼ cups (315 g) Gluten-Free Bread Flour (page 8), plus more for sprinkling
½ teaspoon cream of tartar
2 teaspoons (12 g) kosher salt
1 tablespoon honey
¼ cup plus 2 tablespoons water, at room temperature
Starter

To make the starter, place all the starter ingredients in a medium-size bowl, and whisk until well combined. The mixture will be thick and shapeless. Cover and set the bowl aside in a warm, draft-free location to rise until doubled (about 40 minutes).

Once the starter has finished rising, make the dough. Place the flour, cream of tartar, and salt in the bowl of your stand mixer, and use a handheld whisk to combine well. Add the honey, water, and risen starter to the bowl, and mix on low speed with the dough hook until combined. Raise the mixer speed to medium and knead for about 5 minutes. The dough will be quite sticky, but should be smooth and stretchy. Spray a silicone spatula lightly with cooking oil spray, and scrape down the sides of the bowl. Transfer the dough to a lightly oiled bowl or proofing bucket large enough for the dough to rise to double its size, and cover with an oiled piece of plastic wrap (or the oiled top to your proofing bucket). Place the dough in the refrigerator for at least 12 hours and up to 5 days.

On baking day, line a rimmed baking sheet with unbleached parchment paper and set it aside. Remove the dough from the refrigerator, turn it out onto a lightly floured surface. Knead until smoother as described in the General Shaping Tips in Chapter 3. Divide the dough into two equally weighted pieces. Lightly flour one piece of dough, and cover the other piece with a moist tea towel so that it doesn't dry out. To shape the first piece of dough, follow the instructions on page 35 for shaping baguettes.

Once finished, place the first shaped baguette carefully on the prepared baking sheet and dust with flour. Repeat the process with the remaining half of the dough, placing it about 3 inches from the first baguette. Cover the pan with oiled plastic wrap and set it in a warm, draft-free location to rise until doubled in size (about 1 hour).

About 25 minutes before the dough has finished rising, preheat your oven to 375°F. Once the dough has finished rising, dust both baguettes with flour again, slash from one side into each baguette in three or four places, with a sharp knife or a lame on a diagonal at a 45-degree angle to the bread, just less than ¼ inch deep. Place the baking sheet in the center of the preheated oven, quickly throw a few cubes of ice into the bottom of the oven to create steam, and quickly close the oven door. Bake until the baguettes are lightly golden brown, and the center of each baguette reads about 190°F on an instant-read thermometer (about 30 minutes). Remove from the oven, transfer to a wire rack, and allow to cool for about 15 minutes before slicing and serving.

WHOLE-GRAIN BAGUETTES
MAKES TWO 16-INCH BAGUETTES

AGAIN, WITH JUST A FEW TWEAKS TO THE BASIC BAGUETTE RECIPE (page 169), we have whole-grain baguettes, for when you're looking for that wheaty bite, and an extra hit of whole-grain nutrition.

STARTER
¾ cup (105 g) Gluten-Free Bread Flour (page 8)
¾ cup (105 g) Whole-Grain Gluten-Free Flour (page 10)
2 teaspoons (6 g) instant yeast
1½ teaspoons (18 g) sugar
1 cup warm water (about 95°F)

DOUGH
2 cups (280 g) Gluten-Free Bread Flour (page 8), plus more for sprinkling
½ teaspoon cream of tartar
2 teaspoons (12 g) kosher salt
1 tablespoon honey
3 tablespoons (42 g) unsalted butter, at room temperature
Starter

To make the starter, place all the starter ingredients in a medium-size bowl, and whisk until well combined. The mixture will be thick and shapeless. Cover and set the bowl aside in a warm, draft-free location to rise until doubled (about 40 minutes).

Once the starter has finished rising, make the dough. Place the flour, cream of tartar, and salt in the bowl of your stand mixer and whisk to combine well with a separate, handheld whisk. Add the honey, butter, and risen starter to the bowl, and mix on low speed with the dough hook until combined. Raise the mixer speed to medium and knead for about 5 minutes. The dough will be quite sticky, but should be smooth and stretchy. Spray a silicone spatula lightly with cooking oil spray, and scrape down the sides of the bowl. Transfer the dough to a lightly oiled bowl or proofing bucket large enough for the dough to rise to double its size, and cover with an oiled piece of plastic wrap (or the oiled top to your proofing bucket). Place the dough in the refrigerator for at least 12 hours and up to 5 days.

On baking day, line a rimmed baking sheet with unbleached parchment paper and set it aside. Remove the dough from the refrigerator, turn it out onto a lightly floured surface. Knead until smoother as described in the General Shaping Tips in Chapter 3. Divide the dough into two equally weighted pieces. Lightly flour one piece of dough, and cover the other piece with a moist tea towel so that it doesn't dry out. To shape the first piece of dough, follow the instructions on page 35 for shaping baguettes. Once finished, place the first shaped baguette carefully on the prepared baking sheet and dust with flour. Repeat the process with the remaining half of the dough, placing it about 3 inches from the first baguette. Cover the pan with oiled plastic wrap and set the dough in a warm, draft-free location to rise until doubled in size (about 1 hour).

About 25 minutes before the dough has finished rising, preheat your oven to 375°F. Once the dough has finished rising, dust both baguettes with flour again, slice from one side into each baguette in three or four places, with a sharp knife or lame on a diagonal at a 45-degree angle to the baguette, just less than ¼ inch deep. Place the baking sheet in the center of the preheated oven, quickly throw a few cubes of ice into the bottom of the oven to create steam, and quickly close the oven door. Bake until the baguettes are lightly golden brown, and the center of each baguette reads about 190°F on an instant-read thermometer (about 30 minutes). Remove from the oven, transfer to a wire rack, and allow to cool for about 15 minutes before slicing and serving.

WHOLE-GRAIN BOULE
MAKES 2 ROUND LOAVES

THESE BOULES ARE MADE WITH WHOLE GRAIN DOUGH, BUT COULD just as easily be made with lean bread dough (page 43). The difference is in the technique, so be sure to read the recipe all the way through before you begin, and maybe even go back and reread the section on shaping bread dough (see page 34).

STARTER
¾ cup (105 g) Gluten-Free Bread Flour (page 8)
¾ cup (105 g) Whole-Grain Gluten-Free Flour (page 10)
2 teaspoons (6 g) instant yeast
1½ teaspoons (18 g) sugar
1 cup warm water (about 95°F)

DOUGH
2 cups (280 g) Gluten-Free Bread Flour (page 8), plus more for sprinkling
½ teaspoon cream of tartar
2 teaspoons (12 g) kosher salt
1 tablespoon honey
3 tablespoons (42 g) unsalted butter, at room temperature
Starter

To make the starter, place all the starter ingredients in a medium-size bowl, and whisk until well combined. The mixture will be thick and shapeless. Cover and set the bowl aside in a warm, draft-free location to rise until doubled (about 40 minutes).

Once the starter has finished rising, make the dough. Place the flour, cream of tartar, and salt in the bowl of your stand mixer, and use a handheld whisk to combine well. Add the honey, butter, and risen starter to the bowl, and mix on low speed with the dough hook until combined. Raise the mixer speed to medium and knead for about 5 minutes. The dough will be quite sticky, but should be smooth and stretchy. Spray a silicone spatula lightly with cooking oil spray, and scrape down the sides of the bowl. Transfer the dough to a lightly oiled bowl or proofing bucket large enough for the dough to rise to double its size, and cover with an oiled piece of plastic wrap (or the oiled top to your proofing bucket). Place the dough in the refrigerator for at least 12 hours and up to 5 days.

On baking day, line a rimmed baking sheet with unbleached parchment paper and set it aside. Remove the dough from the refrigerator, turn it out onto a lightly floured surface. Knead until smoother as described in the General Shaping Tips in Chapter 3. Divide the dough into two equally weighted pieces. Lightly flour one piece of dough, and cover the other piece with a moist tea towel so that it doesn't dry out. To shape the first piece of dough, follow the instructions on page 34 for shaping a boule. Once finished, place the first boule onto the prepared baking sheet, seam side down, and dust with more flour. Repeat the process with the other piece of dough. Cover both loaves with oiled plastic wrap and set to rise in a warm, draft-free location until doubled in size (about 1½ hours).

About 25 minutes before the dough has finished rising, preheat your oven to 375°F. Once the dough has finished rising, remove the plastic wrap, dust both loaves with more flour, and slash each a few times horizontally near the base at a 45 degree angle about ¼ inch deep with a sharp knife or lame. Place the baking sheet in the center of the preheated oven, quickly throw a few cubes of ice into the bottom of the oven to create steam, and quickly close the oven door. Bake until the loaves are lightly golden brown, and the center of each loaf reads about 190°F on an instant-read thermometer (about 40 minutes). Remove from the oven, transfer to a wire rack, and allow to cool for about 20 minutes before slicing and serving.

SOFT OLIVE GARDEN–STYLE GARLIC BUTTER BREADSTICKS
MAKES 12 BREADSTICKS

THE BREADSTICKS AT OLIVE GARDEN ARE LEGENDARY, RIGHT? EVEN though this restaurant chain offers a few gluten-free items on its menu, a gluten-free iteration of its breadsticks is not among them. No mind. These breadsticks get most of their flavor from the garlic butter they are brushed with, twice. So, there's no need for a second rise. You know what that means, don't you? It means that they require very little advance planning before you're walking right down memory lane, the Olive Garden edition.

BREAD DOUGH
4¼ cups (595 g) Gluten-Free Bread Flour (page 8), plus more for sprinkling

2 teaspoons (6 g) instant yeast

2 tablespoons (24 g) sugar

2 teaspoons (12 g) kosher salt

6 tablespoons (84 g) unsalted butter, at room temperature

1¼ cups plus 2 tablespoons warm water (about 95°F)

GARLIC BUTTER
3 tablespoons (42 g) unsalted butter, melted

1 teaspoon garlic salt

First make the bread dough. Place the flour, yeast, and sugar in the bowl of your stand mixer, and use a handheld whisk to combine well. Add the salt, and whisk to combine. Add the butter and water, and mix on low speed with the dough hook until combined. Raise the mixer speed to medium and knead for about 5 minutes. The dough will be quite sticky, but should be smooth and stretchy. Spray a silicone spatula lightly with cooking oil spray, and scrape down the sides of the bowl.

Line a rimmed baking sheet with unbleached parchment paper and set it aside. Turn out the dough onto a lightly floured surface. Knead until smoother as described in the General Shaping Tips in Chapter 3. Divide the dough into twelve pieces. With each piece, follow the instructions on page 35 for shaping hoagies (covering the remaining pieces of dough with a moist tea towel so that they don't dry out), elongating each breadstick to about 8 inches long. Place the breadsticks about 2 inches apart from one another on the prepared baking sheet, and dust with flour. Once all the breadsticks are shaped, cover the baking sheet with oiled plastic wrap and set in a warm, draft-free location to rise until the breadsticks are nearly doubled in size (about 1½ hours). About 25 minutes before the dough has finished rising, remove the plastic, preheat your oven to 375°F.

Once the breadsticks have finished rising, remove the plastic, place the baking sheet in the center of the preheated oven and immediately turn down the oven temperature to 350°F. Bake for 5 minutes. While the breadsticks are baking, melt the butter for the garlic butter in a small, microwave-safe bowl, then mix in the garlic salt. Remove the baking sheet from the oven and brush each breadstick generously with the garlic butter. Return the breadsticks to the oven and continue to bake until they are lightly golden brown all over (about another 5 minutes). Remove the breadsticks from the oven and brush again with garlic butter. Serve immediately.

BASIC TORPEDO BREAD (OR BATARD)
MAKES 2 LOAVES

THIS RECIPE IS MEANT TO SHOW OFF ANOTHER OF THE SHAPES that good gluten-free bread can take. A batard is shorter and wider than a baguette but is shaped quite similarly. Once you have mastered one, the other shouldn't be far behind.

STARTER
1¼ cups (175 g) Gluten-Free Bread Flour (page 8)
2 teaspoons (6 g) instant yeast
1½ tablespoons (18 g) sugar
1 cup warm water (about 95°F)

DOUGH
2¼ cups (315 g) Gluten-Free Bread Flour (page 8), plus more for sprinkling
½ teaspoon cream of tartar
2 teaspoons (12 g) kosher salt
1 tablespoon honey
¼ cup plus 2 tablespoons water, at room temperature
Starter

To make the starter, place all the starter ingredients in a medium-size bowl, and whisk until well combined. The mixture will be thick and shapeless. Cover and set the bowl aside in a warm, draft-free location to rise until doubled (about 40 minutes).

Once the starter has finished rising, make the dough. Place the flour, cream of tartar, and salt in the bowl of your stand mixer, and use a handheld whisk to combine well. Add the honey, water, and risen starter to the bowl, and mix on low speed with the dough hook until combined. Raise the mixer speed to medium and knead for about 5 minutes. The dough will be quite sticky, but should be smooth and stretchy. Spray a silicone spatula lightly with cooking oil spray, and scrape down the sides of the bowl. Transfer the dough to a lightly oiled bowl or proofing bucket large enough for the dough to rise to double its size, and cover with an oiled piece of plastic wrap (or the oiled top to your proofing bucket). Place the dough in the refrigerator for at least 12 hours and up to 5 days.

On baking day, line a rimmed baking sheet with unbleached parchment paper and set it aside. Remove the dough from the refrigerator, turn it out onto a lightly floured surface. Knead until smoother as described in the General Shaping Tips in Chapter 3. Divide the dough into two equally weighted pieces. Lightly flour one piece of dough, and cover the other piece with a moist tea towel so that it doesn't dry out. To shape the first loaf, follow the instructions on page 34 for shaping batards. Place the loaf on the prepared baking sheet and dust it with more flour. Repeat the process with the other piece of dough. Cover both loaves with oiled plastic wrap and set to rise in a warm, draft-free location until doubled in size (about 1½ hours).

About 25 minutes before the dough has finished rising, preheat your oven to 375°F. Once the dough has finished rising, remove the plastic wrap, dust both loaves with more flour, and slash each a few times horizontally near the base at a 45 degree angle about ¼ inch deep with a sharp knife or lame. Place the baking sheet in the center of the preheated oven, quickly throw a few ice cubes into the bottom of the oven to create steam, and quickly close the oven door. Bake until the loaves are lightly golden brown all over, and the center of each loaf reads about 190°F on an instant-read thermometer (about 40 minutes). Remove from the oven, transfer to a wire rack, and allow to cool for about 20 minutes before slicing and serving.

HAWAIIAN ROLLS
MAKES 12 ROLLS

I F YOU'VE BEEN MISSING THE SWEET, LIGHT, AND FLAVORFUL TASTE of Hawaiian rolls, you'll want to start doing the happy dance right about now. I like these best as dinner rolls, but if you prefer them made into miniature ham and cheese sandwiches, I'll understand.

INGREDIENTS
3 cups (420 g) Gluten-Free Bread Flour (page 8), plus more for sprinkling
2 teaspoons (6 g) instant yeast
¼ cup (50 g) sugar
1 teaspoon (6 g) kosher salt
4 tablespoons (56 g) unsalted butter, at room temperature
1 large egg, at room temperature, beaten
1 cup plus 1 tablespoon pineapple juice
1 teaspoon gluten-free vanilla extract
Egg wash (1 large egg, at room temperature, beaten with 1 tablespoon water)

Place the flour, yeast, and sugar in the bowl of your stand mixer, and use a handheld whisk to combine well. Add the salt, and whisk to combine. Add the butter, egg, pineapple juice, and vanilla, and mix on low speed with the dough hook until combined. Raise the mixer speed to medium and knead for about 5 minutes. The dough will be quite sticky, but should be smooth and stretchy. Spray a silicone spatula lightly with cooking oil spray, and scrape down the sides of the bowl. Transfer the dough to a lightly oiled bowl or proofing bucket large enough for the dough to rise to double its size, and cover with an oiled piece of plastic wrap (or the oiled top to your proofing bucket). Place the dough in the refrigerator for at least 12 hours and up to 5 days.

On baking day, grease an 8-inch round baking pan and set it aside. Remove the dough from the refrigerator and turn it out onto a lightly floured surface. Knead until smoother as described in the General Shaping Tips in Chapter 3. With a floured bench scraper, divide the dough into twelve pieces of equal size. Shape one piece into a round by following the directions for shaping small, round rolls on page 32. Place the first roll in the prepared baking pan. Repeat with the remaining pieces of dough, placing the rolls less than an inch apart from one another. Cover the baking pan with oiled plastic wrap and set it aside in a warm, draft-free location to rise for 30 minutes. Uncover the pan and brush the rolls generously with the egg wash. Allow the rolls to finish rising, uncovered, until fully doubled in size (about 20 minutes more).

About 20 minutes before the rolls have completed their final rise, preheat your oven to 350°F. Place the baking pan on the lower rack of the preheated oven and bake until lightly golden brown, and the inside of the rolls registers about 185°F on an instant-read thermometer (about 20 minutes). Allow to cool briefly in the pan before serving.

MINIATURE BRIOCHE BUNS

MAKES 16 BUNS

THESE ARE JUST ADORABLE LITTLE MINIATURE VERSIONS OF BRIoche Bread (page 50), all dressed up like you see them in a bakery, with those sweet little balls of dough on top.

STARTER

1 cup (140 g) Gluten-Free Bread Flour (page 8)

2⅔ teaspoons (8 g) instant yeast

1 tablespoon (12 g) sugar

½ cup milk, scalded and cooled to 95°F (not nonfat)

¼ cup plus 2 tablespoons warm water (about 95°F)

DOUGH

3 cups (420 g) Gluten-Free Bread Flour (page 8), plus more for sprinkling

1 teaspoon (6 g) kosher salt

1½ tablespoons honey

3 large eggs, at room temperature, beaten

11 tablespoons (154 g) unsalted butter, at room temperature

Starter

Egg wash (1 large egg, at room temperature, beaten with 1 tablespoon milk)

To make the starter, place all the starter ingredients in a medium-size bowl, and whisk until well combined. The mixture will be thick and shapeless. Cover and set the bowl aside in a warm, draft-free location to rise until doubled (about 40 minutes).

Once the starter has finished rising, make the dough. Place the flour and salt in the bowl of your stand mixer, and use a handheld whisk to combine well. Add the honey, eggs, butter, and risen starter to the bowl, and mix on low speed with the dough hook until combined. Raise the mixer speed to medium and knead for about 5 minutes. The dough will be quite sticky, but should be smooth and stretchy. Spray a silicone spatula lightly with cooking oil spray, and scrape down the sides of the bowl. Transfer the dough to a lightly oiled bowl or proofing bucket large enough for the dough to rise to double its size, and cover with an oiled piece of plastic wrap (or the oiled top to your proofing bucket). Place the dough in the refrigerator for at least 12 hours and up to 5 days.

On baking day, grease sixteen miniature brioche molds well and set them aside on a rimmed baking sheet. If you don't have brioche molds, you can use standard muffin tins.

Turn the dough out onto a lightly floured surface. Knead until smoother as described in the General Shaping Tips in Chapter 3. Divide the dough in half, then each half in half to make four equal pieces, and each of the four pieces into four pieces, until you have sixteen total pieces of equal size. Working with one piece of dough at a time (covering the others with a moist tea towel so that they don't dry out), pull off a piece of dough that is about one-fifth the size of the whole. Shape both the large and the small pieces into rounds between your floured palms. Place the larger round in a prepared mold and place the small round on top in the center of the larger round, pressing down slightly to ensure that they adhere. Replace the mold on the baking sheet, and repeat with the remaining pieces of dough.

Cover the molds on the baking sheet with oiled plastic wrap and set in a warm, draft-free location to rise until doubled in size (about 1 hour). About 25 minutes before the dough has finished rising, preheat your oven to 350°F. Once the buns have finished rising, remove the plastic wrap, brush the tops generously with the egg wash, then place the baking sheet in the center of the preheated oven. Bake the buns for about 15 minutes, or until they are lightly golden brown and register 185°F in the center on an instant-read thermometer. Allow to cool briefly before serving.

7 FLATBREADS

BREADS AND CRACKERS YOU ROLL OR PRESS FLAT

THICK-CRUST PIZZA DOUGH
MAKES 2 THICK 12-INCH PIZZAS

IZZA DOUGH IS USUALLY CONSIDERED TO BE THE EASIEST ENTRY-
point for baking yeast dough as the rising is almost entirely for the purpose of flavor development. Believe it or not, in theory, you can even skip the
refrigerator rise and go right to shaping and baking. Your pizza will still puff
up in the oven during baking, thanks to the oven spring. But (you knew there
was a but, right?), even if you were willing to forgo the flavor that a long, slow
refrigerator rise gives to your pizza, I really don't recommend getting right
to work with this dough. This thick-crust pizza dough is a relatively high-
hydration (wet) dough, so unless it spends some time in the refrigerator, it
can be quite difficult to handle.

STARTER
1½ cups (210 g) Gluten-Free Bread Flour (page 8)
1 teaspoon (3 g) instant yeast
2 teaspoons (8 g) sugar
¾ cup plus 2 tablespoons warm water (about 95°F)

DOUGH
2 cups (280 g) Gluten-Free Bread Flour (page 8), plus more for sprinkling
1⅓ teaspoons (4 g) instant yeast
2 teaspoons (12 g) kosher salt
1 tablespoon extra-virgin olive oil
¼ cup water, at room temperature
Starter

To make the starter, place all the starter ingredients in a medium-size bowl,
and whisk until well combined. The mixture will be thick and shapeless.
Cover and set the bowl aside in a warm, draft-free location to rise until doubled (about 40 minutes).

   Once the starter has finished rising, make the dough. Place the flour and
yeast in the bowl of your stand mixer, and use a handheld whisk to combine well. Add the salt, and whisk to combine. Add the olive oil, water, and
risen starter to the bowl, and mix on low speed with the dough hook until

combined. Raise the mixer speed to medium and knead for about 5 minutes. The dough will begin as a rough ball and become very sticky, but should be smooth and somewhat stretchy. Spray a silicone spatula lightly with cooking oil spray, and scrape down the sides of the bowl. Transfer the dough to a lightly oiled bowl or proofing bucket large enough for the dough to rise to double its size, and cover with an oiled piece of plastic wrap (or the oiled top to your proofing bucket). Place the dough in the refrigerator for at least 12 hours and up to 5 days.

Once the pizza dough has finished rising in the refrigerator, it is best to work with it cold. Place a pizza stone (or overturned rimmed metal baking sheet) on the bottom rack of your oven and preheat the oven to 400°F. On a lightly floured surface, knead dough until smoother as described in the General Shaping Tips in Chapter 3. Divide the chilled dough into two equal portions, and roll each into a ball. Sprinkle both lightly with flour, and cover one with a moist tea towel so that it doesn't dry out. Using well-floured hands and a rolling pin, as necessary, pat and roll out the first piece of dough on a lightly floured surface into a 12-inch round, rotating the dough and flouring it frequently, to prevent sticking. Roll and pat the dough more thickly as you work from the center of the dough to the edges to create a crust. Transfer the round of dough to a piece of unbleached parchment paper. Repeat with the second piece of dough.

Place each crust, one at a time, each still on its parchment paper, on the hot pizza stone. Bake for about 5 minutes, or until the crust begins to puff and brown. Remove it from the oven. Top your pizza with your desired toppings, then place the pizzas again, one at a time, back on the pizza stone. Bake until the crust is browned and your toppings are cooked as desired (about 7 minutes, but time will vary depending upon toppings and taste). Allow the pizza to set for a few minutes before slicing and serving.

For more ideas on how to use the pizza dough, see Chapter 9.

THIN-CRUST PIZZA DOUGH
MAKES 2 THIN 10-INCH PIZZAS

MAKING A GOOD THIN CRUST PIZZA MEANS MORE THAN ROLLING out the Thick-Crust Pizza, well, thinly. The ingredient proportions in this thin crust pizza are a bit different, making for a stiffer dough that crisps more and rises less.

STARTER
1 cup (140 g) Gluten-Free Bread Flour (page 8)
1⅔ teaspoons (5 g) instant yeast
1½ teaspoons (6 g) sugar
1 cup warm water (about 95°F)

DOUGH
2 cups (280 g) Gluten-Free Bread Flour (page 8), plus more for sprinkling
2 teaspoons (12 g) kosher salt
Starter

To make the starter, place all the starter ingredients in a medium-size bowl, and whisk until well combined. The mixture will be thick and shapeless. Cover and set the bowl aside in a warm, draft-free location to rise until doubled (about 40 minutes).

Once the starter has finished rising, make the dough. Place the flour and salt in the bowl of your stand mixer, and use a handheld whisk to combine well. Add the risen starter to the bowl, and mix on low speed with the dough hook until combined. Raise the mixer speed to medium and knead for about 5 minutes. The dough will begin as a rough ball and will become very sticky and rather stiff, but still stretchy and smooth.

Spray a silicone spatula lightly with cooking oil spray, and scrape down the sides of the bowl. Transfer the dough to a lightly oiled bowl or proofing bucket large enough for the dough to rise to double its size, and cover with an oiled piece of plastic wrap (or the oiled top to your proofing bucket). Place the dough in the refrigerator for at least 12 hours and up to 5 days.

Once the pizza dough has finished rising in the refrigerator, it is best to work with it cold. Place a pizza stone (or overturned rimmed metal baking sheet) on the bottom rack of your oven and preheat the oven to 400°F. On a lightly floured surface, knead the dough until smoother as described in the General Shaping Tips in Chapter 3. Divide the dough into two equal portions, and roll each into a ball. Sprinkle both lightly with flour, and cover one with a moist tea towel so that it doesn't dry out. Using well-floured hands and a rolling pin, as necessary, pat and roll out the first piece of dough on a lightly floured surface into an 11-inch round, rotating the dough and flouring it frequently, to prevent sticking. Transfer the round of dough to a piece of unbleached parchment paper. Roll in the edges of the dough to create a crust, and pinch to secure. Repeat with the second piece of dough.

Place each crust, one at a time, each still on its parchment paper, on the hot pizza stone. Bake for about 5 minutes, or until the crust begins to puff and brown. Remove it from the oven. Top your pizza with your desired toppings, then place the pizzas again, one at a time, back on the pizza stone. Bake until the crust is browned and your toppings are cooked as desired (about 7 minutes, but time will vary depending upon toppings and taste). Allow the pizza to set for a few minutes before slicing and serving.

For more ideas on how to use the pizza dough, see Chapter 9.

THICK-CRUST WHOLE-GRAIN PIZZA CRUST DOUGH

MAKES 2 THICK 14-INCH PIZZAS

BECAUSE WE NOW HAVE THICK-CRUST PIZZA (PAGE 187) AND THIN-Crust Pizza (page 189), it's time to get greedy. This whole-grain pizza dough has that satisfying bite and weight that only whole grains can bring, and the moral superiority that you get when you not only make your own food but make it healthfully, to boot. Home run!

STARTER

1 cup (140 g) Whole-Grain Gluten-Free Flour (page 10)

¾ cup (105 g) Gluten-Free Bread Flour (page 8)

1⅓ teaspoons (4 g) instant yeast

1 tablespoon (12 g) sugar

1¼ cups plus 2 tablespoons water, at room temperature

DOUGH

2¼ cups (315 g) Gluten-Free Bread Flour (page 8), plus more for sprinkling

1⅓ teaspoons (4 g) instant yeast

2 teaspoons (12 g) kosher salt

1 tablespoon extra-virgin olive oil

2 tablespoons (28 g) unsalted butter, at room temperature

Starter

To make the starter, place all the starter ingredients in a medium-size bowl, and whisk until well combined. The mixture will be thick and shapeless. Cover and set the bowl aside in a warm, draft-free location to rise until doubled (about 40 minutes).

Once the starter has finished rising, make the dough. Place the flour and yeast in the bowl of your stand mixer, and use a handheld whisk to combine well. Add the salt, and whisk to combine. Add the olive oil, butter, and risen starter to the bowl, and mix on low speed with the dough hook until combined. Raise the mixer speed to medium and knead for about 5 minutes. The dough will begin as a rough ball and become very sticky dough, but should be smooth and somewhat stretchy. Spray a silicone spatula lightly with cooking oil spray, and scrape down the sides of the bowl. Transfer the dough to a lightly oiled bowl or proofing bucket large enough for the dough to rise to double its size, and cover with an oiled piece of plastic wrap (or the oiled top to your proofing bucket). Place the dough in the refrigerator for at least 12 hours and up to 5 days.

Once the pizza dough has finished rising in the refrigerator, it is best to work with it cold. Place a pizza stone (or overturned rimmed metal baking sheet) on the bottom rack of your oven and preheat the oven to 400°F. On a lightly floured surface, knead the dough until smoother as described in the General Shaping tips in Chapter 3. Divide the dough into two equal portions, and roll each into a ball. Sprinkle both lightly with flour, and cover one with a moist tea towel so that it doesn't dry out. Using well-floured hands and a rolling pin, as necessary, pat and roll out the first piece of dough on a lightly floured surface into a 12-inch round, rotating the dough and flouring it frequently to prevent sticking. Roll and pat the dough more thickly as you work from the center of the dough to the edges to create a crust. Transfer the round of dough to a piece of unbleached parchment paper. Repeat with the second piece of dough.

Place each crust, one at a time, each still on its parchment paper, on the hot pizza stone. Bake for about 5 minutes, or until the crust begins to puff and brown. Remove it from the oven. Top your pizza with your desired toppings, then place the pizzas again, one at a time, back on the pizza stone. Bake until the crust is browned and your toppings are cooked as desired (about 7 minutes, but time will vary depending upon toppings and taste). Allow the pizza to set for a few minutes before slicing and serving.

For more ideas on how to use the pizza dough, see Chapter 9.

DEEP-DISH CHICAGO-STYLE PIZZA
MAKES TWO 8-INCH DEEP-DISH PIZZAS

CHICAGO'S FAMOUS DEEP-DISH PIZZA IS SIMPLY IN A CLASS BY IT-self. Almost like a cross between a piecrust and a pizza crust, it's buttery and flaky but still has some bite. If you've been missing it, or even if you didn't know to miss it, things are about to change for the better.

PIZZA DOUGH
2½ cups (350 g) Gluten-Free Bread Flour (page 8), plus more for sprinkling

¼ cup (33 g) coarsely ground gluten-free cornmeal

1⅓ teaspoons (4 g) instant yeast

2 teaspoons (8 g) sugar

2 teaspoons (12 g) kosher salt

¼ cup canola oil

¾ cup warm water (about 95°F)

PIZZA
2 tablespoons (28 g) unsalted butter, melted

5 ounces thickly sliced provolone cheese

4 ounces cubed pancetta

Leaves from 3 sprigs of fresh oregano or 2 teaspoons dried

1 cup Quick Homemade Tomato Sauce (page 249) or store-bought sauce

2 ounces finely grated Parmigiano-Reggiano cheese

To make the pizza dough, place the flour, cornmeal, yeast, and sugar in the bowl of your stand mixer, and use a handheld whisk to combine well. Add the salt, and whisk to combine. Add the canola oil and water to the bowl, and knead on low speed with the dough hook until combined. Raise the mixer speed to medium-high and knead until smooth (about 5 minutes). Transfer the dough to a lightly oiled bowl or proofing bucket large enough for the dough to rise to double its size, and cover with an oiled piece of plastic wrap (or the oiled top to your proofing bucket). Place the dough in the refrigerator for at least 12 hours and up to 3 days.

On baking day, preheat your oven to 375°F. Grease two 8-inch round baking pans with sides at least 1½ inches high and set them aside. Remove the container of dough from the refrigerator and place on a lightly floured surface. Knead the dough until smoother as described in the General Shaping tips in Chapter 3. Divide the chilled dough into two equal portions, and roll each into a ball. Sprinkle both lightly with flour, and cover one with a moist tea towel so that it doesn't dry out. With a rolling pin, roll out one piece of the dough into a round that is about ¼ inch thick, flouring the dough and the surface and moving the dough often as necessary to prevent it from sticking to the surface. Lift the round of dough carefully into one of the prepared baking dishes and press it into the bottom and up the sides of the pan, as you would with a piecrust. Trim any edges that extend over the top of the sides of the pan. Repeat the process with the other half of the dough, placing it in the remaining prepared baking dish.

To assemble the pizzas, with the two crusts side by side, brush the bottoms and sides of each generously with the melted butter. Divide the provolone cheese between the two baking dishes, covering the bottom surface of each crust completely. Divide the pancetta between the two dishes, scattering it in an even layer on top of the cheese, followed by the oregano leaves and then the tomato sauce in a thick layer. Sprinkle the tops evenly with the Parmigiano-Reggiano cheese. Cover each pizza loosely with aluminum foil, and place together in the center of the preheated oven. Bake for about 30 minutes, or until the sauce is bubbling and the pancetta is very fragrant. Uncover the pizzas and continue to bake until about one-third of the moisture has evaporated from the tomato sauce (about another 15 minutes).

Remove from the oven and allow to cool at room temperature until set (about 10 minutes). Slide the pizzas out of the pans onto a cutting board, cut into slices, and serve warm.

NAAN BREAD
MAKES 8 PIECES

T HE MARRIAGE OF YOGURT AND GHEE IN THIS RECIPE FOR NAAN makes for a very tender flatbread. Serve it alongside your favorite Indian curry, or try layering it with sliced deli meat for the perfect open-faced sandwich.

INGREDIENTS
2½ cups (350 g) Gluten-Free Bread Flour (page 8), plus more for sprinkling
1⅔ teaspoons (5 g) instant yeast
1½ tablespoons (18 g) sugar
¼ teaspoon cream of tartar
½ teaspoon (3 g) kosher salt
⅓ cup plain yogurt, at room temperature
3 tablespoons (42 g) ghee or unsalted butter, melted and cooled
¾ cup plus 2 tablespoons warm water (about 95°F)
Ghee or unsalted butter, for frying

In the bowl of your stand mixer, place the flour, yeast, sugar, and cream of tartar, and use a handheld whisk to combine well. Add the salt, and whisk to combine. Add the yogurt, ghee, and water, and knead on low speed with the dough hook until combined. Raise the mixer speed to medium-high and knead until smooth (about 5 minutes). Spray a silicone spatula lightly with cooking oil spray, and scrape down the sides of the bowl. Transfer the dough to a lightly oiled bowl or proofing bucket large enough for the dough to rise to double its size, and cover with an oiled piece of plastic wrap (or the oiled top to your proofing bucket). Place the dough in the refrigerator for at least 12 hours and up to 3 days.

On baking day, line a rimmed baking sheet with unbleached parchment paper, spray the paper lightly with cooking oil, and set it aside. Remove the dough from the refrigerator. Knead the dough until smoother as described in the General Shaping tips in Chapter 3. Divide the dough in half, then each half in half, until you have eight total pieces, each about 95 grams. Shape the first piece of dough. Flouring the surface as necessary to keep the dough from sticking, and covering the remaining pieces of dough with a moist tea towel

so that they don't dry out, use a rolling pin to roll each piece of dough into an elongated oval about ⅜ inch thick. Repeat with the remaining pieces of dough. Place each piece of shaped dough 2 inches apart from one another on the prepared baking sheet. Cover with lightly oiled plastic wrap, and set in a warm, draft-free location to rise until nearly doubled in size (about 1 hour).

As the dough is nearing the end of its rise, place about 2 tablespoons of ghee in a cast-iron skillet, and melt over medium-high heat. Once the pan is hot, place the first piece of dough in the pan. Fry on one side until large bubbles begin to form (about 1 minute). Continue to fry for another 30 seconds to 1 minute, or until the underside is golden brown. Flip the bread to cook on the other side until browned, another minute or so. Transfer to a paper towel. Repeat with the remaining seven pieces of dough. Serve immediately.

HERB FOCACCIA
MAKES 1 LARGE FOCACCIA

BEFORE DECIDING UPON THIS NEW AND EXCITING WAY OF MAKING gluten-free bread, I had made gluten-free nice focaccia. But as soon as I began to have success baking this new way, I had no choice but to continue to raise the bar. The characteristic dimples serve a necessary function: The dough is meant to rise so much that dimpling is necessary to break any over-sized bubbles not just to achieve the traditional appearance. Now, with this recipe, gluten-free focaccia is crispy on the outside and truly light and airy on the inside, with those big, yeasty holes I never before dared to wish for. Eureka!

STARTER
1 cup (140 g) Gluten-Free Bread Flour (page 8)

1⅓ teaspoons (4 g) instant yeast

¾ cup warm water (about 95°F)

1 tablespoon honey

DOUGH
2 cups (280 g) Gluten-Free Bread Flour (page 8), plus more for sprinkling

1 teaspoon (6 g) kosher salt

¾ teaspoon cream of tartar

1 tablespoon (12 g) sugar

¾ cup water, at room temperature

3 tablespoons extra-virgin olive oil

Starter

TOPPING
¼ cup extra-virgin olive oil

2 tablespoons dried herbes de Provence (or your favorite dried herbs)

To make the starter, place all the starter ingredients in a medium-size bowl, and whisk until well combined. The mixture will be thick and shapeless. Cover and set the bowl aside in a warm, draft-free location to rise until more than doubled in size (about an hour).

Once the starter has finished rising, make the dough. In the bowl of your stand mixer, place the flour, salt, cream of tartar, and sugar, and use a hand-held whisk to combine. Add the water, oil, and risen starter, and mix on low speed with the dough hook until combined. Raise the mixer speed to medium and knead for about 5 minutes. When you raise the dough hook, a trail of dough from the hook to the bowl should be intact for at least the count of five. The dough will be quite sticky. Spray a silicone spatula lightly with cooking oil spray, and scrape down the sides of the bowl. Transfer the dough to a lightly oiled bowl or proofing bucket large enough for the dough to rise to double its size, and cover with an oiled piece of plastic wrap (or the oiled top to your proofing bucket). Place the dough in the refrigerator for at least 24 hours and up to 5 days.

On baking day, line a large rimmed baking sheet with unbleached parchment paper and set it aside. In a small bowl, combine the topping ingredients and mix to combine to create an herb oil. Set the bowl aside.

Remove the dough from the refrigerator, scatter a generous amount of flour on a flat surface, scrape the dough out of the bowl on top of the flour, and sprinkle with flour. Turn the dough over on itself with a bench scraper and transfer it carefully, with the help of a floured bench scraper, to the center of the prepared baking sheet. Drizzle half of the herb oil on top of the dough and, with the tips of your fingers, press and push the dough out toward the edges of the pan. The dough will be very wet and may be difficult to handle. Cover the dough with oiled plastic wrap and place in a warm, draft-free location to rise until doubled in size (about 2 hours). The dough will rise both up and out.

About 25 minutes before the end of the dough's rise, preheat your oven to 450°F and place a pizza stone on the lower rack. Once the dough has finished rising, pour the remaining herb oil over the top of the risen dough. Gently spread the oil around with your fingertips, dimpling the dough if you see any large bubbles, but otherwise taking care not to deflate it.

Place the baking sheet on the pizza stone, and bake for 5 minutes at 450°F. Lower the oven temperature to 400°F and continue to bake for another 15 minutes, or until the top of the focaccia is golden brown and the center of the bread reaches 200°F on an instant-read thermometer. Slice and serve warm.

GARLIC FOCACCIA
MAKES 1 LARGE FOCACCIA

WITH ALL THE DELICATE CRUST AND CHEWY INSIDE OF THE HERB
Focaccia (page 198), the garlic-infused oil is what makes this focaccia
extra special. If you dare, try first sautéing the garlic with the oil before adding the herbs and mixing to combine. Slice into squares, and you won't need
anything else for a seriously impressive appetizer.

STARTER

1 cup (140 g) Gluten-Free Bread Flour (page 8)
1⅓ teaspoons (4 g) instant yeast
¾ cup water, at room temperature
1 tablespoon honey

DOUGH

2 cups (280 g) Gluten-Free Bread Flour (page 8), plus more for sprinkling
1 teaspoon (6 g) kosher salt
¾ teaspoon cream of tartar
1 tablespoon (12 g) sugar
¾ cup water, at room temperature
3 tablespoons extra-virgin olive oil
Starter

TOPPING

5 cloves garlic, peeled and minced
¼ cup extra-virgin olive oil
1 teaspoon kosher salt

To make the starter, place all the starter ingredients in a medium-size bowl,
and whisk until well combined. The mixture will be thick and shapeless.
Cover and set the bowl aside in a warm, draft-free location to rise until more
than doubled in size (about an hour).

Once the starter has finished rising, make the dough. In the bowl of your
stand mixer, place the flour, salt, cream of tartar, and sugar, and use a handheld whisk to combine. Add the water, oil, and risen starter, and mix on low

speed with the dough hook until combined. Raise the mixer speed to medium and knead for about 5 minutes. When you raise the dough hook, a trail of dough from the hook to the bowl should be intact for at least the count of five. The dough will be quite sticky. Spray a silicone spatula lightly with cooking oil spray, and scrape down the sides of the bowl. Transfer the dough to a lightly oiled bowl or proofing bucket large enough for the dough to rise to double its size, and cover with an oiled piece of plastic wrap (or the oiled top to your proofing bucket). Place the dough in the refrigerator for at least 24 hours and up to 5 days.

On baking day, line a large rimmed baking sheet with unbleached parchment paper and set it aside. Make the topping. In a small, heavy-bottomed saucepan, sauté the minced garlic in the olive oil over low heat, stirring frequently, until the garlic is fragrant (about 3 minutes). Remove the pan from the heat, add the salt, mix to combine, and set the garlic mixture aside to cool.

Remove the dough from the refrigerator, scatter a generous amount of flour on a flat surface, scrape the dough out of the bowl on top of the flour, and sprinkle with flour. Turn the dough over on itself with a bench scraper and transfer it carefully, with the help of a floured bench scraper, to the center of the prepared baking sheet. Drizzle half of the garlic oil on top of the dough and, with the tips of your fingers, press and push the dough out toward the edges of the pan. The dough will be very wet and may be difficult to handle. Cover the dough with oiled plastic wrap and place in a warm, draft-free location to rise until doubled in size (about 2 hours). The dough will rise both up and out.

About 25 minutes before the end of the dough's rise, preheat your oven to 450°F and place a pizza stone on the lower rack. Once the dough has finished rising, pour the remaining garlic oil over the top of the risen dough. Gently spread the oil and minced garlic topping around with your fingertips, dimpling the dough if you see any large bubbles, but otherwise taking care not to deflate it.

Place the baking sheet on the pizza stone, and bake for 5 minutes at 450°F. Lower the oven temperature to 400°F and continue to bake for another 15 minutes, or until the top of the focaccia is golden brown and the center of the bread reaches 200°F on an instant-read thermometer. Slice and serve warm.

FLOUR TORTILLAS
MAKES ABOUT 20 TORTILLAS, DEPENDING UPON SIZE

THIS RECIPE IS ADAPTED FROM THE GLUTEN-FREE FLOUR TORTIL-las that I have made in Shoestring cookbooks past. Here, I've set aside the tortilla press in favor of a floured surface, a French rolling pin, and an 8-inch cake cutter, which is pretty much just a really large metal cookie or biscuit cutter. A cake cutter is typically used to trim small cakes, but I think this is an even higher and more noble use: making even, uniform flour tortillas. They make perfect burritos and gorgeous soft tacos.

INGREDIENTS

1¾ cups (245 g) all-purpose gluten-free flour (page 9), plus more for sprinkling
35 grams (about ¼ cup) Expandex modified tapioca starch
1½ teaspoons baking powder
1 teaspoon (6 g) kosher salt
4½ tablespoons (54 g) vegetable shortening
¾ cup warm water (about 85°F)

In a large bowl, place the all-purpose flour, Expandex, baking powder, and salt, and whisk to combine. Add the vegetable shortening and toss it in the dry ingredients. With the tines of a large fork, break up the shortening into small pieces about the size of small peas. Create a well in the center of the mixture, and add the water. Mix to combine. The dough will come together and be thick. Press together into a ball, cover with a moist tea towel, and allow to sit for about 20 minutes. The dough will stiffen a bit as it absorbs more of the water.

Heat a 10- or 12-inch cast-iron skillet over medium-high heat. Divide the dough into five pieces. Begin with one piece of dough, and cover the rest with a moist tea towel to prevent them from drying out. On a lightly floured sur-face, with a rolling pin, roll out the first piece of dough until it is ⅛ inch thick. Cut out as many rounds as you can (should be three or four) with an 8-inch metal cake cutter. Stack the raw tortillas on top of one another, dusting lightly with flour between them, if necessary, to prevent them from sticking. Gather the scraps and set them aside. Repeat with the remaining pieces of dough, including gathering and rerolling all of the scraps together.

Once all the tortillas have been rolled out and cut, place them one at a time in the center of the hot skillet and cook on one side until bubbles begin to appear on the top surface and the tortilla darkens in color a bit on the underside (about 45 seconds). Flip the tortilla over with a wide spatula, and cook on the other side until more bubbles form and the tortilla darkens on the underside (about another 45 seconds). Remove the tortilla from the pan, place on a moist tea towel, and cover gently. Repeat with the remaining tortillas.

If you don't plan to use the tortillas right away, place them, still wrapped in the towel, in a plastic bag to seal in the moisture. Use within a few hours.

WHOLE-GRAIN FLOUR TORTILLAS
MAKES ABOUT 20 TORTILLAS, DEPENDING UPON SIZE

THIS IS THE TORTILLA VARIETY THAT YOU WANT TO USE WHEN YOU are looking for the wrap itself, and not just its fillings, to stand up and get noticed. The addition of a whole-grain blend to these tortillas adds depth of flavor, plus greater nutrition and bite than white tortillas (page 203).

INGREDIENTS
1¼ cups (175 g) all-purpose gluten-free flour (page 9), plus more for sprinkling
½ cup (70 g) Whole-Grain Gluten-Free Flour (page 10)
35 grams (about ¼ cup) Expandex modified tapioca starch
1½ teaspoons baking powder
1 teaspoon (6 g) kosher salt
4½ teaspoons (54 g) vegetable shortening
¾ cup plus 2 teaspoons warm water (about 95°F)

In a large bowl, place the all-purpose flour, whole-grain flour, Expandex, baking powder, and salt, and whisk to combine. Add the vegetable shortening and toss it in the dry ingredients. With the tines of a large fork, break up the shortening into small pieces about the size of small peas. Create a well in the center of the mixture, and add the water. Mix to combine. The dough will come together and be thick. Press together into a ball, cover with a moist tea towel, and allow to sit for about 20 minutes. The dough will stiffen a bit as it absorbs more of the water.

Heat a 10- or 12-inch cast-iron skillet over medium-high heat. Divide the dough into five pieces. Begin with one piece of dough, and cover the rest with a towel to prevent them from drying out. On a lightly floured surface, with a rolling pin, roll out the first piece of dough until it is ⅛-inch thick. Cut out as many rounds as you can (should be three or four) with an 8 inch metal cake cutter. Stack the raw tortillas on top of one another, dusting lightly with flour between them, if necessary, to prevent them from sticking. Gather the scraps and set them aside. Repeat with the remaining pieces of dough, including gathering and rerolling all of the scraps together.

Once all the tortillas have been rolled out and cut, place them one at a time in the center of the hot skillet and cook on one side until bubbles begin to appear on the top surface and the tortilla darkens in color a bit on the underside (about 45 seconds). Flip the tortilla over with a wide spatula, and cook on the other side until more bubbles form and the tortilla darkens on the underside (about another 45 seconds). Remove the tortilla from the pan, place on a moist tea towel, and cover gently. Repeat with the remaining tortillas.

If you don't plan to use the tortillas right away, place them, still wrapped in the towel, in a plastic bag to seal in the moisture. Use within a few hours.

CORN TORTILLAS
MAKES 10 TORTILLAS

CORN TORTILLAS ARE MOSTLY JUST RECONSTITUTED MASA HARINA corn flour, rolled flat and cooked in a skillet, but they're truly one of the most delicious flatbreads you'll ever taste. Just be sure to source reliably gluten-free masa harina, as the most common grocery store brands are almost always gluten-contaminated. I rely upon Bob's Red Mill brand masa, and I order it online as I use it quite a lot.

INGREDIENTS

2 cups (230 g) gluten-free masa harina (corn flour)
¾ teaspoon kosher salt
1 cup plus 2 tablespoons warm water (about 95°F), plus more if necessary

Place the masa harina and salt in a large bowl and whisk to combine well. Add the water and mix to combine. The dough should hold together and be stiff, but not at all dry and crumbly. If the dough is at all crumbly, add more water, about 1 tablespoon at a time, until it reaches the proper consistency.

Cover the dough loosely with a moist tea towel (or place the dough in a bowl and cover it with plastic wrap), and allow it to sit for 10 to 15 minutes, to allow it to absorb some of the water. After it rests, the dough should not stick to your hands as you handle it. Divide the dough into ten pieces, and roll each into a round between your palms.

Heat a 10- or 12-inch cast-iron skillet over medium-high heat. Cut a gallon-size resealable plastic bag along the sides, and then in half along the base to form two equal rectangles. Cut off and discard the zipper top. Press one piece of dough into a disk, and place the disk between the two pieces of plastic. With a rolling pin, roll out the dough into a round about 6 inches in diameter and about ⅕ inch thick. Remove the plastic and place the tortilla carefully in the hot skillet. Allow to cook undisturbed until the edges of the tortilla begin to pull away from the skillet (about 45 seconds). With a wide spatula, flip the tortilla over and cook for about another 30 seconds. Flip once more and cook for a final 15 seconds. Remove the tortilla from the skillet and cover with a moist tea towel. Repeat with the remaining dough, stacking the tortillas together beneath the tea towel.

Corn tortillas will stay pliable for a few hours if stored at room temperature, wrapped in a damp tea towel. They can also be revived before eating by searing briefly on both sides in a hot skillet. They are best eaten the same day that they're made.

CREPES
MAKES 6 TO 8 CREPES

I HAVE MADE CREPES WITH XANTHAN GUM, AND I HAVE MADE CREPES without xanthan gum. Although I typically consider some sort of xanthan gum or equivalent to be essential to nearly every recipe in this book, this recipe is a notable exception. It does not mean that xanthan gum is the devil's plaything. It just means that when you want batter to be readily pourable, as you do for crepes and, say, pancakes, you're best off not having to fight the thickening that xanthan gum does to batter. For light and delicate gluten-free crepes, this is the best and easiest recipe.

INGREDIENTS
1 cup (140 g) Basic Gum-Free Gluten-Free Flour (page 9)
⅛ teaspoon kosher salt
2 large eggs, at room temperature, lightly beaten
2 tablespoons (28 g) unsalted butter, melted and cooled
1½ cups milk, at room temperature (not nonfat)

In a large bowl, place the flour and salt, and whisk to combine well. Add the eggs and butter, blending well after each ingredient.

In a slow and steady stream, add the milk while whisking to combine. Continue to whisk the mixture until the batter is smooth. The batter should be thin and not very elastic, as well as pourable. Add more milk, if necessary, to reach the right consistency.

Heat a 12-inch nonstick skillet over medium-high heat. Once the skillet is hot, ladle ¼ cup of batter into the pan, swirling to spread the batter evenly and thinly. Allow the batter to cook until set but not crispy (1 to 2 minutes), and flip with a wide spatula. Allow the other side to cook for about another 30 seconds.

Remove the crepe from the pan and cover with a moist tea towel. Repeat with the remaining batter and stack the crepes, covered, until ready to serve.

PARMESAN CORNMEAL CRACKERS
MAKES ABOUT 100 CRACKERS

I T'S NOT THAT YOU CAN'T BUY PACKAGED GLUTEN-FREE CRACKERS from many, if not most, grocery stores these days. It's that . . . they're just not worth the coin. This recipe for Parmesan crackers makes snappy and satisfying salty little crackers that can be easily made into any size and shape you like. Personally, I generally find it faster and easier to cut out rounds of cracker dough than it is to cut dough into squares or rectangles (I never seem to get those lines straight!), but . . . to each her own. Square or round, these crackers have the perfect toothsome, buttery bite.

INGREDIENTS

1¼ cups (175 g) all-purpose gluten-free flour (page 9)

1 cup (132 g) coarsely ground gluten-free cornmeal

½ teaspoon baking soda

¾ teaspoon kosher salt, plus more for sprinkling

1 cup finely grated Parmigiano-Reggiano cheese

4 tablespoons (56 g) unsalted butter, melted and cooled

¾ cup buttermilk, at room temperature (not nonfat)

1 tablespoon (14 g) unsalted butter, melted (still warm), for brushing

Preheat your oven to 350°F. Line rimmed baking sheets with unbleached parchment paper and set aside.

In a large bowl, place the flour, cornmeal, baking soda, and the salt, and whisk to combine. Add the cheese, and mix to combine. Add the 4 tablespoons of cooled melted butter and the buttermilk, and mix until combined and the dough begins to come together. Divide the dough into two parts, and press each into a small ball.

Place the first ball of dough between two sheets of unbleached parchment paper, and roll with a rolling pin into a rectangle about ⅛ inch thick (about the thickness of a nickel). The dough should roll out quickly and easily. With a fluted or simple round 1-inch cookie cutter, cut out disks of dough and place them about 1 inch apart, on one of the prepared baking sheets (the crackers will not spread during baking). Gather and reroll the scraps. Repeat with the other half of the dough.

Using a toothpick, poke four evenly spaced holes toward the center of each of the rounds of dough. Make the holes by moving the toothpick in a tight circular motion to create well-rounded holes.

Using a pastry brush, brush the tops of all of the rounds of dough lightly with the remaining tablespoon of melted butter. One tablespoon of melted butter should be enough to cover all of the rounds lightly. Sprinkle the tops of the rounds liberally with coarse salt.

Place the baking sheet in the center of the preheated oven and bake, rotating once during baking, for about 12 minutes, or until the crackers are dark golden brown on the edges and lightly golden brown on top. Allow to cool completely on the baking sheet. Store in a tightly sealed glass container at room temperature. For best results, serve within 2 to 4 days.

RITZ-STYLE CRACKERS
MAKES ABOUT 2 DOZEN CRACKERS

THESE REALLY DO TASTE LIKE THEIR NAMESAKE. BUT UNLIKE those gorgeous buttery Ritz crackers, these have no preservatives because, well, we made them ourselves and I wouldn't even know where to begin to add preservatives! The key to keeping your crackers from getting soggy? Store them in a glass container at room temperature, instead of in plastic. You'll get an extra few days of crispness with just that one little change.

INGREDIENTS

1 cup (140 g) Gluten-Free Pastry Flour (page 8)

1½ teaspoons baking powder

2 teaspoons (8 g) sugar

½ teaspoon smoked Spanish paprika

½ teaspoon (3 g) kosher salt, plus more for sprinkling

4 tablespoons (56 g) unsalted butter, melted and cooled

1 tablespoon vegetable oil

½ cup water, at room temperature

2 tablespoons (28 g) unsalted butter, melted (still warm), for brushing

Preheat your oven to 375°F. Line a rimmed baking sheet with unbleached parchment paper and set it aside.

In a large bowl, whisk together the flour, baking powder, sugar, paprika, and salt, and whisk to combine well. Create a well in the center of the dry ingredients, add the oil, the 4 tablespoons of melted butter, and the water, and mix to combine well. The dough will begin to come together. Press into a disk, and place between two sheets of unbleached parchment paper. With a rolling pin, roll out the dough until it is less than ¼ inch and more than ⅛ inch thick. Place the rolled-out dough in the refrigerator and chill until firm.

Once the dough is chilled, remove from the refrigerator and cut out shapes with a 1½-inch round cookie cutter (for an authentic-looking cracker, use a cutter with a scalloped edge). Place the shapes about 1 inch apart on the prepared baking sheet, and, with a toothpick, poke four small holes toward the center of each cracker. Make the holes by moving the toothpick in a tight circular motion to create well-rounded holes. Return the baking sheet to the refrigerator to chill once more until firm.

Place the baking sheet in the center of the preheated oven and bake for 7 to 10 minutes, or until the crackers are just beginning to brown around the edges. Brush the crackers with the remaining 2 tablespoons of melted butter and sprinkle with kosher salt to taste. Allow to cool briefly before serving. Store in a tightly sealed glass container at room temperature. For best results, serve within 2 to 4 days.

WHEAT THIN–STYLE CRACKERS
MAKES ABOUT 100 CRACKERS

BECAUSE THESE CRACKERS ARE HOMEMADE AND HAVE OUR FAVOR-
ite whole grains (thank you, sorghum and teff), I think it's worth going
for broke and using coconut palm sugar (also known as palm sugar), an un-
refined granulated sugar. I find it in my local health food store, but more
frequently I order it from Amazon.com or Nuts.com, both of which have significantly better prices than the local health food store. It certainly makes
these crackers heartier, and gives them a more authentic Wheat Thin taste
than when they are made with granulated sugar. Either way, they are pretty
darn close to the real thing.

INGREDIENTS
1¼ cups (175 g) all-purpose gluten-free flour (page 9)
¾ cup (105 g) Whole-Grain Gluten-Free Flour (page 10)
¼ cup (40 g) coconut palm sugar or 6 tablespoons (72 g) granulated sugar
1½ teaspoons baking powder
¼ teaspoon baking soda
1 teaspoon (6 g) kosher salt, plus more for sprinkling
6 tablespoons (84 g) unsalted butter, melted and cooled
½ cup milk, at room temperature (not nonfat)

Preheat your oven to 350°F. Line a rimmed baking sheet with unbleached
parchment paper and set it aside.

In a large bowl, place the all-purpose flour, whole-grain flour, sugar, baking powder, baking soda, and salt, and whisk to combine well. Add the butter and milk, and mix to combine until the dough begins to come together.
Knead the dough until it is smooth. Divide the dough into two parts and press
each into a small ball.

Place the first ball of dough between two sheets of unbleached parchment
paper and roll with a rolling pin into a rectangle about ⅛ inch thick (about
the thickness of a nickel). The dough should roll out quickly and easily. With
a pastry wheel or sharp knife, slice the dough into 1-inch square crackers.
Place the squares less than 1 inch apart, on the prepared baking sheet (they
will not spread during baking). Gather and reroll the scraps. Repeat with

the other half of the dough. Sprinkle the tops of the squares liberally with kosher salt.

Place the baking sheet in the center of the preheated oven and bake, rotating once during baking, for about 9 minutes, or until the crackers are golden brown around the edges. Allow to cool completely on the baking sheet. Store in a tightly sealed glass container at room temperature. For best results, serve within 2 to 4 days.

YEAST-RAISED WAFFLES
MAKES 4 TO 5 WAFFLES, DEPENDING UPON SIZE

WAFFLES ARE SPECIAL, GENERALLY SPEAKING, BECAUSE THEY have built-in syrup cups. These waffles are special because they are yeasted, which makes them quite fluffy inside with a bit of a yeasty tang, and as crispy on the outside as any self-respecting waffle should be. Plus—they still have those fancy syrup cups.

INGREDIENTS

2 cups (280 g) Gluten-Free Bread Flour (page 8)

2 teaspoons (6 g) instant yeast

2 tablespoons (24 g) sugar

1 teaspoon (6 g) kosher salt

5 tablespoons (70 g) unsalted butter, melted and cooled

2½ cups milk, at room temperature (not nonfat)

2 large eggs, at room temperature, beaten

In a large bowl, combine the flour, yeast, and sugar, and whisk to combine well. Add the salt, and whisk to combine. Create a well in the center of the dry ingredients, add the butter and 2 cups of the milk, and whisk to combine well. The mixture will be relatively thin. Cover the bowl tightly with plastic wrap or transfer to a proofing bucket large enough for the dough to rise to double its size, and secure the top of your proofing bucket. Allow the batter to sit at room temperature, covered, for at least 2 hours and up to overnight. It will swell, but will deflate easily if the batter is stirred or the bucket is shaken. The batter can also be kept, covered, in the refrigerator for up to 2 days.

When ready to bake, preheat your waffle iron according to the manufacturer's instructions. Uncover the waffle batter, stir it down, and add the remaining ½ cup of milk and the eggs. Whisk to combine well. Once the waffle iron is ready, wipe down the waffle iron grates with a paper towel moistened with vegetable oil. Working quickly so the iron does not cool, pour ¾ to 1 cup of the waffle batter in the center of the waffle iron, spread into an even layer, and cook for 4 to 5 minutes, or according to the waffle iron manufacturer's directions. Waffles are usually done when steam is no longer escaping from the iron. Remove the baked waffle from the iron, and repeat with the remaining batter. Serve warm.

To keep waffles warm while others are being baked, place them in a single layer on a baking sheet in a 200°F oven until ready to serve. Freeze any leftover waffles. You can refresh frozen waffles in a 300°F oven or toaster oven before serving.

8 YEAST-FREE QUICK BREADS

SAVORY AND SWEET BREADS AND PASTRIES WITH NO YEAST

GOUGÈRES
MAKES 12 CHEESE PUFFS

GOUGÈRES ARE THE SAVORY COUSIN OF CREAM PUFFS. GOUGÈRES are made of essentially the same French choux pastry as Cream Puffs (page 223), except this batter is studded with grated Gruyère cheese. Make micro-mini cheese puffs (cut the baking time about in half) and you can serve them as adorable appetizers. I like to make them full-size, as the recipe directs, and serve them as dinner rolls. Not being miniature, they go from adorable to simply elegant. Not really a step down.

INGREDIENTS

1 cup milk (not nonfat)

4 tablespoons (56 g) unsalted butter, chopped

¾ teaspoon (5 g) kosher salt

1 cup (140 g) Gluten-Free Pastry Flour (page 10)

4 large eggs, at room temperature, beaten

4 ounces Gruyère cheese, grated

Preheat your oven to 375°F. Line a rimmed baking sheet with unbleached parchment paper and set it aside.

In a medium-size saucepan, place the milk, butter, and salt, and cook over medium heat until the butter is melted and the mixture begins to simmer. Remove the pan from the heat, and add the pastry flour, stirring vigorously. Return the pan to the heat, and continue to stir vigorously until the mixture pulls away from the pan and comes together in a ball (about 2 minutes). A thin film will form on the bottom of the pan. Set the mixture aside to cool until no longer hot to the touch (about 3 minutes).

Transfer half the dough to a blender or food processor. Pour the beaten eggs on top and then add the rest of the dough. Pulse the blender or food processor until the mixture is smooth and uniformly well blended. Add the cheese, and pulse until it is uniformly distributed throughout the dough.

Transfer the dough from the blender or food processor to a pastry bag fitted with a large, plain piping tip about 1 inch in diameter. Pipe the dough into twelve mounds, each about 2 inches in diameter, onto the prepared baking sheet, spacing the pastries about 2 inches apart from one another. With wet

GLUTEN-FREE ON A SHOESTRING BAKES BREAD

fingers, gently smooth the tops of the pastries so that nothing will burn during baking. Bake the cheese puffs in the center of the preheated oven until pale golden (about 20 minutes). To make sure the pastries hold their shape well, once they are done baking, turn off the oven and remove the baking sheet. Working quickly, slice a small hole in the side of each pastry to allow some steam to escape, and return the baking sheet to the oven. Allow the pastries to sit in the oven, with the oven door propped open slightly, until they are dry enough to hold their shape (about 10 minutes). Remove the pastries from the oven and serve warm.

CREAM PUFFS
MAKES ABOUT 20 PASTRIES

'M PRETTY SURE I HEARD A RADIO INTERVIEW OF MAYA ANGELOU where she recommended making cream puffs for "your beloved," declaring them easier to make than you think. Clearly, there is little daylight between me and Maya Angelou . . . at least on this topic. Easier than you think, impressive as all get-out. Make them for your beloved.

PASTRY
1 cup milk (not nonfat)
4 tablespoons (56 g) unsalted butter, at room temperature
⅛ teaspoon kosher salt
140 grams (1 cup) Gluten-Free Pastry Flour (page 10)
4 large eggs, at room temperature, beaten

WHIPPED CREAM
¾ cup heavy whipping cream, chilled
¼ cup (29 g) confectioners' sugar
⅛ teaspoon kosher salt

CHOCOLATE DRIZZLE
4 ounces dark chocolate, chopped
½ cup heavy whipping cream

First, make the pastries. Preheat your oven to 375°F. Line two large rimmed baking sheets with parchment paper and set them aside. Heat the milk, butter, and salt in a medium-size, heavy-bottomed saucepan over medium heat until the butter is completely melted and the mixture begins to simmer. Remove the pan from the heat, add the flour, stirring vigorously. Return the pan to the heat and cook, stirring vigorously, until the mixture begins to pull away from the sides of the pan and comes together in a ball (about 2 minutes). A thin film will form on the bottom of the pan. Remove from the heat, and allow the mixture to cool for at least 3 minutes, or until it is no longer hot to the touch.

Transfer half the cooled dough to a blender or food processor. Pour the beaten eggs on top and then add the rest of the dough. Pulse until the mixture is smooth and uniformly well blended.

Transfer the dough from the blender or food processor to a pastry bag fitted with a large, plain piping tip (about 1 inch in diameter). Pipe the dough into about 20 small mounds, each about 1½ inches high, about 1 inch apart, onto the prepared baking sheets. Smooth the tops of the pastry dough lightly with wet fingers so that nothing will burn during baking. Bake the cream puffs in the center of the preheated oven for 10 minutes, or until pale golden. Remove the baking sheet from the oven and, working quickly, with a sharp knife, cut a small slit in the side of each cream puff to allow steam to escape. Return the pastries on the baking sheet to the oven, turn off the oven, and prop open the oven door slightly. Allow them to sit in the oven until dry (about 30 minutes).

While the pastries are drying in the oven, make the whipped cream. Place the cream in the bowl of your stand mixer (or in a large metal bowl) fitted with the whisk attachment. Turn the mixer on medium speed (or use a hand mixer on medium speed) and whip until soft peaks begin to form in the cream. Add the confectioners' sugar and salt, and continue to beat on medium speed until glossy and stiff, but not dry, peaks form. If you turn the mixer speed to high, your whipped cream will not be as stable.

Once the pastries are cool and dry, slice them in half horizontally, spoon some whipped cream on the bottom halves, and then top with the remaining halves. To make the chocolate drizzle, place the chopped chocolate in a small, heat-safe bowl and set it aside. Place the cream in a small saucepan and cook over medium heat until the cream begins to simmer. Pour the hot cream over the chopped chocolate and stir until the chocolate is melted and smooth. Drizzle the chocolate mixture over assembled puffs. Serve chilled or at room temperature.

STRAWBERRY SCONES
MAKES 8 SCONES

THE LINE BETWEEN A BISCUIT AND A SCONE IS A FINE ONE. FOR ME, it mostly mirrors the line between savory and sweet. Biscuits are flaky savory pastries, and scones are flaky slightly sweeter pastries. These strawberry scones are just right for when you want to celebrate the beginnings of strawberry season, when those beautifully berries are red through and through and actually taste, well, like strawberries.

INGREDIENTS

2 cups (280 g) Gluten-Free Pastry Flour (page 10)

1½ teaspoons baking powder

¼ teaspoon baking soda

½ teaspoon (3 g) kosher salt

2 tablespoons (24 g) sugar

1 dry pint fresh strawberries (about 2 cups), hulled and sliced thinly

5 tablespoons (70 g) unsalted butter, cut into large chunks and chilled

¾ cup heavy cream, chilled

2 tablespoons milk, chilled, for brushing (optional)

2 tablespoons coarse sugar, for sprinkling (optional)

Preheat your oven to 400°F. Line a rimmed baking sheet with unbleached parchment paper and set it aside.

In a large bowl, place the flour, baking powder, baking soda, salt, and sugar, and whisk to combine well. In a separate, small bowl, place the strawberries. Transfer 1 tablespoon of the flour mixture to the bowl of strawberries, toss to coat, then place the small bowl in the freezer to chill briefly.

Add the butter chunks to the dry mixture, and toss to coat. Press each piece of butter between your floured thumb and forefinger to flatten. Remove the strawberry mixture from the freezer, and carefully fold into the flour mixture. Create a well in the center of the flour mixture, and add the chilled cream. Mix with a large spoon or spatula just until the dough begins to come together.

Handling the dough as little as possible, with well-floured hands, turn the dough out onto a lightly floured surface and pat into a rectangle about ½ inch thick. With a floured bench scraper, cut the dough into eight triangles, or cut out eight circles with a floured biscuit cutter. Place the triangles or rounds about an inch apart on the prepared baking sheet. Brush the tops with a bit of milk, if using, and sprinkle with the coarse sugar, if using.

Place the baking sheet in the freezer for about 15 minutes, or until the scones are firm. Transfer the baking sheet to the center of the preheated oven and bake the scones until they are puffed and slightly brown around the edges (about 18 minutes). Allow the scones to cool for a few minutes on the baking sheet until firm (about 5 minutes). Serve warm or at room temperature.

EXTRA-FLAKY BUTTERMILK BISCUITS
MAKES 8 BISCUITS

I WANT YOU TO KNOW THE BEAUTY OF EXTRA-FLAKY GLUTEN-FREE buttermilk biscuits. So rest assured that what I am about to say, I say with love: You are cheating yourself if you just press together your biscuit dough, cut out rounds, and bake. With the investment of a few puff-pastry-style "turns" of the dough (which just means rolling, folding, then rolling again, and folding again, and so on), you will be richly rewarded with the flakiest layered biscuits. That's a big ROI, for you financial types.

INGREDIENTS

2 cups (280 g) Gluten-Free Pastry Flour (page 10)
1 tablespoon baking powder
½ teaspoon baking soda
2 tablespoons (24 g) sugar
1 teaspoon (6 g) kosher salt
8 tablespoons (112 g) unsalted butter, cut into large chunks and chilled
1 cup buttermilk, chilled (not nonfat)

Preheat your oven to 400°F. Line a rimmed baking sheet with unbleached parchment paper and set it aside.

In a large bowl, place the flour, baking powder, baking soda, sugar, and salt, and whisk to combine well. Add the chopped butter to the flour mixture, and toss to coat. Place each piece of butter between your floured thumb and forefinger to flatten. Create a well in the center of the flour mixture, and pour in the buttermilk. Mix with a large spoon or spatula until the dough begins to come together.

For the flakiest biscuits, turn the dough out onto a lightly floured surface. Then dust the surface with a bit more flour, and roll out the dough with a rolling pin into a thick rectangle. Fold the rectangle in half lengthwise, dust again lightly with flour, and roll the dough out again into a thick rectangle. Once more, fold the rectangle in half lengthwise, and then fold again width-wise to create a much smaller, thicker rectangle. Dust lightly with flour, and roll the dough out into a rectangle that is about 1 inch thick. With a floured, round 2½-inch biscuit or cookie cutter, cut out rounds of dough and place

them, about 2 inches apart from one another, on the prepared baking sheet. Gather and reroll the scraps of dough, and cut out as many more rounds as possible, placing them on the baking sheet.

Place the baking sheet in the freezer for 5 minutes to chill the dough (or in the refrigerator for 10 minutes, or until chilled). Then place the baking sheet in the center of the preheated oven and bake until the biscuits are puffed and pale golden (about 15 minutes). Allow the biscuits to cool on the baking sheet until firm (about 5 minutes). Serve warm or at room temperature.

CREAM CHEESE BUTTERMILK BISCUITS
MAKES 10 BISCUITS

THESE BISCUITS HAVE IT ALL, AS THEY SOMEHOW MAINTAIN JUST the right balance between flaky biscuit and creamy cream cheese. I think of them almost like cheesecake biscuits—they're that rich and indulgent.

INGREDIENTS
2½ cups (350 g) Gluten-Free Pastry Flour (page 10)

2 teaspoons baking powder

¼ teaspoon baking soda

1 teaspoon (6 g) kosher salt

1½ tablespoons (18 g) sugar

6 tablespoons (84 g) unsalted butter, cut into large chunks and chilled

4 ounces cream cheese, chilled

¾ cup buttermilk, chilled (not nonfat)

Preheat your oven to 400°F. Line a rimmed baking sheet with unbleached parchment paper and set it aside.

In a large bowl, place the flour, baking powder, baking soda, salt, and sugar, and whisk to combine well. Add the chopped butter to the flour mixture, and toss to coat. Place each piece of butter between your floured thumb and forefinger to flatten. Add the cream cheese in chunks, and toss to combine. Create a well in the center of the flour mixture, and add the buttermilk. Mix with a large spoon or spatula until the dough begins to come together.

For the flakiest biscuits, turn the dough out onto a lightly floured surface. Then dust the surface with a bit more flour, and roll out the dough with a rolling pin into a thick rectangle. Fold the rectangle in half lengthwise, dust again lightly with flour, and roll the dough out again into a thick rectangle. Once more, fold the rectangle in half lengthwise, and then fold again widthwise to create a much smaller, thicker rectangle. Dust lightly with flour, and roll the dough out into a rectangle that is about 1 inch thick. With a floured, 2½-inch round biscuit or cookie cutter, cut out rounds of dough and place them about 2 inches apart from one another on the prepared baking sheet. Gather and reroll the scraps of dough, and cut out as many more rounds as possible, placing them on the baking sheet.

Place the baking sheet in the freezer for 5 minutes to chill the dough (or in the refrigerator for 10 minutes, or until chilled). Then place the baking sheet in the center of the preheated oven and bake until the biscuits are puffed and pale golden (about 15 minutes). Allow the biscuits to cool on the baking sheet until firm (about 5 minutes). Serve warm or at room temperature.

CORNMEAL BISCUITS
MAKES 8 BISCUITS

CORNMEAL BISCUITS ARE THE ONES YOU CHOOSE WHEN YOU WANT something a bit more substantial than a Buttermilk Biscuit (page 227). And they are better alongside some fluffy scrambled eggs than should be legal.

INGREDIENTS

1½ cups (210 g) Gluten-Free Pastry Flour (page 10)

¾ cup (98 g) coarsely ground gluten-free cornmeal

2 teaspoons baking powder

1 teaspoon (6 g) kosher salt

6 tablespoons (84 g) unsalted butter, roughly chopped and chilled

½ cup plain whole-milk yogurt, chilled

½ cup milk, chilled (not nonfat)

Preheat your oven to 400°F. Line a rimmed baking sheet with unbleached parchment paper and set it aside. In a large bowl, place the flour, cornmeal, baking powder, and salt, and whisk to combine well. Add the chopped butter to the flour mixture, and toss to coat. Flatten each piece of butter between your floured thumb and forefinger. Create a well in the center of the flour mixture, and add the yogurt and milk. Mix with a large spoon or spatula until the dough begins to come together.

For the flakiest biscuits, follow the instructions for folding and shaping the Extra-Flaky Buttermilk Biscuits (pages 227–229). Then, with a floured, round 2½-inch biscuit or cookie cutter, cut out rounds of dough and place them, about 2 inches apart, on the prepared baking sheet. Gather and reroll the scraps of dough, and cut out as many more rounds as possible, placing them on the baking sheet.

Place the baking sheet in the freezer for 5 minutes to chill the dough. Then place the baking sheet in the center of the preheated oven and bake until the biscuits are puffed and golden brown around the edges (about 15 minutes). Serve warm or at room temperature.

MORNING GLORY MUFFINS
MAKES 16 MUFFINS

THERE'S NO GETTING AROUND THE FACT THAT MORNING GLORY muffins have more than a couple of ingredients in them. But they make a truly hearty breakfast that keeps you going all morning long, and, almost as if they knew they had to make themselves more attractive to their would-be bakers, they freeze beautifully. So I like to make a batch, wrap them tightly in freezer-safe wrap, and then defrost a few overnight on the counter at room temperature. That way, they're ready when I am.

INGREDIENTS

1½ cups (210 g) all-purpose gluten-free flour (page 9)

⅔ cup (80 g) certified gluten-free oat flour

1 teaspoon baking soda

½ teaspoon baking powder

½ teaspoon kosher salt

2 teaspoons ground cinnamon

1 cup (218 g) packed light brown sugar

5 tablespoons vegetable oil

⅔ cup (150 g) sour cream, at room temperature

3 large eggs, at room temperature, beaten

1 teaspoon gluten-free vanilla extract

2 cups (180 g) peeled and grated carrots (from about 4 medium-size carrots)

1 cup (110 g) peeled, cored, and grated apple (any baking variety, such as Granny Smith)

½ cup (90 g) raisins

½ cup (40 g) large coconut chips (large flaked coconut)

¼ cup (25 g) whole gluten-free old-fashioned oats tossed with 1 tablespoon melted unsalted butter, for sprinkling (optional)

Preheat your oven to 325°F. Grease or line the wells of two standard 12-cup muffin tins, and set them aside.

In a large bowl, place the flour, oat flour, baking soda, baking powder, salt, and cinnamon, and whisk to combine well. Add the brown sugar, and whisk again, working out any lumps in the brown sugar. In a separate small bowl, place the oil, sour cream, eggs, and vanilla, and mix to combine well. Create a well in the center of the flour mixture, and add the oil mixture. Mix with a large spoon or spatula to combine. Add the carrots and apple, and mix to combine. Add the raisins and coconut, and mix gently to combine. The muffin batter will be thick.

Fill the prepared wells of the muffin tin three-quarters of the way with the batter, and smooth out the top of each well with wet fingers. Sprinkle the top of each muffin with the oat topping, if using. Place the muffin tin in the center of the preheated oven and bake, rotating once, until the muffins are lightly golden brown and a toothpick inserted into the center comes out clean (about 22 minutes). Remove the tin from the oven and allow the muffins to cool in the tin for at least 5 minutes before transferring to a wire rack to cool completely. Repeat with the remaining batter.

CARROT MUFFINS
MAKES 24 MUFFINS

THIS IS NOT A RECIPE FOR CARROT CUPCAKES. IN TWO DOZEN MUF-fins, there is only ½ cup of sugar but 3 cups of grated carrots. If my math is right, that means there is just one tiny little teaspoon of sugar in each muffin—and 2 full tablespoons of grated carrots in each of those same muffins. So you see, they can't be cake. They're too healthy.

INGREDIENTS

2 cups (280 g) all-purpose gluten-free flour (page 9)

1 teaspoon baking soda

1½ teaspoons baking powder

½ teaspoon (3 g) kosher salt

2 teaspoons ground cinnamon

½ cup (109 g) packed light brown sugar

3 cups (270 g) peeled and grated carrots (from about six medium-size carrots)

1 cup (110 g) chopped macadamia nuts

½ cup vegetable oil

4 large eggs, at room temperature, beaten

1 teaspoon apple cider vinegar

½ cup milk, at room temperature (not nonfat)

Preheat your oven to 350°F. Grease or line the wells of two standard 12-cup muffin tins, and set them aside.

In a large bowl, place the flour, baking soda, baking powder, salt, and cinnamon. Whisk to combine well. Add the brown sugar, and whisk again to combine, working to break up any lumps in the brown sugar. In a separate, medium-size bowl, place the grated carrots and chopped nuts. Add a tablespoon of the flour mixture to the carrot mixture, and toss to combine. Set both bowls aside.

In a separate, medium-size bowl, place the oil, eggs, vinegar, and milk, and whisk to combine very well. The mixture should become pale and frothy. Working quickly, create a well in the center of the flour mixture, and pour in the oil mixture. Mix with a large spoon or spatula to combine well. Add the carrot mixture to the batter, and mix until just combined. The batter will be thick, but not stiff.

Fill the wells of the prepared muffin tins about three-quarters of the way with batter, and shake the pans back and forth to distribute the batter evenly in each well. Place one muffin tin in the center of the preheated oven and bake until a toothpick inserted in the center of the muffins comes out with no more than a few moist crumbs attached (about 20 minutes). Remove the tin from the oven and allow to cool in the pan for at least 5 minutes before transferring to a wire rack to cool completely. Repeat with the remaining muffin tin.

BRAN MUFFINS
MAKES 18 MUFFINS

BRAN MUFFINS CAN BE CONSIDERED A BIT OF A DELICATE SUBJECT, considering the reason that most people think to eat them. Instead of having a whole discussion about why a person might think well of a bran muffin as daily constitution, let's talk about stabilized rice bran. Yes, you really do need stabilized rice bran for this recipe (and any other recipe you might come across that calls for rice bran). I buy mine from Amazon.com and Bob's Red Mill has a very nice one. Most good rice bran is stabilized before it is sold. The husk from which rice bran is made is very high in oil, and if it is not stabilized it will become rancid before you have a chance to use it.

INGREDIENTS

1 cup (120 g) gluten-free stabilized rice bran
1 cup (140 g) all-purpose gluten-free flour (page 9)
¼ cup (50 g) sugar
½ teaspoon kosher salt
1 teaspoon baking powder
½ teaspoon baking soda
¾ cup (138 g) raisins or other small, dried fruit
4 tablespoons (56 g) unsalted butter, at room temperature
¼ cup honey
1 tablespoon unsulfured molasses
1 teaspoon gluten-free vanilla extract
3 large eggs, at room temperature, beaten
1¼ cups (300 g) sour cream, at room temperature

Preheat your oven to 350°F. Grease or line the wells of two standard 12-cup muffin tins and set them aside.

In a large bowl, place the rice bran, flour, sugar, salt, baking powder, and baking soda, and whisk to combine well. Place the dried fruit in a separate small bowl, and add about 1 teaspoon of the flour mixture to the bowl. Toss to coat, and set the bowl aside. To the flour mixture, add the butter, honey, molasses, vanilla, eggs, and sour cream, beating well after each addition, until the mixture is smooth. The batter will be thick. Add the raisins, and mix gently until they are evenly distributed throughout the batter.

Fill the prepared muffin cups about three-quarters of the way with batter , and smooth the top of each well with wet fingers.. Place the tin in the center of the preheated oven, and bake for about 22 minutes, or until a tester placed in the center of a middle muffin comes out mostly clean.

Remove from the oven, and allow to cool for at least 5 minutes in the muffin tin before transferring to a wire rack to cool completely. Repeat with the remaining batter.

BROWN BUTTER SAGE CORNBREAD MUFFINS

MAKES 12 MUFFINS

IF YOU HAVE NEVER TASTED PERFECTLY BROWNED BUTTER, YOU might be tempted toward a bit of an eye roll when you hear the name of these muffins. I can assure you that I, too, am an eye-roller from way back when I think that something is merely the Emperor's New Clothes in the food world (or otherwise), but brown butter is the real deal. When the butter solids drop out in the saucepan and toast just lightly, brown butter is nutty and deeply fragrant in the best way possible. Try it in these cornbread muffins, with a pretty little sage leaf on top, and you'll know.

INGREDIENTS

6 tablespoons (84 g) unsalted butter, chopped

1¼ cups (165 g) coarsely ground gluten-free cornmeal

1 cup (140 g) all-purpose gluten-free flour (page 9)

1½ teaspoons baking powder

¼ teaspoon baking soda

½ teaspoon kosher salt

2 teaspoons (8 g) sugar

2 teaspoons honey

1 large egg, at room temperature, beaten

1¼ cups plus 2 tablespoons buttermilk, at room temperature (not nonfat)

12 leaves fresh sage

1 tablespoon extra-virgin olive oil, for brushing

Preheat your oven to 350°F. Grease or line the wells of a standard 12-cup muffin tin and set it aside.

First, brown the butter. Place the butter in a small, heavy-bottomed saucepan, and cook over medium heat, stirring constantly. The butter will melt, and then it will boil and foam. Continue to stir, and watch carefully. The protein solids will separate and drop to the bottom of the pan. As soon as you begin to smell a nutty aroma, and begin to see a golden brown color start forming around the edges of the saucepan, remove the pan from the heat, and continue to stir. Once the bubbles clear, you will be able to see whether

the protein has begun to brown. If not, return to the heat briefly, stirring constantly, and remove once the butter has begun to brown. Continue to stir, as the butter will continue to brown off the heat. Pour the brown butter into a small, heat-safe bowl, and set it aside to cool briefly.

In a large bowl, place the cornmeal, flour, baking powder, baking soda, salt, and sugar, and whisk to combine well. In a separate, medium-size bowl, place the cooled brown butter, honey, egg, and buttermilk, and whisk to combine well. Create a well in the center of the flour mixture, pour in the buttermilk mixture, and mix to combine. Divide the batter evenly among the prepared wells of the muffin tin. Brush both sides of each fresh sage leaf with olive oil, and place one on top of the batter in each well of the muffin tin. Place the tin in the center of the preheated oven and bake until a toothpick inserted in the center of the muffins comes out with no more than a few moist crumbs attached (about 20 minutes). Remove from the oven and allow to cool for at least 5 minutes in the muffin tin before transferring to a wire rack to cool completely.

BROWN BUTTER BANANA BREAD

MAKES 1 LOAF

I DON'T LIKE THE IDEA OF MAKING BANANA BREAD ONLY WHEN YOUR bananas have taken a turn for the worse, but it does seem to be a bit of an inevitability, as nobody buys bananas that are already brown. You can always freeze very ripe bananas for use at a more considered time to make banana bread, but at that point your only option for baking with your frozen and defrosted bananas is to mash them finely. Once they have been frozen, they practically mash themselves. No mind. Even if you only make this banana bread to save your ripe fruit from uselessness, the brown butter in this recipe makes it sufficiently intentional and special, to show everyone just how much you care.

INGREDIENTS

8 tablespoons (112 g) unsalted butter, chopped

2 cups (280 g) all-purpose gluten-free flour (page 9)

¾ teaspoon (5 g) kosher salt

1 teaspoon baking powder

½ teaspoon baking soda

⅔ cup (133 g) sugar

2 large eggs, at room temperature, beaten

1 teaspoon gluten-free vanilla extract

⅔ cup sour cream, at room temperature

2 large ripe bananas

Preheat your oven to 350°F. Grease a standard 9- by 5-inch loaf pan and set it aside.

First, brown the butter. Place the butter in a small, heavy-bottomed saucepan, and cook over medium heat, stirring constantly. The butter will melt, and then it will boil and foam. Continue to stir, and watch carefully. The protein solids will separate and drop to the bottom of the pan. As soon as you begin to smell a nutty aroma, and begin to see a golden brown color forming around the edges of the saucepan, remove the pan from the heat, and continue to stir. Once the bubbles clear, you will be able to see whether the protein has begun to brown. If not, return to the heat briefly, stirring constantly, and remove once the butter has begun to brown. Continue to stir, as the butter will continue to brown off the heat. Pour the brown butter into a small, heat-safe bowl, and set it aside to cool briefly.

In a large bowl, place the flour, salt, baking powder, baking soda, and sugar, and whisk to combine well. Add the cooled brown butter, eggs, and vanilla, then the sour cream, mixing to combine well after each addition. Peel the bananas, and smush them a bit between your fingers as you add them to the batter. Fold in the bananas, breaking them up only a bit, leaving some bigger pieces.

Scrape the batter into the prepared loaf pan, and smooth the top with a wet spatula. Place the pan in the center of the preheated oven, and bake until the banana bread is golden brown and a toothpick inserted in the center comes out with no more than a few moist crumbs attached (about 50 minutes). If the loaf is browning too fast for the center to bake fully, tent the pan with foil while the loaf finishes baking. Allow to cool in the pan for at least 20 minutes before transferring to a wire rack to cool completely.

ZUCCHINI BREAD
MAKES 2 LOAVES

HERE IS A REASON THAT THIS RECIPE FOR ZUCCHINI BREAD MAKES two loaves. You can halve all the ingredients and just make one loaf, but frankly for the life of me, I can't understand why you would do that. It's really the best recipe for zucchini bread you'll ever make, and, just as important, zucchini bread has a job to do. During zucchini season (which seems to go on for six months out of every twelve, even though I know it doesn't really), you have one job: get rid of zucchini. Zucchini plants are simply too prolific, and we all have to do our part.

INGREDIENTS
3 cups (420 g) all-purpose gluten-free flour (page 9)

1 teaspoon kosher salt

1 teaspoon baking soda

1 teaspoon baking powder

2 teaspoons ground cinnamon

1 cup (200 g) granulated sugar

1 cup (218 g) packed light brown sugar

2½ cups grated zucchini

3 large eggs, at room temperature, beaten

1 ripe banana, peeled and mashed

½ cup vegetable oil

2 teaspoons gluten-free vanilla extract

8 ounces semisweet chocolate chips

1 teaspoon (3 g) cornstarch

Preheat your oven to 325°F. Grease two standard 9- by 5-inch loaf pans and set them aside.

In a large bowl, place the flour, salt, baking soda, baking powder, cinnamon, granulated sugar, and light brown sugar, and whisk to combine (working out any lumps in the brown sugar). In a separate small bowl, place the zucchini, eggs, banana, oil, and vanilla, and mix to combine well. Create a well in the center of the flour mixture, and pour in the zucchini mixture. Mix with a large spoon or spatula to combine. The batter will be very wet. In a separate small bowl, toss the chocolate chips with the cornstarch. Pour the chocolate chips mixture into the batter, and mix until the chips are evenly distributed throughout the batter. Divide the batter evenly between the two prepared loaf pans, and smooth the tops with a wet spatula.

Place the loaf pans in the center of the preheated oven, and bake, rotating once, until the tops of the zucchini breads are golden brown and a toothpick inserted in the center of each loaf comes out clean (about 50 minutes). Remove from the oven and allow to cool for at least 30 minutes in the loaf pans. Remove from the pans and transfer to a wire rack to cool completely.

IRISH SODA BREAD
MAKES 1 LOAF BREAD

THIS RECIPE IS ADAPTED FROM . . . ME. I PUBLISHED A VERSION OF this in my first Shoestring cookbook. Too good to leave behind, it is really made even better with a slightly different pastry-making technique and, of course, the use of gluten-free pastry flour.

INGREDIENTS

3 cups (420 g) Gluten-Free Pastry Flour (page 10)

¾ cup (150 g) sugar

2¼ teaspoons baking powder

1 teaspoon baking soda

½ teaspoon kosher salt

¼ teaspoon cream of tartar

6 tablespoons (84 g) unsalted butter, chopped and chilled

2 cups raisins

2 tablespoons caraway seeds

1½ cups buttermilk, chilled (not nonfat)

1 large egg, at room temperature, beaten

Preheat your oven to 350°F. Grease a 12-inch ovenproof skillet and set it aside.

In a large bowl, place the flour, sugar, baking powder, baking soda, salt, and cream of tartar, and whisk to combine well. Add the chopped butter and toss to coat. Flatten each piece of butter between your floured thumb and forefinger. Stir in the raisins and caraway seeds. Create a well in the center of the flour mixture, and add the buttermilk and egg. Mix with a large spoon or spatula until the dough begins to come together.

Turn the dough out into the prepared skillet and, with wet hands, smooth the top, piling it a bit higher toward the center of the skillet. With a sharp knife, slash an X in the center of the dough, about ½ inch deep.

Place the skillet in the center of the preheated oven, bake for 40 minutes, and reduce the oven temperature to 325°F. Bake for another 30 to 35 minutes, or until a toothpick comes out clean. Allow the bread to cool in the pan for about 30 minutes before transferring it to a wire rack to cool completely.

9 USING THE DOUGH

WHAT TO DO WITH ALL THAT GORGEOUS BREAD AND DOUGH

QUICK HOMEMADE TOMATO SAUCE
MAKES 2 CUPS SAUCE

THERE ARE PLENTY OF WONDERFUL GLUTEN-FREE TOMATO SAUCES that you can buy ready-made, and I frequently use them myself. But the fact that those sauces are really quite good doesn't stop my family from clamoring for this quick homemade tomato sauce. Canned, whole, peeled tomatoes are always brilliantly ripe, red and practically bursting with flavor. So, if you have a can of those in the cupboard, you're really already halfway there.

INGREDIENTS
¼ cup extra-virgin olive oil

1 medium-size onion, peeled and diced

¼ teaspoon kosher salt, plus more to taste

3 cloves garlic, peeled and minced

1 (28-ounce) can whole peeled tomatoes, chopped roughly

1 teaspoon (4 g) sugar, plus more to taste

3 tablespoons chopped fresh basil, or 1½ tablespoons dried

1 tablespoon chopped fresh oregano, or ½ tablespoon dried

In a large saucepan, combine the olive oil, onion, and salt. Cook, stirring often, over medium heat until the onion is nearly translucent (about 4 minutes). Add the garlic and cook, stirring frequently, until fragrant (about another 2 minutes). Add the tomatoes, sugar, basil, and oregano, and stir to combine. Cook, stirring occasionally, until the tomatoes are largely broken down (about 3 more minutes). Taste, then add more salt and sugar, in small increments, if desired.

For a smooth sauce, blend with an immersion blender until you reach the consistency you like best. Continue to cook, stirring occasionally, over medium heat until the sauce is reduced by about one-eighth.

CHEESE CALZONES
MAKES 4 INDIVIDUAL CALZONES

NOT THAT I DON'T ENJOY A CHEESE CALZONE THAT IS JUST PIZZA dough wrapped around a few types of cheese in abundance. It's just that I have a harder time justifying that as an actual meal. These calzones have just the right balance of sauce and cheese, and the thick pizza crust keeps everything neat and tidy.

INGREDIENTS

1 recipe Thick-Crust Pizza Dough (page 187), already risen
3 cloves garlic, peeled and minced
2 tablespoons extra-virgin olive oil
¼ cup Quick Homemade Tomato Sauce (page 249) or store-bought sauce
2 tablespoons tomato paste
15 to 16 ounces part-skim ricotta cheese
8 ounces part-skim mozzarella cheese, grated
Leaves from 3 sprigs fresh oregano, or 2 teaspoons dried
1½ ounces Parmigiano-Reggiano cheese, grated finely

Place a pizza stone (or overturned rimmed metal baking sheet) on the bottom rack of your oven and preheat to 400°F.

On a lightly-floured surface, divide the pizza dough into four equal pieces (about 4 ounces each). Cover the dough with a moist tea towel, and set it aside to rest while you make the filling.

To make the filling, in a small, heavy-bottomed saucepan, place the garlic, olive oil, and tomato sauce, and whisk to combine. Cook, stirring frequently, over medium heat until the garlic is fragrant (about 2 minutes). Remove the saucepan from the heat, add the tomato paste, and whisk to combine. Add the ricotta cheese, mozzarella cheese, and oregano, stir to combine, and set the filling aside.

Pat and roll out with a rolling pin the first piece of dough on a lightly floured surface into an 8-inch round, rotating the dough and flouring it frequently to avoid sticking. Transfer the round of dough to a piece of un-bleached parchment paper. Sprinkle some of the Parmigiano-Reggiano cheese on half of the surface of the dough. Place about ½ cup of the filling on top of the Parmigiano-Reggiano cheese, and spread into an even layer, leaving a ½-inch border clean. Sprinkle the filling with a bit more Parmigiano-Reggiano cheese. Carefully pull the other half of the dough up and over the filling, and press the edges tightly to seal. With a sharp knife or lame, cut three diagonal slits on the top of the calzone only deep enough to cut the dough but not into the filling. Repeat with the remaining pieces of dough and the rest of the filling.

Transfer the calzones, two at a time, still on their parchment paper, to the hot pizza stone and bake until lightly golden brown all over (about 12 minutes). Remove from the oven and allow to cool slightly before serving.

CAST-IRON SKILLET PIZZA
MAKES 2 10-INCH PIZZAS

IF YOU DON'T HAVE A CAST-IRON SKILLET (WHY DON'T YOU? THEY'RE inexpensive and last forever), you can of course make this pizza in the manner suggested in the Pizza Margherita (page 255). But, really, nothing compares to a thick-crust pizza cooked entirely on the stovetop. It brings the crust to a whole new level of crisp and chewy. I have included my favorite toppings for cast-iron pizza here, but of course, feel free to make it your own by topping it with your favorites!

INGREDIENTS
1 recipe Thick-Crust Pizza Dough (page 187), already risen
¾ cup Quick Homemade Tomato Sauce (page 249) or store-bought sauce
8 ounces low-moisture part-skim mozzarella cheese, grated thickly

Heat a dry, well-seasoned 10-inch cast-iron skillet over high heat until a bead of water sizzles when it hits the pan (about 5 minutes). The skillet must have a tight-fitting lid, but you won't cover it just yet.

On a lightly floured surface, divide the dough into two equal portions, and roll each into a ball. Sprinkle both lightly with flour, and cover one with a moist tea towel so that it doesn't dry out. Pat and roll out (with a rolling pin) the first piece of dough on a lightly floured surface into a 10-inch round, rotating the dough and flouring it frequently to avoid sticking. Carefully transfer the round of dough to the hot skillet, and cover tightly with the lid. Cook until the dough has begun to puff up and the underside is lightly browned (about 5 minutes). Open the lid and flip the pizza dough with tongs. With a large, wide spatula, press down on the dough in the center. Cover the skillet again, and cook until the side that is now facing down has begun to brown.

Open the lid of the skillet, and lower the heat to medium-low. Flip the pizza dough again, then spread half of the tomato sauce on top. Scatter half of the mozzarella cheese on top of the sauce, and cover the skillet once more. Cook until the cheese is melted and bubbling (about 4 minutes). Repeat with the second piece of dough and remaining ingredients.

Allow the cheese on both pizzas to set for a few minutes before slicing and serving.

SPINACH AND SALAMI STROMBOLI
MAKES 1 LARGE STROMBOLI

ECHNICALLY, A CALZONE IS DISTINCT FROM STROMBOLI BECAUSE the stromboli has tomato sauce tucked inside, and the calzone does not. But my version of a Cheese Calzone (page 251) does have some tomato sauce inside. So the chief distinction in my world is that the calzone is folded; and the stromboli, rolled. Because stromboli tends to be a bit more messy, though, I suggest eating this with a knife and fork—especially when you have company. What you do when you're alone is your business, and mine is not to judge.

INGREDIENTS

1 recipe Thick-Crust Pizza Dough (page 187), already risen
2 tablespoons extra-virgin olive oil
¼ cup Quick Homemade Tomato Sauce (page 249) or store-bought sauce
1½ ounces Parmigiano-Reggiano cheese, grated finely
4 ounces salami, sliced thinly
1 (1-pound) bag fresh, triple-washed baby spinach
½ pound provolone cheese, sliced thinly

Place a pizza stone (or overturned rimmed metal baking sheet) on the bottom rack of your oven and preheat to 400°F.

On a lightly floured piece of unbleached parchment paper, roll out the pizza dough with a rolling pin into a 9- by 12-inch rectangle, rotating the dough and flouring it frequently to avoid sticking. Drizzle 1 tablespoon of the olive oil plus the tomato sauce on top of the dough, and spread it into an even layer. Sprinkle the dough evenly with the Parmigiano-Reggiano cheese, then with an even layer of the salami slices, the spinach leaves, and finally, the provolone, leaving a ½-inch border clean around the perimeter. Beginning at the 9-inch width of the dough, roll the dough away from you gently but firmly, using the parchment paper to help roll and ending with the *stromboli* seam side down on the parchment. Brush the top and sides of the *stromboli* with the remaining tablespoon of olive oil. Trim the excess parchment paper from around the roll, and transfer the *stromboli* to the hot pizza stone. Bake until lightly golden brown all over (about 25 minutes). Remove from the oven and allow to cool slightly before serving.

PIZZA MARGHERITA
MAKES TWO 10-INCH PIZZAS

Y OU KNOW HOW YOU LIKE YOUR PIZZA. BUT I WOULD BE REMISS IF I didn't at least give you a few pizza ideas to kick around, seeing as how Chapter 7 gave you a virtual cornucopia of pizza dough recipes to choose from. I like my pizza old school, so a simple Pizza Margherita is where it's at for me.

INGREDIENTS

1 recipe Thin-Crust Pizza Dough (page 189), already risen
1 cup Quick Homemade Tomato Sauce (page 249) or store-bought sauce
½ cup fresh basil, torn roughly
¼ cup chopped fresh parsley
2 ounces Parmigiano-Reggiano cheese, grated finely
8 ounces low-moisture, part-skim mozzarella cheese, sliced into ¼-inch-thick rounds

Place a pizza stone (or overturned rimmed metal baking sheet) on the bottom rack of your oven and preheat to 400°F.

On a lightly floured surface, divide the dough into two equal portions, and roll each into a ball. Sprinkle both lightly with flour, and cover one with a moist tea towel so that it doesn't dry out. Pat and roll out the first piece of dough on a lightly floured surface into an 11-inch round with a rolling pin, rotating the dough and flouring it frequently to avoid sticking. Transfer the round of dough to a piece of unbleached parchment paper. Roll in the edges of the dough to create a crust, and pinch to secure. Repeat with the second piece of dough.

Place each crust, one at a time, each still on its parchment paper, on the hot pizza stone. Bake for about 5 minutes, or until the crust begins to puff and brown. Remove it from the oven. Divide the tomato sauce between the two pizza crusts, and spread it over the bottom of each crust. Scatter the basil and parsley, and then the Parmigiano-Reggiano cheese, on top of the sauce. Scatter the mozzarella cheese on top.

Place the pizzas again, one at a time, back on the pizza stone. Bake until the cheese is melted and bubbling and the crust is browned (about 7 minutes). Allow the cheese to set for a few minutes before slicing and serving.

MEATBALL SUBS
MAKES 5 SANDWICHES

I F YOU ARE FEELING VERY, VERY GENEROUS, WHEN YOU MAKE THESE meatball subs for dinner, package one up for lunch the next day for your favorite person (whoever that may be—I won't tell). Because the Hoagie Rolls (page 135) are lightly crispy on the outside, they're hearty enough to stand up well to being reheated, and the sauce keeps the meatballs moist enough that they won't dry out.

FOR THE MEATBALLS

2 large eggs, at room temperature, beaten
½ cup Quick Homemade Tomato Sauce (page 249) or store-bought sauce
2 tablespoons tomato paste
2 teaspoons gluten-free Worcestershire sauce
½ teaspoon kosher salt
2 teaspoons dried oregano
2 teaspoons dried basil
½ teaspoon garlic powder
¾ cup fresh gluten-free bread crumbs
4 ounces Parmigiano-Reggiano cheese, grated finely
1½ pounds lean ground beef
2 to 3 tablespoons extra-virgin olive oil, for drizzling

FOR THE SANDWICH

5 (6-inch) gluten-free Hoagie Rolls (page 135)
½ cup Quick Homemade Tomato Sauce (page 249) or store-bought sauce
6 ounces low-moisture part-skim mozzarella cheese, sliced thinly

Preheat your oven to 350°F. Line a rimmed baking sheet with unbleached parchment paper and set it aside.

In a large bowl, place the eggs, tomato sauce, tomato paste, Worcestershire sauce, salt, oregano, basil, and garlic powder, and whisk to combine well. Add the bread crumbs and three-quarters of the Parmigiano-Reggiano cheese, and mix again to combine. Add the beef, and mix with your hands until all the ingredients are well incorporated and evenly distributed. With wet hands, form the meatballs into twenty-four pieces of roughly equal size (about 1½ inches in diameter), roll them into balls, and place them 2 inches apart from one another on the prepared baking sheet. Drizzle the olive oil over the meatballs, spreading the oil evenly over each meatball. Sprinkle the meatballs with the remaining Parmigiano-Reggiano cheese, and place them in the center of the preheated oven. Bake the meatballs until cooked through and golden brown all over (about 40 minutes). Remove from the oven and set aside to cool briefly, until no longer too hot to handle.

To assemble the sandwiches, slice the hoagie rolls lengthwise without slicing all the way through, so that the halves stay together. Remove about half of the doughy inside of each roll, spoon a tablespoon of tomato sauce on the bottom half of the inside of the bread, and cover with two to three slices of mozzarella cheese. Slice three of the meatballs horizontally through their center. Place the meatball halves on top of the tomato sauce on one roll, overlapping each half on the other. Spoon another tablespoon of tomato sauce on top of the meatballs, and place thin slices of mozzarella cheese on top of the sauce. Wrap the sandwich, open side up, in a piece of aluminum foil, and set it aside. Repeat with the remaining rolls.

These sandwiches can be made ahead up to this point, wrapped tightly in plastic wrap over the aluminum foil and refrigerated until ready to eat. When ready to eat, remove the plastic wrap and place the sandwiches in a preheated 250°F oven until heated through. Open the foil to expose the cheese, and place the subs under your oven's broiler for a minute or so until the cheese is melted and bubbling and the bread is crisped on the edges. Serve hot.

PHILLY CHEESESTEAKS

MAKES 5 SANDWICHES

M Y HUSBAND IS FROM PHILADELPHIA, SO I CAN'T MESS AROUND IN
the cheesesteak department and expect to get away with it. I am proud
to report that he deputized me, for the purpose of this recipe only, to say that
this recipe produces a completely authentic-tasting Philly cheesesteak, one
worthy of the name. And, what's more, our crispy on the outside, soft on the
inside Hoagie Rolls (page 135) have also been deemed worthy by His Philly
Highness.

INGREDIENTS

1½ pounds (24 ounces) steak (rib eye, eye roll, or flank steak work well),
    frozen for about an hour before slicing
½ teaspoon kosher salt
4 tablespoons vegetable oil
1 large yellow onion, peeled and diced
10 ounces white mushrooms, cleaned and sliced thinly
8 ounces provolone cheese, sliced thinly
5 (6-inch) gluten-free Hoagie Rolls (page 135)

Remove the steak from the freezer, and slice it widthwise (against the grain),
as thinly as possible. Sprinkle ¼ teaspoon of the salt evenly over the slices.

In a large sauté pan with high sides (or a large Dutch oven), heat 2 tablespoons of the oil over medium-high heat. Carefully place some of the slices
of steak in the pan in a single layer, making sure they don't overlap. Sauté for
a minute, and then flip the slices with tongs. Cook for another minute or so,
and remove the cooked slices from the pan. Repeat with the remaining slices,
taking care not to overcrowd the pan. Set the beef aside.

Add the remaining 2 tablespoons of oil and the onion to the pan, and lower
the heat to medium. Cook, stirring frequently, until the onion is translucent
but has not yet begun to brown (about 6 minutes). Remove the onion from the
pan and set it aside. Add the sliced mushrooms to the same pan, so they can
cook in the onion and beef juices. Add the remaining ¼ teaspoon of salt and
stir to combine. Raise the heat again to medium-high, and cover the pan for
3 to 4 minutes to sweat the mushrooms. Uncover the pan, and cook, stirring

occasionally, until the mushrooms are soft and fragrant (about 4 minutes more). Remove the mushrooms from the pan.

To assemble the sandwiches, slice the hoagie rolls lengthwise without slicing all the way through, so that the halves stay together. Remove about half of the doughy inside of each roll, and divide the beef among the bread. Layer in the mushrooms and the onion. Top with the sliced cheese and serve warm.

CHICKEN CHEESESTEAKS
MAKES 5 SANDWICHES

I AM PAINFULLY AWARE THAT, BY MAKING A CHICKEN CHEESESTEAK, I run the risk of completely ruining all of the street cred I worked so hard to cultivate in making an authentic gluten-free Philly Cheesesteak (page 258). But this sandwich is, put simply, worth it.

INGREDIENTS

4 tablespoons (56 g) ghee or vegetable oil
1¼ pounds skinless boneless chicken breasts
½ teaspoon kosher salt
¼ teaspoon freshly ground black pepper
2 shallots, peeled and diced
2 cloves garlic, peeled and minced
5 (6-inch) gluten-free Hoagie Rolls (page 135)
3 pieces prepared roasted red peppers, sliced thinly lengthwise
6 ounces sharp white Cheddar cheese, sliced thinly

In a medium-size heavy-bottomed skillet, heat 2 tablespoons of the ghee over low heat until melted. Blot the chicken dry, and sprinkle salt and pepper on both sides. Place the chicken breasts in the hot skillet in a single layer and raise the heat to medium. Cook the chicken for 5 minutes on one side, then flip it over and cook until opaque throughout (about 5 minutes more). Remove the cooked chicken from the pan and set it aside. Add the remaining 2 tablespoons of ghee to the pan. Once it has melted, add the shallots to the pan and cook, stirring frequently, until the shallots are mostly soft and translucent (about 5 minutes). Add the garlic, and cook until fragrant (about 2 minutes more). Slice the cooked chicken thinly and add it to the pan. Toss everything together.

To assemble the sandwiches, slice the hoagie rolls lengthwise without slicing all the way through, so that the halves stay together. Remove about half of the doughy inside of each roll, and divide the chicken, shallot, and garlic mixture among the rolls. Layer in the red peppers. Top with the cheese and serve warm.

CLUB SANDWICH
MAKES 1 SANDWICH

I T MUST BE OBVIOUS BY NOW, BUT I'M DEAD SET ON REVIVING EVERY last memory of diner sandwiches you could possibly have. When you can make great gluten-free bread every which way, which you most certainly now can, I am willing to bet that you feel inspired to bring back club sandwiches, too. Just because you can.

INGREDIENTS
1 tablespoon mayonnaise
3 slices Soft White Sandwich Bread (page 45), lightly toasted
1 leaf romaine lettuce, cut horizontally into 4 pieces
2 slices beefsteak tomato
2 slices thinly sliced deli roasted turkey
2 strips crisp cooked bacon, each broken in half horizontally

Spread mayonnaise on one side of each of the three slices of toasted bread. On one slice of bread, layer two pieces of lettuce, one tomato slice, one turkey slice, and two halves of one strip of bacon. Top with another slice of toasted bread (mayonnaise side up), followed by two pieces of lettuce, one tomato slice, one turkey slice, and one strip of bacon, cut into two halves. Top with the remaining slice of toast, mayonnaise side down. Press the sandwich down firmly to seal.

With a sharp knife, with the sandwich already assembled, slice off all of the crusts. Insert a toothpick into each of the four quadrants of the sandwich, pressing it all the way through, to anchor the sandwich elements together. Slice the sandwich into quarters diagonally, from corner to corner to create triangles. Serve immediately.

REUBEN SANDWICH
MAKES 1 SANDWICH

WE GLUTEN-FREE PEOPLE GENERALLY KNOW WHAT WE'RE MISSing. And we're missing a Reuben sandwich. It is with great excitement that I share this recipe for an authentic-tasting gluten-free Reuben. It may be all about the No-Rye "Rye" Bread (page 101), but the right fillings bring this favorite all the way home.

INGREDIENTS

2 one-half inch thick slices No-Rye "Rye" Bread (page 101)
1 tablespoon (14 g) unsalted butter, at room temperature
2 tablespoons Thousand Island dressing
1 ounce sliced Jarlsberg cheese
¾ cup sauerkraut, drained well (optional)
4 ounces thickly-sliced pastrami or corned beef

Lay out both slices of bread, and butter one side each generously. Next, spread 1 tablespoon of the dressing on top of the butter. On one slice, top with half of the cheese slices, then the sauerkraut (if using), pastrami, and finally the rest of the cheese. Top with the other slice of bread, dressing side down.

Press the sandwich down to seal, slice in half, and serve . . . with a dill pickle spear and an ice-cold gluten-free beer (if I may be so bold as to suggest one).

MONTE CRISTO
MAKES 1 SANDWICH

ARE YOU ONE OF THOSE PEOPLE WHO INSISTS THAT SHE DOESN'T really go for the whole salty-sweet thing, especially in a sandwich? All of those people have never, ever had a good Monte Cristo sandwich. I can prove it.

INGREDIENTS

1 teaspoon Dijon mustard

1 teaspoon strawberry jam

2 thick slices Brioche Bread (page 50), toasted lightly

3 slices thinly sliced Swiss cheese

2 slices thinly sliced deli ham

2 slices thinly sliced deli roasted turkey

1 large egg, at room temperature, beaten

1 tablespoon heavy cream

1 tablespoon (14 g) unsalted butter, melted and cooled

1 tablespoon (14 g) ghee or more unsalted butter

Place the mustard and jam in a small bowl and mix to combine well. Spread the mixture on one side of each slice of toasted bread. On one slice of bread, layer a slice of cheese, then a slice of ham, then turkey, followed by cheese, ham, turkey and ending with the final slice of cheese. Top with the remaining slice of toast, mustard mixture side down. Press the sandwich down firmly to seal.

In a shallow dish, place the egg, cream, and butter, and whisk to combine well. Place the ghee in a cast-iron skillet over medium-high heat. Once the ghee has melted and the skillet is hot, dip both sides of the sandwich in the egg mixture, and place the sandwich in the hot skillet. Cover the skillet and fry the sandwich for 2 minutes on one side. Uncover the skillet, flip the sandwich with a wide spatula, and press down on the sandwich firmly with the spatula. Fry until the second side of the sandwich is golden brown (about 1 minute more). Remove the sandwich from the skillet, slice it in half, and serve immediately.

GRILLED CHEESE PANINI
MAKES 4 SANDWICHES

DON'T KNOW ABOUT YOU, BUT I DON'T HAVE A PANINI PRESS, AS IT'S so easy to approximate its effect with the use of a second heavy skillet. Here, I have chosen to use the Ciabatta Bread (page 121), as its large holes and plentiful crust make for a beautiful presentation, but thick slices of tangy Pain au Levain (page 91) also pair beautifully with these cheeses. Or, if you dare, the actual Cheese Bread (page 52) itself?!

INGREDIENTS

2 loaves Ciabatta (page 121)
4 tablespoons (56 g) unsalted butter, at room temperature
8 ounces Gruyère cheese, sliced thinly
4 ounces Parmigiano-Reggiano cheese, sliced thinly

Heat a dry, well-seasoned cast-iron skillet or heavy grill pan (or heat your panini press) over high heat until a bead of water sizzles when it hits the pan (about 5 minutes). Unless you are using a panini press, have ready another heavy skillet to place on top of the sandwich during grilling.

Slice each loaf of bread lengthwise, and then in half to make four sandwiches. Open the sandwiches and butter all eight open sides. Divide the slices of Gruyère and Parmigiano-Reggiano cheese among the sandwiches, close the tops, and press down gently to seal.

Butter lightly the outside of two of the sandwiches, and place them in the hot skillet (or panini press) and place the other heavy skillet on top of the sandwich (or close the panini press). Cook for about 4 minutes, or until the cheese is melted and the bread is crisp, flipping the sandwiches halfway through. Press down on the top skillet occasionally to ensure that the sandwiches are compressing.

Repeat with the remaining two sandwiches. Serve warm.

HAM AND BRIE TEA SANDWICHES
MAKES 12 TEA SANDWICHES

I HAVE ALWAYS BEEN FASCINATED BY TEA SANDWICHES. IT NEVER occurred to me, as a child, to demand sandwiches without crusts. That is, until I experienced tea sandwiches. I didn't suddenly lose my appreciation for the crusty part of bread. It's just that it felt so elegant to eat delicate tea sandwiches, with their precise, even edges. Very impressive, and an excellent use of the fluffy centers of our Soft White Sandwich Bread (page 45).

INGREDIENTS

6 slices Soft White Sandwich Bread (page 45), crusts removed

3 tablespoons (42 g) unsalted butter, at room temperature

Kosher salt, to taste

6 ounces smoked deli ham

6 ounces Brie cheese, sliced thinly, at room temperature

Lay out all six slices of bread, and butter them generously on one side. Sprinkle the buttered slices lightly with kosher salt, to taste. Layer the ham and then the Brie cheese on half of the buttered slices of bread, taking care not to allow any of the sandwich fillings to hang over the sides of the bread. Top with the remaining slices of bread. Press the sandwiches down gently to seal, and slice each sandwich in half, and then in half again, leaving twelve small rectangular tea sandwiches.

Serve immediately at room temperature.

PITA CHIPS
MAKES 32 CHIPS

HERE'S WHAT YOU DO WITH ANY OF THAT PITA BREAD (PAGE 133) that you didn't get a chance to eat when it was fresh.

INGREDIENTS
¼ cup extra-virgin olive oil
1 tablespoon dried oregano
½ teaspoon dried basil
1 recipe Pita Bread (page 133)
Kosher salt and freshly ground black pepper

Preheat your oven to 400°F. Line a rimmed baking sheet with unbleached parchment paper and set it aside.

In a small bowl, place the olive oil, oregano, and basil, and mix to combine. Brush the mixture on all eight pita breads, on both sides. Slice the pitas into quarters, and place them in a single layer on the prepared baking sheet. Sprinkle with salt and pepper, to taste. Place the baking sheet in the center of the preheated oven and bake until the pita chips are lightly golden brown (about 6 minutes). They will continue to crisp as they cool. Serve warm or at room temperature.

BREAD CRUMBS
MAKES ABOUT 3 CUPS BREAD CRUMBS

GIVE ME THE WRETCHED REFUSE OF YOUR EARLY BREAD ATTEMPTS, the I-forgot-it-was-on-the-counter-cut-side-up partial loaf and the crusts-of-children-who-won't-eat-crusts, and make bread crumbs. And never pay a retail price for prepared gluten-free bread crumbs again! Store your fresh bread crumbs in the freezer and you'll never be without.

INGREDIENTS
4 to 5 slices gluten-free bread, any kind
½ teaspoon kosher salt (optional)
Dried seasonings, such as oregano and parsley (optional)

Preheat your oven to 325°F. Line a large rimmed baking sheet in an even layer with aluminum foil and set it aside.

Break up the slices of bread into chunks and place in the bowl of a standard 7-cup food processor fitted with the steel blade. Cover the food processor and pulse until coarse crumbs form. Open the lid and add the salt and seasonings, if using. Close the lid and pulse again until combined, or until the crumbs reach the desired consistency (I prefer coarser panko-style crumbs, but you may like to grind them finely).

Transfer the bread crumbs to the prepared baking sheet and place in the center of the preheated oven. Bake for about 8 minutes, and then remove from the oven and stir the crumbs to redistribute them. Return to the oven and bake until the bread crumbs are lightly golden brown all over (about another 7 minutes). Remove from the oven and allow to cool on the baking sheet before transferring to a freezer-safe container. Seal tightly and place in the refrigerator or freezer until ready to use. The bread crumbs can be used directly from the refrigerator or freezer, without defrosting, and will stay fresh for months when frozen.

CINNAMON SUGAR FRENCH TOAST
SERVES 1

LEARLY, THIS RECIPE CAN BE MULTIPLIED—OR SHARED AS IT IS. But I present it as a recipe for one, mostly because it's so easy to make that it's worth making just for yourself, or perhaps someone else for whom you are taking some extra special care. This recipe calls for the Crusty White Sandwich Bread (page 43), as it is a lean bread and soaks up the eggs and milk in this recipe so well. For richer French Toast, try Brioche Bread (page 50), after it has been sliced thickly and left out at room temperature overnight. Once stale, even enriched bread will absorb the eggs and butter in this recipe.

INGREDIENTS

2 large eggs, at room temperature, beaten
¼ cup milk, at room temperature (not nonfat)
1 teaspoon gluten-free vanilla extract
2 tablespoons (28 g) unsalted butter, at room temperature
4 thin slices Crusty White Sandwich Bread (page 43)
1 tablespoon (14 g) ghee or unsalted butter, for frying
Sugar and ground cinnamon, for sprinkling

In a 9- by 12-inch baking dish, whisk the eggs, milk, and vanilla until well combined. Butter the slices of bread on both sides, and add them to the egg mixture. Allow the slices of bread to soak for 1 to 2 minutes per side.

While the bread is soaking, place the ghee in a medium-size cast-iron or nonstick skillet. Melt the ghee over medium heat until it begins to shimmer. Place the egg-soaked bread in the skillet. Fry until golden brown on the underside (about 2 minutes). Flip and fry the other side for about 1 minute more or until golden brown. Transfer the French toast to a plate lined with a paper towel. Repeat with the remaining slices of bread.

Sprinkle the cinnamon sugar on a plate, and press both sides of each slice of the still-warm bread into the mixture to coat. Serve immediately.

RESOURCES

Alice.com: This is where I buy Red Star Quick Rise Yeast by the jar. Go to www.alice.com.

Amazon.com: Often, Amazon is still the best source for many products, such as Authentic Foods superfine rice flours, particularly if you are an Amazon Prime member, as the superfine rice flours are usually available to ship for free to Prime members. I also order Bob's Red Mill certified gluten-free products from Amazon when it has the best price. Amazon is also my source for such products as If You Care unbleached parchment paper, a pizza stone, pizza peel (Epicurean brand is durable and well priced), cutting boards (again, Epicurean brand), and Cambro brand 2- and 4-liter food storage containers (which I use as proofing buckets). You can also find Rodelle Gourmet Baking Cocoa, a gluten-free Dutch-processed cocoa powder, at Amazon.

Authentic Foods: Authentic Foods' online shop, http://www.glutenfree-supermarket.com/, is one of only a few sources for Authentic Foods superfine rice flours (and Authentic Foods is the only company I am aware of that manufactures truly superfine rice flours). If you are not a member of Amazon Prime, be sure to check the shipping rates directly from Authentic Foods to where you live. It may be cheaper than ordering through Amazon.

Bed Bath & Beyond: This is the one brick-and-mortar store that I recommend for large appliances, such as a KitchenAid stand mixer, since the store will allow you to use its own discount coupon (you know you have a bunch of those, and it has been my experience that the store willingly accepts expired coupons even for a large purchase like that). No need to wait for a sale, unless you are able to bide your time and wait out one of the blowout sales at such department stores as Macy's and Bloomingdale's. Order at www.bedbathandbeyond.com or visit any of the company's many stores. If you want to use a coupon, though, you will have to use it in the store.

Better Batter: If you are buying Better Batter Gluten Free Flour, the best price is always on their website, www.betterbatter.org, particularly if you buy in bulk.

Bob's Red Mill: Some of this company's products, such as gluten-free masa harina, are frequently unavailable at Amazon.com, so I buy them directly from the company at www.bobsredmill.com.

Expandex: Click on "Where to Buy Expandex" at www.expandexgluten-free.com for a list of retailers. The company that makes Expandex, Corn Products International (don't worry—Expandex does not contain corn), sells it in bulk to retailers, which then repackage it. So be sure to purchase it from a source that repackages it in a gluten-free facility.

Growing Naturals: You can buy Growing Naturals Rice Protein Isolate (Original Flavor) directly from the company's site, at www.growingnaturals.com.

King Arthur Flour: I buy certified gluten-free buckwheat flour directly from www.kingarthurflour.com. King Arthur Flour is also a good source for proofing baskets, pizza stones, plastic "double bread bags," bench scrapers, English muffin rings, and even a Brød & Taylor bread proofer (just search for "bread proofer").

Netrition.com: This is my primary source for NOW Foods Whey Protein Isolate, although I do also order it from Amazon.com. I am forever in search of the best current price. Netrition is also a good source for NOW Foods Pea Protein Isolate.

Nutrition calculators: SparkRecipes has a popular nutrition calculator at http://recipes.sparkpeople.com/recipe-calculator.asp. You will have to create an account to use the site, but it's easy to do and you can remain relatively anonymous. I have an account under the name "NICOLEGF1" on the site, and I have entered the recipe for my mock Better Batter blend (see page 9) in a public recipe collection called "Gluten Free Flour." Hopefully, that will help you get started. Another site with a good nutrition calculator is http://caloriecount.about.com/. Similarly, you must create an account to build a recipe using the calculator, but it's simple to do.

Nuts.com: I order tapioca starch/flour, cornstarch, sweet white sorghum flour, teff flour, potato flour, and masa harina all from www.nuts.com, which typically has the best prices on those products. All those products are certified gluten-free when you buy them from Nuts.com (as of the writing of this book). However, the shipping costs tend to be expensive when you buy in small quantities, so I generally order more product, less often.

Williams-Sonoma: I really like the 1-pound (8 by 4½-inch) loaf pans from Williams-Sonoma's Goldtouch line. Go to www.williams-sonoma.com.

ACKNOWLEDGMENTS

REMEMBER WHEN HILARY SWANK WON THE OSCAR IN 2000 FOR *BOYS Don't Cry,* and forgot to thank her then-husband of three years, Chad Lowe? Well, this isn't the Oscars, and I'm no Hilary Swank, but in the right light you could say that my husband . . . okay, fine, he doesn't look like Chad Lowe. But I'm not going to forget to thank him, all the same. My husband is the reason that these books exist. Well, to be fair (to me), there was some eye rolling (from him) when I first came up with the name for the blog. I tried and tried to come up with a different blog moniker, but I just kept coming back to Gluten-Free on a Shoestring. I went with it, he got on board, and he's been my safety net ever since. This whole writing-a-book thing is something I can handle. It's the putting-it-out-into-the-world part that might have killed me, if it weren't for Brian. So, thank you thank you, Brian.

To my children, who are immensely proud that I write cookbooks, even though they're nearing the age where they realize that I am, most decidedly, not famous. I keep telling them I'm not, but it hasn't seemed to dampen their enthusiasm much. It's sweet, though, and it somehow seems to bring the whole business full circle, being as I started the blog in the first place with them in mind. Making them proud has become very important to me. And, with any luck, they are growing up with the understanding that they are many different ways to forge a career, even when you have young children. You just don't get much sleep, is all. No biggie.

To my agent, Brandi Bowles, who is everything I need her to be: She doesn't mince words, and she goes to bat for me every single time. If it can be made to happen in this world, Brandi is going to get it done. So when things don't go as I had hoped, which inevitably happens from time to time in publishing, as in life, I have the peace of mind that comes from knowing that I have the best at my side. Actually, I'm standing behind the best. It's safest there.

To my editors, Christine Dore and Renée Sedliar. By now, they both know the high esteem in which I hold the thorough line edit of a manuscript. They each bring a perspective to the work that I have inevitably lost months ago, mired as I am in the details. And they put up with my intensity and impatience with grace and, yes, charm. They are my champions on the inside, from both coasts. I've got everything I need.

To my in-house publicist, Kate Burke, for always staying ahead of what needs to be done. She is a true team player who keeps her eye on the prize, and handles even the stickiest situations with style and grace. There's no denying that Kate is good at the publicity game!

To Lindsey Triebel and Kevin Hanover of the in-house marketing department, for, quite simply, getting the job done. Always on top of everything from the word go, they get my books on shelves, both physical and virtual, and into the right hands every time.

To Allyson Acker and Crystal Patriarche and the rest of the crackerjack team at BookSparksPR, for putting me at ease and taking this book franchise to a whole new level. They have become the trusted advisers whom I reflexively seek out when I want to know whether an opportunity is right for me, as they have the knowledge, experience, and foresight to see both the forest and the trees. Visit them at http://www.booksparkspr.com/.

To Stephen Gross of Stephen Scott Gross Photography, and his assistant Jason, for just taking the most gorgeous food photography with pitch-perfect aesthetic. Being able to trust that Stephen will "shoot the hell" out of every photo, no matter how peripheral it could be considered, was tremendous comfort. And from the cover all the way through to the final page of this book, the photos simply speak for themselves. Plus, there's also the matter of author photos that even *I* can admire, that Stephen managed to get done, despite my less-than-accommodating manner. Now that is amazing. Visit Stephen at http://ssgphoto.com/.

To Treva Chadwell, food stylist extraordinaire. She's a classically trained chef, and food stylist to the food stars. And even though I thought I'd be intimidated, instead, she put me at ease with her warmth, sense of humor, professionalism, and, of course, her skill. Treva is the reason that the food in this book is beautiful. And a big thank-you to her husband and daughter, too, who ate a lot of gluten-free bread shoot food (and probably still have some in their home freezer). Visit her at http://www.beehiveoven.com/ for a taste of her Southern charm.

To all the other professionals at Perseus Books, from the designers who got the book cover up and at 'em so early this time to the production team who are the best at what they do, and everyone in between, thank you for your skill and patience.

And to my blog readers, who support me every step of the way, in every way possible. You are the ones who come to visit me every day on the blog. And I know it's a cliché to say, "I couldn't do it without you," so I won't say exactly that. But, really, I wouldn't want to do it without you (not to mention that I couldn't). It would be lonely, and there's nothing particularly gratifying about doing everything only for oneself. Contentment comes not from looking inward, but from the connections we make with one another. I may kid, but it's not a game to me, and your loyalty and patronage are not anything I take for granted. Every time you tell me that you danced in the kitchen with your son or daughter while you baked and ate together, I get choked up. But don't tell anybody I'm such a mush. You'll totally ruin my street cred (of which I have precious little).

INDEX

Parmesan Cornmeal Crackers,
210–211
Pastrami
Reuben Sandwich, 263
Pastry dough, troubleshooting, 26–27
Pea protein isolate, source for, 270
Pectin, powdered
High-Quality All-Purpose Gluten-
Free Flour, 9
Peppers, red
Chicken Cheesesteaks, 260
Philly Cheesesteaks, 258–259
Pineapple juice
Hawaiian Rolls, 181–182
Pita Bread, 133–134
Pita Chips, 267
Pizza
Cast-Iron Skillet Pizza, 253
Deep-Dish Chicago-Style Pizza,
193–194
Pizza Margherita, 255
Thick-Crust Pizza Dough, 187–188
Thick-Crust Whole-Grain Pizza
Crust Dough, 191–192
Thin-Crust Pizza Dough, 189–190
Pizza dough, rolling out, 38
Pizza peels
defined, 16
sources for, 269, 270
Pizza stones
defined, 16
sources for, 269, 270
Plain (or Seeded) Bagels, 123–124
Plain Sourdough Bagels, 113–114
Poppy seeds
Braided Challah Bread, 62–63

Crunchy Levain Breadsticks, 93–94
Potato Bread, 57–58
Potato flour
High-Quality All-Purpose Gluten-
Free Flour, 9
source for, 273
Potato starch
Basic Gum-Free Gluten-Free Flour,
9–10
High-Quality All-Purpose Gluten-
Free Flour, 9
Make-It-Simpler All-Purpose
Gluten-Free Flour, 9
Potatoes
Potato Bread, 57–58
Pretzel Rolls, 153–154
Pretzels, Sourdough Soft, 107–108
Proofers
defined, 14
source for, 270
Proofing, 12
Proofing baskets
defined, 11, 16–18
source for, 270
Proofing buckets
defined, 18
sources for, 269, 270
Protein powders, 6, 10
"Pumpernickel" Bagels, 111–112
"Pumpernickel" Bread, 105–106

Q

Quick breads
Bran Muffins, 237–238
Brown Butter Banana Bread,
242–243

ABOUT THE AUTHOR

NICOLE HUNN IS THE PERSONALity behind the popular *Gluten-Free on a Shoestring* blog and book series. She has been featured in high-profile national print and broadcast outlets, including the *New York Times*, *MSN Money*, Epicurious.com, *The Daily Meal*, *BetterTV*, and the *Dr. Steve Show*. In addition, she is a regular contributing gluten-free expert for SheKnows.com Food and a guest blogger for several other influential food and lifestyle outlets. Nicole believes that, with the right tools and instruction, anyone can learn to bake fresh, artisan, gluten-free bread at home with great success—without relying on a bread machine or other expensive tools. She lives in Westchester County, New York, with her husband and three children. For more information and recipes, please visit www.glutenfreeonashoestring.com.